TREE

RALPH LEMON

TREE

BELIEF/CULTURE/BALANCE

WESLEYAN UNIVERSITY PRESS

Middletown, Connecticut

Published by
WESLEYAN UNIVERSITY PRESS
Middletown, CT 06459
© 2004 by Ralph Lemon
All rights reserved
Printed in China
5 4 3 2 1

Library of Congress Cataloging-in-Publication Data
Lemon, Ralph.
Tree : belief/culture/balance / Ralph Lemon.
p. cm.
ISBN 0-8195-6699-3 (cloth : alk. paper)
1. Lemon, Ralph—Diaries. 2. Lemon, Ralph—Asia—Description and
travel. 3. Choreographers—United States—Biography. 4. Tree
(Choreographic work : Lemon) I. Title.
GV1785.L385A32 2004
792.8'42—dc22   2003022479

Tree was co-produced by Yale Repertory Theatre and Cross Performance, Inc. It was commissioned by Yale Repertory Theatre and premiered in New Haven, Connecticut. Commissioning support was provided by San Francisco Performances and Yerba Buena Center for the Arts and the University of Texas, Austin.

Tree was funded, in part, by The Rockefeller Foundation, the National Endowment for the Arts, Asian Cultural Council, Arts International's Inroads Program, Africa Exchange program of 651 ARTS and the National Theatre Artist Residency Program administered by Theatre Communications Group, the national organization for the American theater, and funded by The Pew Charitable Trusts. Tree was also made possible through the Doris Duke Fund for Dance of the National Dance Project, a program administered by the New England Foundation for the Arts, with lead funding from the National Endowment for the Arts and the Andrew W. Mellon Foundation. The ninety-minute performance directed and choreographed by Ralph Lemon featured a cast of 12 performers from Côte d'Ivoire, China, India, Japan, Taiwan and the U.S. It premiered in April 2000 at Yale Repertory Theatre, New Haven, CT and toured to the Walker Art Center, Minneapolis, MN; University of Texas, Austin; Krannert Center for the Performing Arts, Urbana, IL; Yerba Buena Center for the Arts & San Francisco Performances, CA; and the Brooklyn Academy of Music, New York. The tour of Tree was sponsored by Philip Morris Companies Inc.

[In the writing of this book I have referred to these sources: Famous Minnesota Winter Storms/Minnesota Climatology Working Group/2003. Storms/Nathan Fisher/2003. National Climatic Data Center. Zen Keys/Thich Nhat Hahn/Thorsons/HarperCollins. Sadhus/Dole Hartsuiker/Thames and Hudson. Ka/Roberto Calasso/Knopf. Associated Press. The Times of India. Hindu News.]

All drawings and photographs are by Ralph Lemon, with the exception of the eleven black-and-white performance photographs at the back of the book, which are © by T. Charles Erickson and are used with his permission.

TREE

"Narration presupposes the loss of the reality narrated—it makes no sense to tell a story to someone who has witnessed-but when the real has slipped away in space and time—all that is left is a dark room where words ring in the ear." Ka/by Roberto Calasso

December

The morning after Christmas we drove back to New York the same way we came, the most direct route, Victoria, Minnesota, off County Road 11, where her mom and step father live, eastward. Tearing across Minnesota, Wisconsin, Illinois, under a national gray sky. Listening to A Perfect Storm on audio tape and Mary Gordon's first memoir, the two most interesting book tapes at Books in the City, an uptown Minneapolis bookstore. We talked about the movie Jackie Brown which we had seen on Christmas day. Not a very good movie. Or we read a day-old Minneapolis Star and Tribune to each other. Switching off, entertaining, announcing the more unusual blurred moments out the passenger's seat window. First she then me, driving. Or thoughtfully uncapping and passing bottles of water to one another.

"Ice crystals. A snowstorm consists of an almost infinite number of ice crystals. Odd, there must be a constant and profuse inflow of moisture and below freezing temperatures simultaneously. Did you know that 'blizzard' comes from boxing. Meaning, barrage of punches?"

No, I didn't know that.

"A small town newspaper in Esterville, Iowa, coined the term in the 1870s. Minnesota's worse blizzard was recorded in January of 1888. Started out a mild day and then an abrupt cold wave struck with overwhelming snow. The temperature dropped to –37. Children were sent home early from school, many froze on the way."

That was a dumb move.

We talked about the duality of nature, weather, that it is never mundane and always becoming something more or less. With the exception of the dead heat of summer.

"Sammy Sosa held his team record for strikeouts this year, 174. The Cubs signed him to a huge contract during the season, now everyone is wondering if he's worth the money. Give the guy a break, he stayed healthy, played in 162 games and hit 40 home-runs. And all that after missing the last month of the 1996 season with a broken hand."

Geez.

Eight hours later we stopped at a motel outside Gary, Indiana. Starving. Got a room, parked our bags and exited, by foot into the dark strip scenery, disappearing, along the four lane highway to a Ponderosa Steak House. A huge sprawling restaurant with five patrons sitting placidly on their banquettes, at three separate tables nearest the kitchen. We ordered to go from a tall skinny waiter dressed in soiled black and white, a bow tie, greasy hair, who placed us at an empty banquette at a table symmetrically positioned not far from the other tables, who then disappeared, for a long time, as we waited for our food. I don't remember exactly what we got except that the choices were many, most having to do with steak, and each steak, we thought, because it was entertaining to think about it, must have been cooked identically, but each steak had a little red or blue or yellow or green colored plastic marker anyway, a flag indicating how it was ordered. Came with a baked potato and a salad, from a giant salad bar. We didn't get steak. Baked potatoes, yes, two apiece, not sure what else. Maybe grilled chicken and most likely salad.

Back at the motel, in our room she ate with her chopsticks and I ate with a plastic knife and fork. She ate everything with chopsticks, even ice cream, but used my plastic knife to cut through the potato skins.

Where do you think they're from?

"India, I'm certain it's India."

The motel was managed by a very friendly couple from India, Gujurat. Earlier, our television wasn't working and the managers came to fix it, he and she. He would say something in what I could only assume was Gujurati and his wife would respond and then he would proceed by tweaking a cable. The private discussions and tweaking went on for fifteen minutes until they solved the problem. And then it was working.

"Where you headed?" he asked, before leaving our room.

New York, we're from New York.

"Oh, you live there?" she asked.

Yes, we live there. We're headed home. And you, how do you like Gary, Indiana?

"Very good. Very nice. We are fine here, business is OK."

We sat, eating on our beds, wondering aloud how they decided to be there, just outside the unappreciated skyline of Gary, Indiana, of all places, that life decisions aren't that simple, are about not so wide choices and the challenge of free will, especially for people with accents. "Where you headed?" It sounded so midwestern.

I took a shower and then switched channels to a basketball game, Michael Jordan, the Chicago Bulls and another team, I don't remember.

After she finished her shower we made love, inches away from the television screen, because that's where it was, right at the foot of the bed nearest the door, Jordan and Pippen. She doing what she loved to do and what I found so sexy, hanging her head off the side of the bed. We both liked that the basketball game was on.

We got up early the next morning, early for me, early was never early enough for her, demanding caffeine. So we stopped at a Seven-Eleven or maybe a Dairy Farmer and both got watery tea, in Styrofoam cups, tea that tasted like Styrofoam, whatever that is, that taste. For sure the same kind of tea we got at a rest stop on our way to Minnesota, in Sandusky, Ohio, which is halfway between Cleveland and Toledo on Route 80 West, where she was born and lived for three years. She reminded me of this at the rest stop, had told me before but I'd forgotten.

We sped the rest of the way home, now ridiculously fast, Indiana, Ohio, the landscape indicating few idiosyncracies until Pennsylvania, ordained quirky and graceful because otherwise the drive would create hallucinations, dangerous, almost as dangerous as driving through the entire prosaic landscape of Texas, which has no panoramic remorse.

Switching off, speeding. Eating turkey jerky and baby carrots. I drove during the bright winter sunset and could barely see in front of me, sunglasses no sunglasses, and wearied of moving so fast and then moving and barely seeing. Always when we got close to where we were going we'd get crabby, suddenly and bitch at each other, losing our appreciation for the odd even parity arrangement of our car architecture. Reading to each other, listening, was no longer interesting, tolerable. She drove into

Manhattan and would honk the horn frequently and I'd tell her to chill out and then she'd get even more irritable. Not this time but once on our way back to Manhattan we crossed the George Washington Bridge by mistake, into New Jersey and got stopped by the police for trying to make a right-hand turn from the left lane to rectify the mistake. All the while I'm cautioning her under my breath not to appear as unhinged as she seemed, to the New Jersey policeman, not to say things like, "No, I don't know where we're coming from, officer, can't you see we're fucking lost!"

We filled up the tank on Houston and Broadway. By now I was speechless. Definitely better not to try and express what I was feeling, loathing everything in sight, especially the excessively lit Amoco gas station/car wash/parking lot in Soho at 11 p.m. on Saturday night, an orgy of taxis, a suspicious island bombarded with stalled yellow cars and brown men, the drivers, this fluorescence, surrounded by all sorts of tourists, swaying as they walked along in many directions.

We dropped off luggage at our East Village apt. And then drove up to Budget at east 43rd St. and dropped off the car. Walked a bit down Lexington Avenue in complete silence. Took the subway home in silence, sitting, holding hands. I stared straight ahead at an ad in Spanish, a college correspondence course, and thought to myself how almost impossible it is to calculate the derivative of distance with respect to time on a subway late at night, speed. Once inside our tiny fourth floor apartment we could talk again, it was always like that, that and retrieving our cat from the neighbors.

L left her favorite nightgown behind in the motel room, probably the bathroom, was so upset. It was heavy German linen, second hand. She'd bought it in France many years ago. She'd wear it to bed every night, where she had a distinct life, reading, thinking, whatever, but would remove it right before she fell asleep, that was the sequence. We called the motel the next day and the friendly Indian couple reported, "We are so sorry but it seems to have disappeared."

What is love?

Huh?

What is love, to you?

I'm sorry, I was thinking about something else. Wondering how much we can really know of ourselves, and how far away that unprovable measurement is from knowing someone else.

You think too much, honey.

Yes, a lot about who I am, would like to be, am not.
Certainly it informs my work. I know I've told you this already, many times.
Talking about one's self is not one's self, it's talking about one's self. Talking is talking. If you were to follow me around 24 hours a day, riding my shoulder, all of my life, you would know a lot more about me, perhaps. But of course that's impossible.

Now you're talking too much. Not listening, dear.

My body functions essentially, moves out of the way when it needs to. My spirit? Ah, there is the profound secret. Made more complicated by how I was brought up to see God, as it cannot be seen. After spirit, which came first the body or mind? Of course they grew together. Mind-heart.
Thinking, wondering, imagining is a diversion I found early, one that gave me peace, play. As an artist that play is all. And it's supported, sort of.
And so the real stuff becomes questionable. Creating is never unreal to me. Love, compassion, selflessness, devotion, intimacy, honesty towards someone I love, sometimes is.
So when you ask, "Who am I?" it becomes another contest. I've learned out of necessity to create peace and play every day of my life.
Now, this moment? I'm considering the ramifications of equipoise. An assumption of quiet. To be where I am. Just that. All of it. Fluid and clear, in all the complexity. Where I imagine these questions simply don't come up, or if they do it doesn't really matter to my life. And to the life of those around me. Amusing, right?

That was not my question, "Who are you?"

January 10 1998

Dear Mr James Lo

I'm a great admirer of your work. Missed your most recent work with John Jasperse but did see and loved your work with Donna Uchizono at DTW not so long ago, the one with the cement mixer and pile of shoes. I have a solo residency at the Miller Theater in March and wondered if you'd like to join me to workshop some ideas in an empty theater? I will have just returned from traveling abroad. I'm sure my head will be spinning. Should be an entertaining time.

Let me know if you're interested and I'll go over the details.

R

January 12

Dear Ralph

I think you're confusing me with someone else. I didn't do sound on that particular Donna show, the one with the cement mixer.

JL

I left for India, in search of L's nightgown. A metaphor.

February 1998
Hours of Water. There is a man sitting in front of me, he is an old black man, and I imagine, no, construct him as someone who looks like he is from America but who also looks like he has spent many years in Europe. He wears a brown pin-striped suit, from the forties and a dusty gray beret. A wedding ring on his left hand. He is alone. Intently reading the folded airline menu for a long time. Patches of thin hair traipse out from under his beret like a newborn. He disembarks at the Schiphol Airport in Amsterdam, a perfect destination, I think.
For the next ten hours I completely forget about him. I've brought along quite a few books.

North
Arrive late to a surprising calm, murky. Stand in a prepaid taxi line and then exit the airport to a dark taxi pool full of thin blanketed covered drivers. One picks me.

Cars shake and rattle drive on the left side of the road. Very fast. I could not yet see the logic, that headlights directed the architecture of lanes.

The hotel is a YMCA with the yellow indoor light of modern rooms I had rented in West Africa but less apologetic.
I have lost two days. Sleep is even more puzzling.
In the morning I walk out of the YMCA and into the taxi of a driver who just happens to be there, regularly, who wants to be "my friend" and transport me to his merchant friends so that he can get a commission on things such as travel plans and emporium goods. "It is too early for me to shop," I tell him.
So he guides me through heavy traffic to the city's basic spectacles: Red Fort, Gandhi Memorial, Parliament. The best is the "sick temple" where those in pain in the middle of the city can go, which is not on any tourist map. This stop was not really for me, my driver wanted to do puja. So far India is horizontal.

Day 1
Delhi. Ceremonies happen quickly and disappear. Chants are abrupt or they go on and on. Groups seem to be connecting in song ritual and then they break away. And there is traffic.

Day 2
The Nepalese taxi driver gets a commission. I hire a car. It is spelled, "R-a-j-e-s-h" but I will call you Raj. My driver, beyond Delhi. Will you be my vehicle to some Vedic forest I've heard of, for two hundred US dollars? A forest where I'm quite sure some queer fig tree wears my lover's nightgown. Stolen. Veda undressed. Unknowledge. Dangerous, yes, of course. You must keep me safe, that's why I'm paying you. I don't want to die in this short time. Neither do I want to muddy my shoes or step in any shit. Do you understand?

On the road.

The first sign that I see. "Little Paradise Bowling Centre Fun For The Whole Family." I think of Indiana.

Then we are stopped by the police. Haryana. Checking for something. There is no whiskey allowed here.

2. "Caution—Accident Prone Area."

Women on scooters sitting side saddle.

Agra. We pick up Bobby, Rajesh's friend, a student and part time guide who also "has a big property." He owns a tennis shoe factory. Who whisks me away and guides me through the many breathtaking monuments of Agra, capital of the Mughals. "The Taj Mahal was accidently dropped to earth by heaven, and has yet to be reclaimed."

Bobby and Raj take me to a restaurant for lunch and I ask if they will be joining me. They decline saying that they would rather eat some "Indian food in the back." I wondered what I would be eating in the "front." They join me later, sit and watch me finish my beer.

We say goodbye to Bobby.

Day 3

Black smoke fills the air, roads of India like.......

Roadblocks due to the elections. No water for fields so a disruption of public services. So we took another route and again a roadblock. This time due to a dead boy lying in the middle of the road, with most of his head missing. The lorry that he ran into, on his scooter, head on, was later used to block the road because the family of the boy had not yet removed his body from the road. (There were actually three boys riding on the scooter. The two survivors sat in the road next to their friend's body, crying, huddled, neither of them were hurt, they had been thrown off to the sides of the road on impact.) The driver of the truck was handcuffed and taken away.

We took another route, right through someone's planted field.

3. "New Japanese Machines."

Three more very violent-looking after the moment accidents.

We ourselves have two very close near missed collisions. I sit in the front seat of a van with no front hood, barely metal and no seat belts. Raj asks me why I look so worried.

Fear. The driving I've encountered in the short time I've been here is either reckless or unafraid of death or naive or resigned to karma or these drivers simply don't care or it is better to move through the streets and roads as quickly as possible, not stopping at danger but speeding straight towards it.

I sit sweating and curiously don't ask questions about Brahma, Shiva, Vishnu, Ganesh, elephant, son of Shiva, god of benevolence, a power different to that of compassion. Religion for Raj, who is Hindu, is not a moral relationship. It is fundamental and pedestrian. Every time we pass an accident he prays to Shiva who happens to sit garlanded on his dashboard, a place I am not allowed to prop my feet.

It is Sunday when we arrive in Jaipur. I ask Raj to take me to a temple, assuming that he would join me. He did not and leaves me at the front gate of a very cold white marble sanctuary. I want to hear chanting, to sit. I ask if perhaps there were not a service later. He tells me that there is no Hindu service on Sunday.

Day 4

This time there is a dead camel on the road, giant entrails exposed, like black hoses displayed in an outdoor American super mart.

And a beautiful leopard cat limping onto the road, stopping right in the middle.

Pink City. Jaipur. At Amber Fort there is no traffic. I ride an elephant. A city palace garden. At dinner Raj's friend, Raj has friends everywhere we go, another driver, says that he had been driving for four years and had seen approximately one hundred dead bodies on the road. And whenever he sees an accident, for fifteen minutes, he thinks that he has chosen "a very terrible life" but then he gets past that and thinks of all the nice people he gets to meet. He says that if I spoke Hindi he would assume that I was Indian. At the moment his clients are Japanese. He and Rajesh complain about the Japanese, that it is hard communicating with them. I meet them, two students. They seem happy to be able to try to speak English with someone who is not confused with the language. We talk about Irabu, they say that he was better when he played baseball in Japan. They explain to me why the Japanese are so good at throwing and hitting baseballs, and then not, that they practice too much.

Today the Meherangarh Fort, overlooking the blue city, Jodhpur. Painted blue so that the Brahmins were Brahmins and no one else was because their house was not, could not be blue.

Another version: Actually, the blue wash serves only to protect against termites, and other insects.

At the Fort, I watch Rajastan musicians playing wild desert soul music.

While Raj explains the inevitable jauhar (collective suicide). Men fighting to the death and their women throwing themselves onto the funeral pyres.

Day 5

Jaisalmer, "the golden city," another fort, inhabited by tourist and old families. The largest number of white tourists I see to date. I run into Bill and Mary Buchen from NYC. Their ninth trip to India. Bill played tablas for my first dance classes in Minneapolis. Bill has had malaria and swears he doesn't have it anymore. Mary argues that that is impossible.

We meet again the next day at a desert festival. An outdoor folk show. The gypsy connection. Mideast here also, a delicacy apart from Africa, more vertical. Here is more mixed up. These Âryans were Persian not German. I knew the German swastika before I knew the Indian Satya—"Insistence on truth."

Watching a camel race I ponder a moral question of truth and beauty: That man has an inherent knowledge—desire for platonic beauty, truth, morality. What?

An artist in Jaipur, very brown, who does yoga exercises every morning for his eyes, says that "artists prefer painting the flesh of men and women white because it is preferable for paint and light."

Here I am almost bored with the Mughal storytelling. Here forty five is old. Most I meet are teenagers.

There is the space of the desert. I stop counting the days.

Raj is nowhere in sight. I shit in sand. Glorious the covering of sand on top of shit, a magic spectacle to the audience of flies. I could not stop. A small boy waited.

Me and a little brown boy like I was, in another country, riding a single camel inside of nothing but white dunes, sun, he singing songs in his desert language, me singing the Temptations. In perfect English he says, "Oh, I like that music very much, very much."

When a camel runs it trys to break the rider's pelvic crest.

We ride through the early night, a star blue black. To Mathaar's house. Branches. His wife crouched and busy. Keeping the fire alive. Making chapatis and then tea. The men and boys are quiet, more quiet than wind. Eat and drink and then smoke a rolled-up leaf. Whispering about the day. Camels sing all night. A bell. Featureless faces although the moon creates an unfamiliar glow and gives a different surface to who was who before. In the morning they all play a game with their goats, all of them. In the morning his father has—a red hennaed beard. I wonder where they all slept the night before. With me in the sand? Mr. Mathaar, his wife, son, nephew, father. The little boy had disappeared, belonged to someone else.

Smoking bidis, we talk.

"In your country you have stone?"

Yes

"Desert?"

Yes

"You have houses? Made of stone?"

Yes, and wood.

I sleep in the desert under a full moon, eternal, camels farting, bellowing with a single goat bell. Sitting under branches thickly woven, I eat, no light but what comes from the cooking fire and the moon. Watch washing dishes with sand. I woke up twenty times, the moon continuing to look at me from its ever curving perspective.

In the desert I saw sunset, sunrise and a moon that would not let me sleep.

Weeks pass.

Rajesh finds me. Not sure how long I've been waiting, smoking, slightly sheltered inside the skeletal concrete beginnings to a new home, right off the road, outside the desert. I imagine I look pretty dirty. I also imagine an air of gratification. He looks me up and down, shakes his head and asks if I would like to have a girl tonight. If he should find me a girl. We drive and watch them walk the roads, faces covered, heads piled high. He tells me to take my pick. I don't believe him. I tell him that I am married. I am not. I show him a photograph of my daughter.

Now only old women, Jains, walking walking walking mouths covered not from the swirling dust and exhaust fumes but to protect the insects (from flying into their mouths) walking walking walking wearing white to the Karni Mata Temple to let themselves be covered by rats fed by fevered other priests and then walking walking walking home again.
Nothing as dark and as inscrutable as the Karni Mata Temple at 7am
But I am confused. Aren't they actually walking to a basti, their own temple and not a Hindu temple? "No it doesn't matter, in India every belief system came from the same system a long time ago and so it is always really all the same."

Rajesh talks incessantly. I understand every 13th word.
Side through.
What city is this?
"Mandawa. Do you know Mandawa?"
No.
Jhunjhunu. Khatri Mahal and Bihariji Temple.
I see my first Sādhus in their natural conclusion of temporal life in Jhunjhunu at the Bihariji Temple. One young man one older man. Long hair beards fine faces featured unbothered mouths refined softly dirty more dusty. Dull but still orange saffron and white cloth that stayed white after all the dirt. Sacred Filth. Sitting in mud and shit "head in the golden heavens"—or in delirium. Begging like children with requisite bowls. Just sitting on the ground crouching squatted oh oh oh the immaculate fold. Outside the temple not inside making noise and praying like all the other people just sitting outside and looking with quick keen eyes and begging. But just outside the door of the temple and not far away.
One walks up to us and puts his bowl through our window and says something in Hindi. I do not give him money. I will not give him money.

And returned to Delhi. Valentines Day.
I call L. It is raining, how odd. An old woman walking in the gorgeous gray of wet earth and cement, a back alley. So far India has never looked more beautiful, just like a popular rainy New York City day. She is singing and crazed. Her eyes see me and then spirits, mostly in the trees that cover her. She wears a blanket and keeps rhythm with a cane. No, she is not wearing a nightgown under the blanket, I tell L.

It is Sunday and all the Hindu temples are locked. I say goodbye to Raj. Pay him less than his most recent favorite client. It is enough. I also give him my favorite shirt. I think of religion. The Vedas. Raj would touch various parts of his torso and lips whenever we saw some mangled mass of car metal abandoned on the road. The human bodies had already gone to heaven. 177 people die in traffic accidents every day in India. That makes 64,604 people a year.

"Where are you from?"

New York.

"Oh, I hear New York is very nice. Do I have nice eyes, could I be a movie star there? Once I had an opportunity to come to America. A marriage arrangement with a wealthy Indian family there. But the girl was very fat so I didn't go. Now I regret it."

Yes, but being in love is important.

"Yes, but so is eating."

There is a hawk landed lost in the old city in a narrow street. Small boys jump for joy but are more intrigued than curious, afraid to give it its unnatural space, the alley. Hearing the commotion an old man walks right up to it and the hawk large now cowers. The old man puts one foot on its right wing and grabs the other wing with his left hand, specific and then spreads both wings wide, lifts it up to his waist height and carries it off. As though he has done this act many times before. Small boys running, following, practicing.

When I arrive in Varanasi there is no traffic only bikes motorized or naturally pedaled. "It is election day so no one will die on the roads today because everyone loves to vote."

I take a bus from the airport that stops three times on the way to the Central Station where I find a rickshaw bike that doesn't want to take me all the way to my hotel so he stops three kilometers away and I hire a boat to row me down the Gaṅgā and pass the city's many ghats to my ghat and hotel.

"It takes three hours for a body to burn to ashes. A man's sternum will not burn and is thrown into the Gaṅgā. A woman's pelvic bone will not burn and is thrown into the Gaṅgā. They burn bodies twenty–four hours a day seven days a week." I pay someone to tell me this. At the main ghat, Manikarnika, one night they burned twelve bodies at once. This I see with my own eyes. "On the average they burn 29,000 bodies a year at this ghat. It cost 6000 rupees or one hundred and fifty-seven dollars a body so only the rich dead are burned here."

A lizard scales the outside of my window as I watch a body burning, head exposed. The face eventually fries, turns a true shiny black for only a moment and quickly exposes a brief white skull that too disappears. Human flesh, burning inside massive pieces of wood, smells like fleeting barbecued meat. The stillness of a burning body. The power of fire.

On the steps of the Gaṅgā

A young German man quite dirty keeps his travel guide neatly wrapped in a plastic baggie.

I drink nothing but the water and sugar of chai and seven-up and orange soda.

There are dolphins in the Gaṅgā but I have never seen them.

Even the boats come here to die, transform.

But Sarnath. A remarkably peaceful hamlet near Varanasi. Dharmachakra Temple, the original name or Dharmekh Stupa. Sight of the first sermon given by the Buddha in

Deer Park. There are deer here and a zoo. King Ashoka made Buddhism relevant. Mauryan period—200 BC. Sarnath is a perfect metaphor for how Buddhism differs from Hinduism. The quiet and peaceful air of this hamlet compared to the wild unstoppable passion, physical, musical, shouting of Varanasi, the Hindu holy spot. In Sarnath most of the Buddhists I meet are Tibetans and Bhutanese, a handful of Indians, as far as my naive eyes can discern.

"It is the Tibetan's karma to be forced out of Tibet for keeping their dharma all to themselves sequestered up in the Himālaya. Because their dharma is so beautiful and therefore for everybody." The Indian government has provided the Dalai Lama with a large tract of Indian land, land which it desperately needs for some of its billion poor people. Buddha has become part of the Hindu Veda. That is love.

February 20. At the train station. But thinking back to a traffic jam that was so tangled and stuck, like a metropolis metal maze, with wheels, which occasionally would shift to a new impenetrable puzzle design. My driver kept saying we were only two kilometers away. Not true. And then, finally, a breakthrough, due to his use of horn, dexterous driving and car free space off the actual road, space were there was just as complex a puzzle of pedestrians. No one was hurt. I was overjoyed.

The train arrives and brings a different puzzle. Trying to find my car I am sent one way and then another, watching the minutes continue to tick away towards 10:10, the time of departure. The train bolted forward an inch, paused, directionless, I found my car, lucky. I found my seat, #23. At first no one comes to check my ticket so I don't really know that I am in the right place.

I sit across from a small boy, blue black, alive with travel, looking out the window, fighting sleep, traveling alone, eating fruit apples that were dirty with his dirty hands and frosted candy out of a white plastic bag, which also carried the rest of his belongings.

Last night I finished The God Of Small Things and dreamt of making love to a dark skinned woman, a stranger, holding a gray flower the whole time.

Bodhgaya, February 1998.

Dorji, a monk, invites me to stay at the Bhutan Monastery. I decline, in need of an expensive hotel, hot water.

"Here, come join our prostrations."
No thank you, I would rather watch.
"Yes, I think that is a good idea."
What number are you on?
"Only nine thousand. I have ninety one thousand left."
Oh, so you are just a baby monk.
"Yes."
And you, what number are you on? The other one, sitting listening, smiling.
"I have not begun, I am still in the womb."

And then back to the first one.

"One must take it easy or you can kill yourself. There are some here who do four thousand a day. They're at break at the moment, eating something. Are you a Buddhist? Do you know the 'string'?

No, not really. Maybe I'm a small Buddhist, I only know a little dharma. I like the parts about "nothingness."

"Oh, that is good. Little but deep misunderstood dharma is the best."

Best, because you don't have to do prostrations, I think to myself.

4. 'Welcome to Sujata Restaurant good for test good for helth cost much less'
5. 'Middle Way Travel'

At night. The queer fig tree. No, it's not here either: I visit the Mahabodhi Temple, twice. The second time, while I sat meditating under the "Bo" tree, someone stole my boots which I had left at the front gate. They were new boots bought specifically for this journey. I had admired those boots every day of my trip. It occurs to me that I could not have had them confiscated at a better time and place.

Dorji comes to visit, after I've walked back to my room, shoeless, dodging Tibetan women in carts flown by decorated horses. Feeling rather liberated I tell him the story and he cautions that "Indian people are very bad." He stares at all of my other various possessions, intrigued.

Two new friends. Dorji, has been a monk for twenty one years. Himalaya is a shopkeeper, he is 21, Indian. Dorji doesn't do very much during the day, stands around a lot, rides his bike, eats very little, rests.

Do you meditate?

"Before, yes, not now."

I took him out to dinner and he ate like he was starving, like me.

I had started the day meditating under my mosquito net. Then I went to visit Himalaya at his junk store. Sitting and talking, picking out old stones for a long time. I eventually bought some very old relics "found" at the site of the Mahabodhi Temple. Himalaya: "Mahabodhi was my playground when I was a boy, my father's house was right next door, here." He draws a map in the dirt with a stick. "Until the government relocated us. I was very lucky."

Then he took me on a journey, first to what seemed a deserted ancient Hindu temple and estate, as quiet as anything Buddhist. Shahkarachary Math. Then a walk across the dry river bed of Falgu, a beautiful country landscape, delicate and soft. Himalaya tells me that there are three possible places where the Buddha could have received the scriptured hand full of milk. Dungeshwari and Suraya temples are two of them.

At night I sit at Mahabodhi Temple again, listening to various male and female chanting tones, from different Buddhist schools, wearing different colored robes, all with shorn hair. I am very glad that I came here.

Gaya, the train station. I hop onto the closest car and a conductor brusquely waves me off, his hands signaling that my car is "farther down there."

Where? He wouldn't be specific. I run hauling the ever growing weight of my bags, shifting them as pointers, when it is possible.

This one?

"No, farther."

This one?

"No, farther."

Finally, he disappears inside the train and I continue to look for a car that hides within a transit system I will never know. By this time all the doors of the train are closing, closed, locked. The train starts to move, slowly, keeps moving. Suddenly a man behind me runs up and begins banging on the door of the car nearest me. Someone I couldn't acknowledge, opens the door, I throw my bags in and hop on. Once on, pushing through a mass of standing bodies, I hold my ticket aloft, my identity, grunting for assistance. A young man comes forward, a passenger, out of the heaving human crowd, confronts me, unsmiling, nods and I follow him as he leads me through three more narrow cars full of bodies in every conceivable traveling, waiting position, soiled heat and no light. In the fourth car there are bunks, he hands my ticket back to me, smiles, quickly turns and walks away. I put my bags on what seems like the only space left on the train, climb onto my bunk and curl into a fossil rock. Crying in my sleep.

West Bengal is lush and beautiful.

Calcutta is more ordered than I imagined. Great 19th century architecture obliterated by smog and blaring auto horns, people crumpled underneath. I wanted to splurge and find lodging that had maid service and CNN. Not to be. No rooms available.

A room at Central Guest House. Another small dark room with bad plumbing and sheets that look soiled but are clean.

The next day I wake to my body flushing black water.

Days pass. I cannot leave my room, don't want to and none of the people I came to Calcutta to contact are reachable, most of the phone numbers that I have are wrong numbers. I leave messages, my phone number and whereabouts, wherever I get an answering machine.

On my last day, three hours before I am scheduled to leave for the airport, one of my contacts shows up at my door, Swapan Kumar Bhattacharya. Swapan is the director of the Indian Council of Cultural Relations. He walks into my room and immediately apologizes for a large bandage that wraps his right big toe, harnessd ingeniously within his sandals. He suggests that we visit a friend of his in the city, in between a trip to the airport, in the short time that I have left.

I feel better, barely. Both of us moving slowly, sharing the weight of my luggage, he takes me to meet Ananda Shankar, son of the celebrated Indian dancer Uday Shankar, nephew of Ravi Shankar. I watch his company perform Indian modern dance in between trips to the toilet. "This is not traditional Indian dance even though there are references. This is modern, from the tradition of my father."

Modern. In Rajastan I saw a boy of nine or ten years who danced something I assumed was traditional that incorporated every bone in his body and it seemed his only objective, besides making a few rupees from tourists, was to never repeat a move that came before. A perfectly modern human science. He also danced bored and couldn't wait to finish his "song" so that he could run away and play. Later Raj described the boy's dancing as a mix of traditional styles and disco. Newly common.

As we leave and say good-bye, Ananda hands me a card, "He is a yoga teacher in Beverly Hills, California, a teacher to the stars. Since you are going back to America, you never know."
Thank you, Ananda. It was a pleasure to see your work. And yeah, you never know, the next time I'm in LA maybe I'll check out this guy.
Swapan asks if I would walk him to where he can catch a train back to his home, "Also a good place for you to catch a taxi to the airport."
Yes, of course. It was very thoughtful of you to come by today, Swapan, especially with your injury. Thank you very much.
He nods and helps me carry my out-distanced belongings to his train stop.

I am more than ready to be home. A thirty hour flight. With nothing to read, have finished all my books, then given them away.

There is a ragged man in a men's room of the Schiphol Airport in Amsterdam. I imagine he is Eurasian (someone who dresses European but whose eyes, lips and movements could belong elsewhere). He stands in front of a mirror refining his disheveled hat, crumpled blue shirt, jacket, hair underneath hat. Smiles, zips up his bag, which rides on wheels and walks away. I see him in another men's room two hours later repeating the exact calculations to his image, being. Zips up his bag and walks away. When I arrive home I want to be married.

March 7

Dear Ralph Lemon

At first you take my heartest love. Then I want to know how do you do? I am well here. I think you are same.You gave me shirt and tea shirt. When I use it I remember you very much. Then I think left India and stay in your country. I always handle many tourist in my life but I never have your type many. So I think you are my best friend. I wait to welcome India for you and your family. Thinking yours. Best friend. Rajesh.

Dear Ralph,

I'm very glad to have received your letter. Thanks a lot for your kind motivation. Hope, enjoyed the tour you did in India. It is really not untolerable movement we shade together, so it always remains in my folly mind.

However it is nature that every things in this external world it gradually meets and parts itself with-out any difficulties. In brief, I'm really not annoyed to come across a person like you. You did mention for my goodness, but I'm really sorry I couldn't help you much while your stay in Bodhgaya. As we have lots of time to come across so we await to true and meet again and hustle together. To remember everlasting each other please send one of your photos to me. For I'm sending mine to you in this letter.

I hope this year I can go home to Bhutan. If I can I will write you. However write me clearly about your coming to Bhutan. So then we can make fix time. Hope to hear from you soon.

Thanks!   Yours Faithfully
20th March 98'   Dorji Wangdi

When I arrived home L had vanished, just like her nightgown.

Two months before, I didn't know anything was wrong, neither did she, really, I mean, the nightgown was unfortunate but, the whole month, we couldn't tell. Our holiday was over, we were busy again. And January can be so apparitional. I know she's still upset about it.

So, dragging my feet, head hanging, I walked all the way uptown, alone, to a friend's theater, needing someplace to think, Columbia College's Miller Theater, for a two week workshop. Me and James Lo. I stood still on stage, for hours at a time, like Dorji in Bodgaya, or threw rocks at my feet and quoted from Rajesh into a microphone, while James provided sonic dramaturgy in an empty theater and then in front of an audience. Workshop 1. It was all rather baleful, I think.

A month later I wanted to return to India, in search of Rajesh and Dorji, to apologize for despising, loving and then co-opting their stories, theirs and others. Hello, remember me? I'm Ralph and although I'm an American, and better yet, even though our skin color is somewhat analogous, I don't think I belong here. But here I am anyway. And I really love this place. I promise.

And since I'm here why not continue, Indonesia, China and Japan, for more complicated cultural discomfiture. I'll create an art map, where I get to dance my fraught humanness.

And, like my father always says, "A job deceptively begun is half started."

My father is a Jehovah's Witness, a religion straight out of America. But he becomes the Buddha whenever I need him to be. My father saw a part of Asia as an American soldier, a black American soldier. A long time ago, when he would bring home Korean street painted portraits of himself, wearing an American military uniform, smiling, with the eyes and lips of an Asian, Negro, that compilation. At that time one could see the resemblance, not now.

Now, like Siddhārtha, he who has reached the goal, he is cared about by others and can afford to forget the styles of shoes, shirts, adrenaline, clothing and weight. And there are enough televisions to go around in his house, where he can watch as many ball games as his memory will permit. True American Dhyan, Chan, Zen. To each a practice.

Date: Sat, Apr 4, 1998 5:57 PM EDT
From: Katherine
Subj: Re: saturday
To: Ralph

Hey ralph. I'm sorry I went so blatantly incommunicado last week – that was not my intent. i just ran out of the miller theater to catch the last train back to new haven, and then found myself in a whirlwind of activity... i had meant to write you and email the very next day, but kept putting it off because of not-enough-time-to-do-it-right.

I was inspired and engaged by all the physical rituals you came up with for that concert/showing. The ones I remember the most powerfully are the rocks dropped towards the feet (intense, and great resonance with Geo I, of course), the holding the mic up in the air and mouthing words away from it (and later without the mic, hands becoming a prayer position), and a certain very ritualistic section of dance, with repeated movements, bowing the head and more – did it accumulate, or did it just repeat? The water being poured over your feet was great too, though I wanted it to spin off into something more, or happen again later... And that whole section of floorwork, variations on sitting and lying – I don't know if you consider that a ritual or not, but I found it mesmerizing.

My only hesitancies would be about the text. You warned it would be a little too much like a travelogue, and I agree. The way I saw it, you used the India travel experience to let the scales drop from your eyes, and see things fresh, but India in all its own self-knowledge couldn't get a voice in the piece. Which would be a difficult (impossible?) thing to do after an intense but short visit. But there has to be a way, ultimately, to allow elements that aren't entirely mediated by your point of view into the piece, like there was in Geo I. In the end the whole piece is framed by you, but there have to be more elements that give up that power, however provisionally.

I know that you're trying to acknowledge and even embrace the extent to which the piece is about YOUR experience of Asia. I'm trying to think through how you can do that and yet at the same time not make a piece about being a tourist. Maybe the answer is just more time, more time for the narratives to settle, and feel a little deeper than the descriptive "and then this, and then this" of a travel journal. I think the intensity with which one observes even the most everyday things in a strange new place is actually a bit of a red herring.

A few days later I talked about the showing with a friend of mine, an anthropology student at Columbia, who saw it as well. We were talking about the way you set the sacred and the profane in sharp contrast, what with the rituals juxtaposed with stories about shitting in sand and the voracious sexual habits of your guide. She said something I thought was interesting – she said she thought that contrast didn't really portray India as she understood India, because in India the contrast wouldn't be possible, the whole point is that sacred and profane there (or what we Westerners see as sacred and profane) are inextricably blended. So for her the attempt to set up the contrast was the most Western-oriented part of all.

I wonder why all these issues of cultural interpretation came up for me with the text, but not with the movement. Perhaps with the movement it was much clearer to me that you had been inspired by the India experience but weren't attempting to represent it in a definitive way.

In any case, I hope my thoughts are helpful. I'd love to keep talking about it with you, and especially to know how you yourself felt about the showing.

best,
Katherine.

And then, a miracle. I hear from L.

Hello. I'm in Brooklyn.

Oh, how is it there?

It's good. Green, a nice place, for sure.

A real neighborhood and real trees, shit! I'm so jealous. I've imagined you with big high ceiling rooms and windows on all sides, south, east, west. More space than you probably know what to do with. Although one can always use more closets, right? And probably a place outside to park a car? Maybe that'll be the next move, buying a car. Sounds really good.

Yeah, maybe. It is a nice place, don't worry, lots of light.

You know, I've been thinking about your question. The one I never answered. Been thinking about it a lot. A great question, really. Still thinking about it.
Listen, I'll be leaving again soon, a weird pilgrimage, I've discovered this new and marvelous anonymity. Anyway, wanted to know if you'd like to take the cat, actually adopt her? I think it would be better for her. And you're so much more patient.

Yes, of course. Will you write?

Yes, yes of course.

SAOLENE
NALANDA
CAMBODIA
MALAYA
CEYLON
SUMATRA
SRIWIJAYA
PALEMBANG

April 23, 1998

Dear Ralph,

For me, I am interested how will you contact Chinese artists, ordinary Chinese, and Beijing city by your English, your body. I guess it'll first time in China for you, you must have a lot of different question, problem and not knowing what to do, etc. It is just aim of my camera. I like to show the process when you do something, with interview, or with discussing between us. I know you aren't just a ordinary traveler, but be a explorer with your eye and thinking. So I'm interested what have you found, how did you found, what have not found by you.

I'm sorry that I can't express myself very well in my poor English.

If you like Wen Hui and me will be pleased to let you enter different circle of people in Beijing.

If there be possible I will often stay with you, bring my camera when you be Beijing. How long will you plan to stay Beijing?

Best, Wu

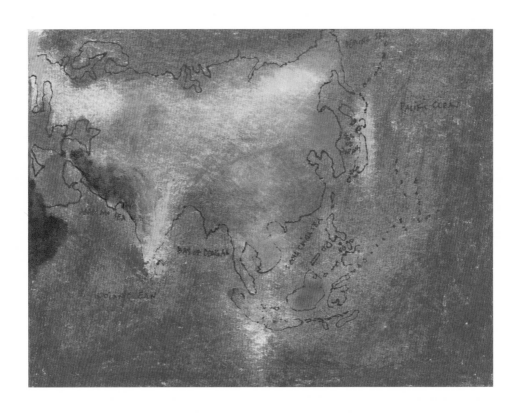

August 1998

I have lost Europe. Only know it now as airports. Feeling quite comfortable with that, where Europe is.

I wait for a free stall. A man opens the door to a closed toilet and as he walks out of the stall we look at each other. I wait until he has completely exited. The door closes behind him. I try to open the door but it is jammed, not locked. I could open it enough to see another body. There is another man behind the door. Partially cleaning up, finishing up. I wait again. Later he exits and we look at each other. The empty stall is immaculate. No semen, no condoms, no shreds of toilet paper.

A monk asks Zen master Chao Chan, "What was Bodhidarma's intention in coming to China?"
Chao Chan replied, "Look at the cypress in the courtyard."

I now travel with a larger piece of luggage. It rides down the conveyor belt towards me broken and slashed, clothes spilling out. Feeling a scream swelling in my throat I force the thought of my stolen boots in Bodhgaya. A signal. I pause. I report the damage to someone in a uniform of white and blue, universal airport colors. He leads me down a series of corridors to a small office. There I perfectly position the bag, to the slash and spillling clothes, to a man with a Swiss accent. He looks at me for a few seconds and not so much at the bag. Then he looks into a manual lying on his desk. Hands me $100 US dollars. The bag cost twice that much. Wu Wenguang thinks this is a good deal, "You can buy a new bag or have the damage repaired."

In the news: "Moderate traffic hums along one of Beijing's city expressways on another rather toxic, heavily polluted day, Thursday. Vehicle exhaust levels in the country's capital have reached dangerous highs as fume-belching cars take to increasingly congested roads. According to preliminary statistics collected by China's state environmental protection administration, Beijing could soon become the world's worst air-polluted city, ahead of São Paolo, Bangkok and Mexico City."

And then it was Tuesday.

Lying in a small bed looking at the ceiling, turning over in no hurry.

The Bamboo Gardens Hotel. Outside my window there is a courtyard but no cypress tree.

Wu Wenguang greets me with his camera turned on. And for the entire Beijing journey he follows me with this extra body part.

Wu Wenguang is a documentary film-maker. Born in 1955, in Yunnan Province. For one week he will guide me through Beijing, introducing me to his friends, videotaping my being lost and silent, unable to speak.

Wen Hui is Wu Wenguang's life long girlfriend, collaborator. Born in 1960, in Yunnan Province. She takes over, leading the way, the few times that Wenguang cannot. Wen Hui is a dance artist and actress.

There is not much of a public for artists in China. The visual artists make their work and have it photographed and or videotaped, pass the images along to their friends and other artists. There are apartment exhibits. Self-contained and self-supported. Even when it is government sanctioned art, the government gives nothing. A dance company pays the government a yearly tax to exist.

I wonder if they call themselves modern artists? "Since 1990," they have been working with performance and installation. Taking it on with a passion, and a particular translated understanding, and no audience, other than each other and that appreciative, curious audience of the West. Where sometimes they go to live. Remain for a while, until they miss home. Some of the younger ones will not leave, setting up a fortress in the outskirts of Beijing, an East Village. But paying for food and life with cash from Paris, Vienna and New York City.

I speak of tradition with Zhang Huan. He is happy that he has his tradition. He has Chairman Mao toys, portraits and busts all over his flat. He showed me photographs of his performances, his work, photographs, otherwise his work would not exist. One photograph pictures him sitting in a filthy Chinese public toilet, his naked body covered with flies, his body smeared with fish oil. A single moment out of the hours he sat there.

Wang Jian Wei is a remarkable painter, trained by Russians, like most of his generation. An enlightened technique that no longer interests him. Now he makes art out of farming. He actually farms, measuring grass. He is more scientist than artist, interested in the complete narrative of experiments.

Today he is in his studio showing me drawings and photographs. Some of his work is plastic. In one work he gave away plastic ears, black and flesh colored ones, in exchange for whatever an audience wanted to barter. He gives me a black ear but I have nothing I want to swap, so, I give it back.

Wu Wenguang smokes and smokes, refuses to let me pay for anything. "The Chinese way." Which? The smoking or the graciousness?

He looks through the eye piece of his camera, sits and listens, translates, invisibly, as I ask all sorts of questions of his friends.

"She has many boyfriends all over the world." Jin Xing is the first publicly advertised transsexual in China. She is a choreographer and has a dance company. Jin Xing's left leg barely supports her. During one of her four operations, an apparatus used to prop her leg in a straddle position slipped down into her calf, burying itself into her skin and muscle, for sixteen hours. Before someone noticed.

If she had had the operation in New York City she could have sued and never walked again. In China it is not possible to sue. But she kept her leg from completely dying by way of Chinese acupuncture treatments. The "modern medicine" doctors at the hospital told her that the leg was dead, useless. She told them, "I don't think so." She was a beautiful dancer before and now moves beautifully, elegantly positioning herself wherever she happens to be. "I am opening up a bar. With music. A lounge. So, that I can sing. I just closed the deal, I walked in with a bag of money. The Chinese way."

Ma Liu Ming has a girl face and a boy body. When he was in college he let his hair grow and his friends told him he looked like a girl. So he made looking like a girl, but being a boy, his project. He is not gay. He has a Spanish girlfriend who now lives in London. Ma Lui Ming is one of the most successful performance artists in China. He has never made any "Chinese money." Along with his performance art, he also makes his living, outside of China, by painting himself as an infant with a grown-up girl face. Ma Liu Ming was arrested while performing with a girl face and a boy body, nude, cooking potatoes. He was arrested in his back yard, "The East Village," where he was performing. He was in jail for two months.

Zhang Huan was also arrested in a famous performance work in China. Hanging from the ceiling in a room, bound in chains, with real doctors administering an IV into his arm, and letting blood drip into a single pan on top of a stacked pile of sparkling white mattresses.

I don't know how long he was in jail. I do know that he was beaten badly in a bar brawl, that was not a performance. But the very young photographer who takes most of the photographs of performance works in Beijing and elsewhere in China, took a photograph of Zhang Huan at the hospital, his head completely bandaged, blood soaked.

The young photographer wants to take a picture of me posing with Ma Liu Ming. He asks me to take off my shirt, because Ma Liu Ming is shirtless. I refuse. He takes a photograph of us sitting, arms around each other's shoulders, in the dark, in Ma Liu Ming's back yard.

Ma Liu Ming, Zhang Huan, and Jin Xing are all physically beautiful and are all deeply interested in their bodies. I do not experience any of that interest as exercises in ceremonial concupiscence, which is how I think of the maleness of my art body much of the time. I cannot translate their sex. As I cannot translate the written Chinese alphabet. How one begins to know.

Lama Temple. At the time I write it is in the Guinness Book of World Records. The world's biggest Buddha.

Beijing Massage Hospital. All are blind. Women, men walking around the complex with footsteps memorized. I am told that I'm the first black man/person ever at the hospital. "Where you from?" A master with breath that smells like death, wearing black sunglasses, asks. The charge is 200 yuan for me 35 yuan for Wu Wenguang. Wu Wenguang argues. I argue that I can't even be seen, recognized as a foreigner. Finally, 100 yuan for me. A great massage.

Dinner with Qing Qing. An installation artist who trained as a traditional Chinese doctor but now likes art better. She works mostly with small installations that incorporate electricity and light, like the energy of Chinese traditional medicine. She still practices acupuncture on her friends. She has a house in Beijing but lives primarily in Vienna.

"In China, rock and roll began in 1985 and died in 1990." Or, maybe how black music never became Chinese.

Why build a wall that defends in the mountains when there are mountains?

Wu Wenguang doesn't understand my question, and therefore can't answer.

The Great Wall. Actually, it is too foggy to see. We walk a few yards of it and take photographs of Chinese, Korean and Japanese tourists falling up and down the steps. Remarkable diagonal bodies. At first Wu Wenguang did not want to come, but once here he became excited. "This is a very special day." Wen Hui didn't come, "Today I do not want to be a tourist."

An Hong is another brilliant Russian trained painter who considers himself another performance artist. He shows me photographs of a work where he's disguised as Krishna sexually impaling his Chinese Radha. He speaks very good English, "Because my father is a teacher who is always suspicious." We talk for hours of the new politics of Chinese art, a freshness of purpose that I find inspiring.

In most cases the artists here are naive to the current Western notions of modern art, as well they should be. They do seem to completely understand the ever-changing rules of the system. There is some genius in this reaction.

Wen Hui is forever putting on makeup. She has little mirrors set up everywhere in her home.

Wu Wenguang is without the element of tiring. The most present person I've ever met. But he immediately falls asleep whenever he's riding in an automobile or taxi.

Tiananmen. 7:20pm flag down. 4:00am flag up. "Even me," says Wenguang, "When I first came to Beijing from Yunnan, I came at 4:00am to see the flag go up."

Chinese tourists wait for hours. Children, food, kneeling, standing. It is 5:30. In two hours it goes down.

The people of Beijing who see me cannot take their eyes off of me. An unapologetic examining. Beyond racial. In New York City this kind of staring would bring a death sentence, or a very bad argument.

I continue to remind Wu Wenguang that in English it is the "Forbidden City." Outside, we stand against a wall of a bridge looking at other tourists.

"Twenty years ago I believed in the Communist Party. Ten years ago I believed in myself. Today I don't know what to believe." Later he says. "Japan face quiet, reserved. Chinese face more nature, animated. Taiwan face like Chinese." They all have umbrellas protecting them from the sun. "Black Americans, they like talking, yes?" This is what he had experienced in New York City. Wu Wenguang will only smoke 'Scarlet Camellia' cigarettes.

I think it was Wen Hui who said, "In school we were told that we must be 'Red Children.' We felt like garbage, to be tossed any which way."

I ask Wen Hui if Wu Wenguang was ever in the army, "No, he was a farmer." And what about you, Wen Hui, what about you? "When I was a young girl I was told that if I even accidentally and slightly brushed against a boy's pants that I would become pregnant. It was a nightmare."

Before leaving Beijing. I taught a workshop for what I would describe as an arts collective. There were two writers, one painter, one theater director, two dancers, one choreographer, one filmmaker, one performance artist, who rode his bicycle twenty miles to attend, and one actress. Jin Xing translated, walking into the space with long flowing black hair and stylish blue dress and heels.

I gave a standard workshop warm-up, something I've done many times before, very boring to me, but it seemed appropriate. The participants seemed to enjoy it, especially the part about the "body disappearing." Then I explored an exercise I recently re-discovered about moving and talking. It seemed appropriate. Before, during and after the workshop there was a lot of talking, uninvited talking, talking that seemed to have very little to do with my suggestions on moving and talking, which had very little to do with their cultural priorities. Necessary and untranslatable. Chinese, they like talking. Yes.

These artists are not starving for information but are energetic about the possibilities that now exist, and that do not exist for them. A vital patience.

Wen Hui took my damaged travel bag to a man sitting on a street corner surrounded by raw pieces of leather, torn shoes, shoe laces, coats and watches. A shoe repairman, for lack of a more sophisticated description. He repaired the damage without elegance and charged her twenty-five cents.

An order that can change rapidly, as boarding gates shift back and forth. Chaos directed. At the airport, a man from England, who stands in a line waiting for a delayed airplane says, "A country of 1.2 billion ignorant people."

I say nothing but think, "No, not ignorance, in the racist choice fashion of the West, but, yes, perhaps a nescience that has more to do with a long tradition of exquisite privacy."

Today I look at the Chinese. The faces are impenetrable to me. I stare and they look back and don't move, eyes hard, direct, not confronting, not looking to understand, but alive. Looking at something that I don't understand, that I can't comprehend. Men, women, children. They do not resent my face, my being here. But somehow I see in their eyes that this is China, a place where I could not possibly be from.

Edmund from Congo. He and I and thirty or so Chinese are traveling to Kunming. Where you from brother? At first he does not answer. A conditioning. I ask again. Where are you from? He begins to talk, softly. He works for Unesco. Has lived in China for eleven years, first as a student. He asks me where I'm from, and I say America. He tells me that in the Chinese language America is, "Mei Guo, Beautiful Country," and that Africa is, "Fei Zou, Continent of Nothing." Edmund seems to accept the tension of living in China. He understands the Chinese way. Going back home, to Congo, is not a translatable option.

(A year later I asked a Chinese court interpreter in America to translate "Fei Zou." "Africa Continent," she answered, "that's the only translation." I asked how someone could have translated it differently. She had no immediate answer.)

When the Buddha came to China he became porcelain.

Two days later Wen Hui meets me in Kunming. Wen Hui and Wu Wenguang are both from Kunming, Yunnan. Wen Hui does not recognize it anymore. When she was a child there were traditional wooden homes and a landscape that you could see, not "one that you can now only imagine." I do see a few traditional wooden homes in several states of eradication.

In Kunming the blind are on the street corners. Wearing white medical coats, set up with little stools. Massaging within crowds of passersby. The massage is better here than in Beijing. "In Kunming it is the best." It cost $1.30 for Wen Hui and $2.50 for me. Afterwards we wobble down the street, muscles and bones falling to the pavement. Later, Wen Hui got car sick.

6:30 am. I wake up and everyone in the city is running around in a giant circle.
The elders practice tai chi in Green Lake Park. And then dance socially, in large groups. In the afternoon, a man from some English speaking country, pacing anxiously in the hotel lobby, assuming I speak English, says to me, "I think there is a problem with all the free time they have here. No one seems to have a job. And when I do see "working," there seem to be twenty people for what could easily be one position."

Tea House. An all day gathering for the elders not dancing. Smoke dense from the wood stove that keeps the tea ready, and sitting, laughing and original music played on a ten year old boom box.

Yuantong Temple. Over one thousand years old. Desecrated during the Cultural Revolution. Now it is buzzing with renovations. Women monks standing guard against anyone with a camera.

Mao Xu Hui. "The most successful painter in Kunming." A beautiful monk man. Living in the most luxurious apartment I have yet seen in China. He has a wife and a daughter. His work is obsessive. Monographic images painted again and again. He spends approximately five years working on an idea. Until it disappears and he is able to see something else. At present he paints Chinese scissors. Are you a formalist, Mao? "I think so, maybe." He lived for a while in Beijing but found it too difficult.

Yunnan Minority Nationalities Protective Zone of Cultures.
Forty-five minutes out of Kunming, in the countryside, is a folk dance music institute. A village set up by the composer Tian Feng. On this day there are nine "minority tribes" represented. Ethnically costumed boys and girls, students, sitting at the feet of master musicians and dancers, all of them also farmers. Many are as brown as me. Stunning darkness. Flesh smells of burned wood.
One teacher beckons me into his room, one he shares with another teacher. And soon there are four old men sitting, playing music, improvising on various handmade

instruments. One, a string instrument in hand, gets up and dances, Wen Hui joins him, knowing the particular skipping steps.

I'm taken with two musicians in particular, their joy. I ask Wen Hui if she would gather names for me, who's who. I hand her my notebook and she paints. Marks, names with no sound, interesting.

I try to buy a tiny reed instrument from one but he says no, that they are too hard to make.

A Chinese tourist, another man visiting, pulls an ocarina like instrument from out of his briefcase. "I made this myself. They played an instrument like this one thousand years ago. But no one knows what kind of music they played." So, he plays a few bars of a Bach concerto instead.

Later there's a public performance. The music is powerfully arcane, breathing within this landscape, these mountains. The dancing is choreographed, for us, staged, outside of the mountains. The young dancers are passionate, they do not know that there is a difference between what they are doing and what they're not, in front of our audience. At the end they feed us and then everyone dances. I know none of the steps and most of the village laughs at my attempt. A girl dancing next to me hugs my arm, and when I say good-bye there are tears in her eyes. The whole village sings as we drive away.

Did I mention a delicate elegantly dressed old woman walking a street in Kunming City? Almost teetering, with a handsome cane supporting her almost non-existent feet. Unusual in the crowds and dirt of this season. Wearing tiny well-built shoes, pointed at the ends, protecting the structure of her feet. She is very old.

I am reminded that I have seen no guns throughout China, not at cross streets, banks, nor airports. No interpretation of the violence that does exist.

Wen Hui returns to Beijing and I continue without guidance.

A landing with no airline traffic control, no tower, pristine when the pilot can see, surrounded by more beautiful mountains. Almost Tibet.
And then a long drive into Lijiang. The air here is stunning, after Beijing and Kunming. Saw an old man walking backwards along the side of the road with his eyes closed, heavy strides.
In a four star hotel. I unpack and then roam in the rain. A traditional Chinese village, welcomed. A village that relates to modernity. Modernity protects it. Good for Chinese tourists, and tourists. The people here are not dark like those in the Kunming countryside. Dressed in folk wear. City Naxis. Almost Tibet.
I meet an American at breakfast. He has been in China for two weeks. He is "fed up from being ripped off," and not understanding the language. Mostly, he is disappointed that China is no longer a culturally exotic place to travel. "It is so industrialized." "And smells like gasoline." "I want to go home." But later he finds the old town of Lijiang and is happy. For a few hours no one rips him off, and it is a pretty place.
In the evening he and I sit through an eternity of amazing music, listening to the old men of the Naxi Music Association. Most are in their eighties. And in between numbers they sit erect, asleep, or pause elsewhere in elder bliss.
Each traditional selection lasts from one to three minutes. A young woman gives an introduction to each piece, each introduction lasting ten minutes. Nine minutes and forty-five seconds of the ten minutes are in Chinese, the final fifteen seconds are in English, announcing the title of what's to come.
We leave after an hour and a half, walk across the street to eat something. Twenty minutes later I see the old men leaving, hobbling carefully in the dark. Tremendous music.

In these mountains, and beyond, they practice Dongba (the sage). A primitive religion of the ethnic Naxi tribe. Dongba is influenced by Shamanism, Taoism and Buddhism. The main activities of Dongba are worshipping, praying, driving out disasters. Dongba is also a practice of witchcraft, medicine, literature, arts and crafts. The Dongba is the important carrier of the culture.

More from the same pamphlet: "Mr. Xuan Ke, a Naxi scholar, says that music and dance originated as rites of exorcism." And that, "Tradition is in danger of being wiped out by the "corrosive" influences of popular culture."

Here modernity is nothing more than active decay. Dongba is also farming and this is completely understood.

Wearing knee high rubber boots a woman stands in a market wading pool, ten feet by six feet, filled with water and neurotically swimming fish, eyes bulging. She occasionally catches one, shows it off, screaming its quality, tosses it back into her ocean. Occasionally she makes a sale.

The Grand Lijiang. Young Chinese businessmen and their mates have breakfast in the dinning room of this four star hotel. Everyone eating with knives and forks.

"Would you like a girl or a boy?"

A man, please.

At 12:00 noon, back in my room, a very pretty and petite boy knocks at my door. Thai, I think. An hour later, after pinching, punching and literally having my body tossed every which way, I announce, "This may not have been the best, but by far it is the most rigorous massage to date." I ask him to come again the next day.

Gone temple walking. I take the wrong road and end up in the middle of a small village. Old men playing a board game. I watch for a while. No one looks back.

Went temple walking. Yufeng Monastery. Baisha. Dabaoji Hall. Dr. Ho. Hired a car this time. Remarkable frescoes in Dabaoji Hall, in Baisha. In Baisha, Dr. Ho, in verbatim, pulled me into his home from the middle of the street. A nice man and a nice garden. Yes, I gave him twenty yuan for a packet of his "healthy tea."

At the Yufeng Monastery I looked at the ten thousand camellias out of bloom. Saw the old man "who risked his life secretly watering them during the Cultural Revolution." Walked down the path behind the camellia garden and then back up the path and then down again. Yes, it was that mysterious and beautiful. Helped by the drizzling light of the sky. Ate walnuts along the way.

Puji Monastery. Driving in what seemed like miles of mud in ancient villages, passing peasants, workers, mostly women, walking along in high rubber boots, carrying twice their weight.

Women carrying bundles of giant grass. Men riding tractor mowers behaving as if they were truck drivers.

Driving, then not being able to go any farther because of mud. Getting out of the car, leaving it in the middle of the road. Walking in mud, following my driver, who really didn't know where he was going, only that "it was up there somewhere." For thirty of the forty-five minute walk I wanted to turn around and go back down into the other mud because I did not believe that there was any place up there and if there was it was only another dilapidated temple ruin, small, dark and lifeless. We continued climbing. Looking through a clearing I saw the colors of brick and concrete, tile. We were at the top. A monk greeted us at a clearing, but made us walk yet around to the front of the temple, through more forest. Ten minutes later, at the front of the temple, the monk was standing there, back to us, urinating.

Then he gave us a tour. "HELLO," only, "HELLO," when he wanted to get my attention. Otherwise he spoke to my driver. At one point he disappeared and another monk took his place, younger, dressed in an old blue double breasted suit jacket, soiled tan pants. He then continued the tour of frescoes, sanded imageless, the renovation work of the People's Liberation Army. A hundred years ago there were many other things to see. He took us to the upstairs, where he and the older monk lived, amidst slanted junk filled rooms, dead wood, and piles of incense ashes. The older monk would occasionally scream "HELLO," from unknown and ever-changing points on the temple grounds. Never saw him again. We said good-bye to the younger monk and I took his photograph. Hands in his pockets, smiling.

We drove back to Lijiang, through same mud, villages and intensely beautiful countryside, with the driver blaring a pirated cassette tape of Black American house music. The most notable was Two Live Crew's, We Want Some Pussy.

Basically, the white people that I meet here, Europeans and Americans, traveling, hate their traveling here, China. "The arrogance and primitive modernity are unbearable." Is threatening.

"They hate us, and they hate you even more."

What?

"We went to see the terra cotta village, they have a museum there, of primitive people, the origins of man, and I expected to see Neanderthals, etc., seeing as how we know these things, humankind's history. What they had there were models of people who look like modern day Africans, with the exception that they were carrying spears and wearing bark diapers." He paused. "And the goddamn spitting!"

The plane is delayed. In the small waiting room there are seventeen groups of card games going on simultaneously.

Hong Kong

"Island of tranquillity, in a very turbulent government." Ex-pats and Chinese in well-tailored suits. At the moment, losing jobs. But still plenty of money and telephones. "When you come to Hong Kong, you must buy a tailored suit, a mandatory protocol." At the bank. The one hundred Hong Kong dollar notes were counted twice, the five hundred dollar notes were counted three times.

Victor Ma and Mandy Yim are my hosts. I met them in Miami, Florida, while they were visiting America, two months before I came to China. I tell Victor and Mandy that I always assumed that Hong Kong was China. They find this assumption curious but not worth debating. Primarily, I've come to Hong Kong to dance with them, to improvise. "But there are many places that we want you to see, especially the Chinese Opera."

We visit the harbor, where the skyline is best showcased.

Hong Kong makes Manhattan seem like a quiet little village.

Victor has a brother who is an architect. "Chinese architecture is built to last maybe fifty years, and then another idea comes along, or not, leaving old badly built structures. But the real problem with modern Chinese architecture is that it is built for a new societal separateness. A movement away from Chinese tradition. There is no communal element to the verticality of modern living structures, no space for children, parents, grandparents and great grandparents. We have borrowed from the West."

Victor and Mandy structure my days around meal times. And there are many names for the variations on noodles and vegetables and meat. "The Malaysians are known for their various drinks."

On many street corners, during this season, they burn colorful money in old pots, flames dancing, and leave food out for the ghosts. Men and women wearing tuxedos, taking a break, a pause from another formal work. "The old people here live with the invisible." But they are not all so old.

Some days later I see an interesting object on the street.

"It is not a good idea to pick that up because it was left for the ghosts." Yes, I understand. It is for someone's ancestors.

"No, not just the ancestors, but for ghosts who will protect that establishment, to keep that shop's business from harm. Just ghosts, ghosts without families, the ghosts of the streets." I put the object back into its charred and hallowed place.

There are many items to buy for the ghosts. Paper watches, eyeglasses, shirts, ties, dresses, shoes, and of course gold and silver painted paper, serving as money. There is everything that the dead could possibly want. And many places to buy these items. Visiting the Wan Temple I bought some gold paper from three men counting a very large stack of real money.

Akira Kurosawa died during the Festival of the Ghosts. In Japan I imagined that they were also celebrating.

Chunking Building. Where all the black people in Hong Kong seem to live. A similar Hong Kong throng, but no Chinese. Cheap rooms and one of the few places to see the police, hovering.

Wong Tai Sin Temple. Buddhism, Taoism, Confucianism. People kneeling, shaking cans full of prayer sticks. "Think of what you would like to have." I kneel and shake my can and think of many things. But decide on one word. "Don't you want to ask for a few more things?" No, it is enough. A stick rises out of the midst of the others and softly floats to the ground.

It was translated as "Lucky." "Everything will be good." "There will be a lot of money and everything will be lucky, with a lot of money." "A lot of good things and money." "Do you want to try another can, and sticks, another prayer?" No, this is enough.

Well Dressed Hong Kong. For a while I live in a district that resembles mid-town Manhattan, as a cartoon. Personal space must be rented.

The City Chain watch shop. Displayed in cases. All watches drastically reduced to "give away prices." Perhaps two hundred bodies crammed in a store maybe two hundred square feet. Choosing and then writing down the numbered code of the watch they want to buy. Then waiting in line. No one just looking. All two hundred bodies, or so, bought a watch. And then the sold watches were replaced.

Wu Wenguang and Wen Hui arrive in Hong Kong. Passing through. A performance here, and then off to New York. It is good to see them.

We all stay at the home of Victor and Mandy. A place outside of the civilization of shopping. A modern concrete shelter situated in a broad green field. I sleep in their dance studio. A little frog, and some rain, joins me in the middle of the night.

We have breakfast. And then Mandy cleans, sweeps, washes clothes, dishes. And then serves tea.

Wen Hui puts on makeup and brushes her beautiful hair. She is from another China, older.

Wu Wenguang smokes. Wenguang "learned how to smoke, and fuck," when he was eighteen, after Mao sent him to work on a farm. He learned these skills from other farmers.

Hong Kong is a great place to shop. Wu Wenguang buys a new camera. His new toy and "first wife." Wen Hui also seems pleased.

What did you think of the Cultural Revolution? Was it a bad thing?

"No. To me Mao was a big man. No, he was a God, is a God. What happened during the Cultural Revolution was a Chinese phenomenon. It cannot be judged outside of China. Yes, people died, and things fell apart. But most people were happy, satisfied. I wrote in my journal, when I was ten years old, that this time, 1966, was "my festival.""

Wu Wenguang and Wen Hui perform. An evening titled, Living Together/Toilet. There is a large piece of transparent plastic that covers the entire stage floor. There is a toilet center stage. Wen Hui and Wu Wenguang eat soup together. Making discriminate choices, Wen Hui places empty plastic shopping bags onto the larger plastic floor. Wenguang picks up the empty bags indiscriminately. Wenguang has a video camera strapped around his waist, projecting whatever arbitrary images it picks up, onto a screen hung on the back center wall of the space. They speak in Putonghua, a Southern Chinese dialect. No one in the audience understands any of it. Later, in their dressing room, they speak of what it is like to live and work together, their sexual experience, "their private narration." Their synopsis doesn't matter. I was fascinated with what I saw and didn't understand.

I help them strike the stage, carefully following their instructions to save all the clearly marked plastic shopping bags that they had brought from the Mainland, tossing the others away.

A few days before in the same space, there was a performance by The Eternal Kids. A theater group from Nagoya, Japan. An intriguing hybrid theater. I was reminded of Imogene Coca, George Burns, Jerry Lewis, and Vaudeville, by way of Japan, in the nineties. Also the Ed Sullivan show starring Robert Wilson and the Wooster Group.

"You must see the Chinese Opera."

There is a restaurant in Yeung Long, near where Victor and Mandy live. Where waitresses wear headset microphones, taking orders and then calling them back into the kitchen, in a space the size of a small American coffee shop. Before this technology they had to scream over the compressed bodied cacophony of the common Hong Kong din.

"We Chinese have a hard life. The only thing we know that we can control is our food, our eating. We cannot care about much else because anything is possible, any change."

And it rains a lot. Today my guide is Wei Mai, flatfooted and beautiful eyes that slant upwards, a friend of Victor and Mandy. Her house sits on a hill top, across from a modern designed structure that stores the ashes of the dead. Victor says, "That is why her rent is so cheap." From her window you also see mostly lush green jutting out from surrounding slopes. Making the light traveling through the window green, golden.

On the way to the Temple of Ten Thousand Buddhas there is a bee farm. A striking older woman. Photographs of her communing with the bees. Wearing a smile and a straw hat. Her son, who does most of the work, wearing a beard of bees, showing off. "It is raining now, so the bees are locked in their boxes. When the sun is out I let them visit the flowers," she explains.

At the Temple of Ten Thousand Buddhas there are two tiger striped cats and five kittens, three of them completely white, frightened by our interest, scampering and then hiding underneath the undusted labyrinthine altar.

Walking down from the temple we intermittently stop so that I can brush away the pilgrimage of mosquitoes that light onto the nape of Wei Mai's neck.

What is the difference between your Asian bodies and my American body?

Here is what the improvisation with Victor and Mandy was like, for me: We gave a performance in a small studio. I exploited my compositional knowledge. Open space. Controlling, my knowledge of improvisation. It was difficult dancing with them, because they dance with different reasons. They are more dramatic, so I barely danced. It was nothing like we had rehearsed, where all three of us seemed to understand that movement is movement, beyond language and culture. "Look at me," I whispered, because she wouldn't and finally did. I jumped on Victor near the end and fell off. Fractured my foot. And spent the final few minutes standing still.

Dr. Yim says that it is dangerous to have acupuncture when one is hungry. So I had breakfast before, breakfast noodles.

Dr. Yim, Mandy's father, places three cups on my lower back, one descending onto my sacrum. He manipulated the suctions left and right. And placed a fourth cup at the bottom of my neck vertebrae. All the cups pulling and shifting to the force of internal and external pressure. Dr. Yim walked away and the cupped points began to burn.

Dr. Yim rides his bike to and from work. Gets up early and jumps rope, one thousand times each morning. His office sits across from a food market. The smell of fish wafts through the single room. He opens at 8:30am and closes at 2:30pm, Tuesday through Sunday. He leaves the office at 2:35pm and returns to his house to prepare herbs, drying and grinding them into little black balls, placing them into little plastic packages. He buys the herbs from mainland China. "The air in Hong Kong is hard on herbs because it is so wet." When Mandy was a young girl her father would take her to the mountains to pick herbs. Now it is illegal to pick herbs in the mountains because it is primarily park reserve land. Monday is his day off.

The Chinese body built China, its "engine." The African body built America, its slavery. And so did the Chinese body, but for a little more reward.

Chinese Opera. Sitting outdoors in aluminum chairs, watching elaborate gesturing and singing in immaculate costumes, at 2:00 in the morning, a humid, flood-lit night, watching with a sprinkle of others, all older viewers who smoke and talk and walk around to talk to others, having already memorized the performance. Backs turned away, drinking, happy, awake on this hot night, entertained. The young performers are undeterred. And sing precisely, sweating.

Victor suggests that he and I go watch the events behind the stage action, where the "real theater is," where the actors live. While Mandy sleeps, sitting in a white plastic chair.

Backstage is simply another open proscenium. The actors, half dressed, half made-up, half eating, half sleeping, washing, kissing, laughing. Theater, the flip side to the precision of an exact hand movement. Tradition. Mortal.

At 4:00am I begin to fall asleep.

What is the geography of flying, being airborne? I think: And feel every second of descent and the painless splintering of all but fluids, disintegration.

I have fallen in love with China.

Wu Wenguang had asked me, "How does one exchange language, music, performance, culture? Perhaps it is important to never know each other." Respecting the impenetrability of another culture.

But I think: I might know the Chinese, that they are a poor people, brilliant, could be "niggers." I have seen nappy hair. And menthol cigarettes are popular. I saw ghettos and inner inner inner cities.

Mandhala.
Man. Ball that bounds, holds.
Dhala. Energy
Mandhala.

Back to the beginning then again.
First. Dhyan. Attention.
And then. Chan. Attention.
Third. Zen. Attention.

South
"My grandfather, I believe, set fire to his Western clothes, as did millions in every hamlet of India, reverting to khadhi, the cotton cloth spun in the seed and toil of the Indian earth. India was rediscovering its beaten-down authenticity. Ordinary men were transformed into gods."
Avanthi Meduri

I stand on a street corner looking for Rajesh, foolishly wondering if he ever drives this far south, if he is still alive. Bangalore. Principal city of Karnataka.

Immediately, as though I had never left, little girls pawing my pant legs, pleading for money with their young sophisticated eyes. And older boys following for blocks, selling bodyloads of the same imaginative object. Or twenty rickshaw taxis in unison asking for their service. "You're my first customer so I give you special price." "Please buy something because I have had no business today." "You will not believe what I can show you." One boy completely covered with drums of various sizes followed me for half an hour asking me which drum I would prefer. Finally, I tell him to "fuck off." He then asks if I would like to buy the smallest drum, to travel with. No thanks, I tell him.

I buy a pair of cheap leather sandals.
I sightsee.
6. The Indian Coffee Worker's Cooperative Society Ltd. Approved by the coffee board. Salmon walls fading downward to brown.
7. Government Soap Factory
8. Government Porcelain Factory
9. Hindusthan Air Craft
Bangalore is the technological center of India. They have many cyber cafes. The computers are often down because of electrical problems. Technology and the ether, the space before information becomes coherent.
There is a pizza place that plays American black music, and every thirty minutes or so the waiters stop serving to create an Indian hip-hop chorus line dance. The dancing rarely moves below the knees, down into the floor. Black American hip-hop makes love to the underworld of gravity. Of course, all of the world's young watch, imitate how black Americans dance, and do not translate, care to, the danger, the body dying, the freedom.
Ah, but Karnatic music! More profound than hip-hop. But hip-hop is all over the world, and sounds funny in French, Hindi and Mandarin.

In the news: "Bangalore. Four school children were killed when a private bus smashed into a jeep in which they had hitched a ride, in Soladevanhalli in Bangalore North on Monday evening. The boys have been identified as Goverdhan (10) and Jagagish (14) from Chikbanavara, Somashekar (14) from Soladevanhalli and Perumal (25). Two of the boys died immediately and two others died minutes after the accident.

A large mob of local residents gathered at the accident soon after the crash and began throwing stones at the bus. The driver and passengers left the bus and took to their heels immediately. A little later several hundred of them torched the bus. Soon, thousands more started to pour in from the two nearby villages of Chickbanaswara and Hurulichickanahalli and erected blocks with burning tyres and large boulders. Later in the evening, about three to four thousand people gathered at the site and went on a dhana, demanding that the police commissioner himself come to the spot."

I hire a car to Nrityagram.
And Protima is buried under the Himalayas. Another pilgrim under the mountain, never found, only a couple of personal items, a purse with identification. She was not yet fifty. Protima Gauri, Odissi danseuse.

"Odissi is a classical dance style from North-East India, dating back to the 2nd century BC, making it the oldest codified dance form in India." A version goes: Originally performed in temples by Maharis as sacred ritual dedicated to Lord Jagannath.
Sixty years ago a guru began to try to recover what was lost of this tradition and, from the sculptures of the period began to re-create the dances with an innovative intent. He took on small boys to dance the newly created roles, boys dressed as young girls. Traveling around India spreading this re-created faith. Sexless, but dressed as sex, dancing seduction. The small boys are now the elder gurus of India, and Nrityagram.

Another version: In the early 1950's royal and religious patronage disappeared and with it the end of temple dancing. The dancers lost their spiritual purpose and so danced as courtesans. The original form lost its sacredness, its role changed, perhaps became more seductive.

Another version: Due to the Indian reformer movement the people stopped caring about the temple dancing. And it ceased to exist. There was an intellectual movement to put dance in a modern context, a public context. Odissi was reconstructed by dance gurus and scholars from the Maharis and Gotipua traditions with materials taken from sculpture and text.

Another version: In the 40's, after Independence, the government encouraged a cultural movement of the arts. There was more than one guru involved in the development of modern Odissi. A combination of Gotipua, "boy's dance," a tradition of boys dancing female roles outside the temples, and Mahari tradition, dancers and singers in service of a temple. Along with these traditions was a research of Orissa temple sculptures and palm leaf text about dance. Young men and women learned the form from the original gurus in the early 60's, each guru imparting their own vision, some of whom were from the Gotipua tradition, small boys now elder gurus.

Another version: The original form did not lose its sacredness and was perhaps as seductive as it is today, if not more.

Version 6. "Odissi is a dance of love and passion, in an everlasting synthesis of divinity and humanity."

To get there we have to take a side road. There has been an accident between a bus and a jeep.

The village is beautiful. Quiet and designed. Nrityagram Dance Village. A girl land. And in these days, moody and intimidating.

Where are the men?

"We found that men were not good for our method, our isolation."

And something about how the men were limited in the roles that they could dance. But I met one young man there, Bharat, who told me that he had learned all the dances, but "I am just a boy, still in school, dancing only in the evening."

The women in the village dance twelve hours a day. Beginning at 6am with eye exercises and finishing at 6pm with "personal practice." Throughout the day they study Sanskrit.

"Rub sandalwood paste around my breasts," Surupa, nine years in the village, chants. She is a remarkable dancer. Bijayini, another of the first disciples of Protima, has a boyfriend in a nearby village, this is exceptional. She visits him on the weekends. He picks her up in a car. An unusual act. She seems happier than the others.

There is a young woman from Japan, Masako, from a wealthy Japanese family. She had seen Odissi dancing on television in Tokyo. She left Japan and came to the village to study, the only non-Indian. She wonders if the other girls accept her. They laugh at her Sanskrit. "I don't know if they will let me stay, it is very closed. I was here once before and left for a while, now I am back and think that I would like to stay for three years." Once she performed a Michael Jackson routine for the village and everyone cheered.

She used to be a famous actress, Protima, the founder, Surupa's teacher, is under mud, Himalayas. A pilgrimage and then a mud-slide. Maybe that is why the girls seem so intimidating.

Another version: "At first she was a go-go dancer. Everyone knows that."

On the road back we pass the remains of the accident. A burnt out bus lying on its side. A burnt out shell. Surrounded by twenty men nodding.

Farther down the road there is fifty yards of tiny shattered glass.

The Indian Coffee Worker's Cooperative Society Ltd. I'm obsessed. A man smoking and drinking coffee, holding his cigarette and hands as though he were an ex-boy dancing as a young girl seducing Krishna. Holding his hands, moving his hands without accompaniment, except for the din of the coffee shop, inhabited by many more younger men. Older men, waiters, dressed as colonial cartoons from the period of British pomposity, kind, humiliated, happy. The man's lips refine his dancing hands, making him a joy to look at.

At night in front of the Indian Coffee Worker's Cooperative Society Ltd., the boys selling drums and wooden snakes and the old women sitting with old coins, are replaced by night eclipsed young mothers, holding babies, or letting the tiny quiet naked figures lie deathlike on blankets on the sidewalk. Mothers crying, tearless, pretending.

During the day there are bookstores on every block, sometimes two.

Cubbon Park. Couples sit on concrete benches, submerged in overgrown grass covering them up to their seated torsos. Relaxing. No one finds sitting in the midst of a jungle strange. It is a park. One patch of lawn, around a fountain near the entrance, is manicured.

In the news: "Suicide. Dejected by the failure of a marriage proposal, an 18-year-old diploma student, Vasantha, allegedly set herself on fire at vacant site in Basavanagudi, on Tuesday morning. She died at The Victoria Hospital. On hearing her cries, a beat constable alerted the Shankarpuram Police and called a Hoysala (mobile patrol) squad for help. Police said that she told them that the prospective groom rejected her because of a disease in her feet."

Habitat, a music shop. The owner is a jazz lover, says that there is a very small clientele for jazz in India. But his shop is primarily jazz, because he "likes the music," and likes to keep the volume of his stereo at full blast. He has a small selection of traditional Indian music in the back of his shop, but says, "most of it is crap." He has a son in the US, going to school in Ohio.

A small crumpled ageless woman, selling whatever it is she is selling, sits on the sidewalk, on MG road, with her son, or her guide, three blocks from The Indian Coffee Worker's Cooperative Ltd.

Only sclera, brown, glowing, her pupils and irises have completely disappeared, perhaps never there to begin with. She's excited about whatever it is she's selling, more excited than her son, or guide. She is also missing all the tips of her fingers.

Later I discover that the man is her husband, I suppose this by the way he helps her pack up whatever it was she was selling.

The dirt in the air is massive today. I feel my lungs growing a layer of black breathless fiber.

In the news: "Man Held. The Peenya Police have arrested Santhosh Kumar on a charge of cheating people on the pretext of polishing their jewelry. Kumar was caught by the public after a housewife in T. Dasarahalli raised an alarm on Monday. The accused had reportedly approached her offering to polish her gold bangles, police said."

A friendly young priest chants and puts red powder on my forehead,
and then hands me his card:

Vidwan N. Seshadri
Bull Temple
Bangalore-560-05
(080)6672618
I walk around the black bull, the cramped temple, the wrong way. Vidwan tenderly leads me in the other direction.

Tiyan, an assistant manager at the pizza place, Tibetan who's never been to Tibet, a Buddhist. "But I cannot practice all the Buddhist precepts. They do not work so well in these modern times. Like lying. Sometimes you have to lie to survive here. There are moments when I find my life very difficult here, and my friends tell me that I must lie to get ahead. Otherwise nothing is possible. So, yes, I am a Buddhist, but I have to survive."

I hire a driver for $50 for the day. A three hour drive to Mysore. Temple cruising with Kumar, beginning at 8:30am.

The drive is not pleasant. Sightseeing dirt, dust, smog. It's too hot to close the window. In a pouch in the back of the sedan there's a magazine of pornographic confession stories from America. Women and men speaking in excited tones about sexual escapades. Lots of "wet red pussys," and "ram rod hard dicks." I read five stories.

It is Sunday and contradicting what Rajesh had told me months ago, there are many families out, lined up at community temples along the way, temples outside of tourbooks, worthless outside of puja. I see my first graveyard in India, actual tombstones and a stone wall enclosing the buried dead. The few in all of India not burned.

Road kill become little animal rugs. Never removed. Eventually pounded invisble into the asphalt.

10. "Dead slow work in progress."

First stop is the summer palace of Tippu Sultan, who, for a moment, beat up the British in the 18th century. A freshly painted vacation home inside and out.

The second stop is the Sri Ranganatha Swamy Temple. One thousand years old. A cavernous lair of assorted god closets. Administered by slow moving suspicious looking priests who take money for every single prayer. I stand in lines, pushing forward, front to back, pressing forward. A haunting dark cave full of gods, for everyone. Old and young kneeling, drinking holy water, blessed red blood dye. And marigolds everywhere.

I secretly tape priests chanting, prayer and for donation, no difference in tone, that I can discern.

Third stop is Chamundi Hill Temple. A young boy finds me, says that he is not a guide but an employee of the temple, and therefore knows the temple's one major secret. He leads me to the slight remain of a wall, gives some description of the abandoned space that surrounds the wall, and then suddenly says that he has to run off to school, and asks if I could give him a little money, to help pay for schoolbooks.

What I give him is not enough, and school becomes a non-issue as he follows me for another hour, providing more informational history of different plots of dirt and covered stone, and reasons why he needs more money. I try to ignore him, for half an hour.

Without warning, I scream, No. I'm startled. He walks away. I walk back to the wall alone and take photographs.

Our final stop is the Palace of Mysore. I do not go inside, suddenly refuse to take my shoes off again. The free Godly Museum is closed.

It gets dark. I buy Kumar dinner. He tells me that he is Jainist. That he is vegetarian and that he is not allowed to eat after sundown.

Why vegetarian?

"Because eating meat is killing and we cannot kill even insects. But since I am working and it is late I will eat after sundown. Sometimes you have to break the rules. God understands."

We drive back and I want to fall asleep but cannot. Some vehicles have their lights on, some do not, sometimes one cannot tell. Dark shadows moving towards our car and away. Horns loud, screaming contradictory signals, "I am in your path, but so what, I will not slow down."

When we arrive at the hotel Kumar confesses how dangerous it is to drive at night. He's happy to be off the road. He has the next three days off and plans to spend it with his wife and children at a mountain resort outside of Bangalore.

And South
Ganesh Everywhere
A little boy sitting under a red umbrella, on airport tarmac, in the grass before the runway. Chennai.

I think of having my fortune told. Over the phone, Nadi, a famous predictor, says that it will take six to seven hours, because it's a very laborious process. I would like to see his process but I don't really want my fortune told. So I stop thinking about it. In China I was "Lucky." Here I don't want to press my luck.

In the news: Sosa, 65. McGuire, 65

But I do and standing, frozen, in front of Hotel Orient I concede and walk across Anna Salai to the Government Museum. I recognize hell, what I recall from images of childhood bible stories, this dense heaving maze of traffic, noise, bodies, heat. In the Paranas, this is only more of life.

On the other side of Anna Salai there is a quiet and stunning collection of Chola bronzes and stone carvings. And room after half empty room of half lit, remarkable broken pieces of antiquity.

Obsolescence? In old dusty pamplets there are Indians with wide afros. Kadar and Saora tribes. "...Medium height, faces rather flat, thick lips, with broad and flat noses and slightly oblique eyes. They live in small huts and have elaborate ideas about religion, particularly about the 'other world.' They have nappy hair..." They also hammer nails into wooden sorcery figures.

In the news: "Chennai, Sept. 24. The entire cosmos is subject to the vicissitudes of time and hence whatever has an origin at a point in time has to come to an end."

"I am not a guru. I am not a celebrity. I do not accept it. I work to be ordinary," she said right off.

Sitting on a wooden bench swing in her front room, holding court for three hours, later sharing leftovers from her breakfast. My dinner with Chandraleka.

She was a star of Bharat Natyam, and stopped dancing for fifteen years. Then began to work again. Became the center of modern dance in India.

Her presence and stories are compelled by long white hair and thick kajjal, glamorous eyes outlined in the charcoal of lamp wick, eternal gender theater for Shiva.

She lives on the ocean.

"When we first moved here there was no street, traffic or lights, just sand and the ocean."

It is a balm, to see an ocean, the Indian Ocean. A completely empty beach. "Indians do not like to swim in the ocean. They prefer fresh water rivers, lakes."

But there are always the fishermen. Like the beauty of the empty beaches of West Africa; Grain Coast, Ivory Coast, Gold Coast, Slave Coast. That same subjective contradiction.

Chandraleka is preparing for performances in New York.

"When we tour we live, eat, sleep in the theater, where we also perform. It maintains a unity."

She sits swinging.

"I had hoped to do something spectacular in New York, with sets and fancy costumes, but the presenters refuse to pay for anything. So we will do what it is we do here in India."

In the news: Chennai, Sept. 26. "The Bhagavad Gita is a gospel of action."

In the news: "Hyderabad, Sept. 26: The driver of the bus whose utter negligence resulted in the death of 19 persons including many school children in the rail-bus collision at Bothapalem in Nalgonda district "should be hanged," Railway Minister Nitish Kumar, has said."

I hire another car and driver and escape Chennai.

More temples. I no longer care when something was built, nor by whom. The ocean encourages my apathy, my weariness, leisure. Surrender. Mahabalipuram. Charming coastal village. Young stone carvers. Ageless men selling bright rocks and guidance, more enlightened intrusion. At the shore temple I burst into sweat. Frightening, the heat this south.

There is David, a born again Christian, a handicraft dealer, standing in the middle of the road, who "would not lie to me," but desperately tries to sell me something from his three shops.

I begin our conversation by saying "Good-bye." David replies, "Jesus loves you brother. Jesus is coming. Jesus loves you, brother." He grabs my arm and drags me into one of his shops. He walks into a back room and brings out a small object wrapped in faded newsprint. A dog with a red penis having intercourse with a woman. "A village piece, bronze, maybe two hundred years old."

In the news: Sosa, 66. McGuire, 66

The Sea Of Bengal. Not caves but shallow rock carvings, internal figure sculptures. Quiet, soothing, for brief moments. Indian tourists, not yielding, as they move into these shallow rock cut halls, not actually pushing, but if you stop you are passively trampled, the "gospel of action."

1. PRARABDA KARMAPALA : IF someone to do anything today and than karma came later.

2. SANCITA KARMA PALA : if someone to do anything today and than karma came today

3. KRYAMANA KARMAPALA: if someone [Before] to do anything Before. and than karma came today.

I wander for solitude. And become lost, and try to climb a large rock formation. I see an adult monkey, my size, a few feet away, preening itself. I decide not to disturb it, and go back the way I came.

Mr. Swarna a master of Ayurveda massage is employed by the Ideal Beach Resort in Mahabalipuram. He has been practicing for thirty-five years, mostly in Kerala. He began when he was eight years old. Now he is old, the resort receptionist informs me, "Is that OK?"

He seems old (but probably not much older than forty-five). He kneels on the floor, beside my prone bedded body. The massage is either a massage or vaudeville. My body is entertained, as he drops his various bottles of oil, forgetting to massage the respective right or left side of a particular anatomical extension or general body area. He is earnest. His touch is that of someone re-examining their own sense of touch, and the loss of sensation.

It's raining in the South, and still the music of crows.

I visit a fishing village and meet a young fisherman. A handsome man, missing a front tooth. Without invitation, he confesses to me that he is having problems with his girl-friend of two years. She has been married twice before. He has never been married. He does not like her anymore. "She is not a good person. Now I think that men are good, women are not so good."

We walk to his family home. A large white building of cement, built by his father. He lives with eighteen family members. No one is there when we enter. In one room there is a single sheet and pillow lying neatly on the concrete floor, a bedroom. Inside the puja room he hands me a well-used brass pot, a gift. And then tells me that he was in a motorcycle accident, lost his front tooth, damaged his left arm, had to go to the hos-pital. There is more to the girlfriend story but I can't quite translate the details. Finally, he asks if I could help him out with some money. I am pleased that he finally does and give him a few rupees. He asks where I will eat dinner and invites me to have dinner with him in a little yellow house, a shelter near his family's big house that he has taken over, "which is all broken, but is a place that I can come and be alone."

I tell him that I'm not sure where I will have my dinner, knowing that I will eat at the resort, at a table with linen and tableware, and waiters. Inaccessible. Where I will pay more than a few rupees, and watch other foreigners eating and talking in isolation, near the ocean.

The next morning I walk the beach, taking a last long look at the ocean, the only world, rhythm that is truly common. During the ride back to Chennai I actually fall asleep.

"Master, what is home?"

"Hello, Ralph? Were you sleeping?
A phone call from the US. It's 1:00am Saturday.
My father is in the hospital. A bleeding colon. "Since he is a Jehovah Witness and we can't stop the bleeding, we need to remove his colon, now, in minutes," the doctors announce. My father's small intestine was connected to his rectum. "He won't have to wear a bag. He will have to use the toilet two to three times a day, instead of the two to three times a week, like before." He is seventy four. Recovery will be complicated. He could die.
My mother is tired, my father is in pain, crying. They have been married for fifty years. Unimaginable.
He began bleeding in his stool on Wednesday, the day I sat on Chandraleka's floor, like a student, in awe, audience to her inflamed wisdom and tantric protest. Those eyes.
His operation was Friday. I was walking the beach of Mahabalipuram, experiencing more peace than I have for two months. The ocean.

This news is very hard being so far away. Did not pack for this. I am poised to go home. My father's breaking down becomes my own.

In the news: McGuire 68. Sosa 66.

There are moments when I see my father in his intensive care unit as myself. My father's name is also Ralph. I can call the hospital but I cannot speak to him directly.

"Oh, you're back."

I went to Mahabalipuram. It is a nice place.

"It is a strange place. I used to live there, but got out just in time. It is important not to be seduced by the seductive ease of that place. When I lived there I met a lot of old people who did not have good hearts."

What do you mean?

"The place makes it hard to make roots, while at the same time making it hard to leave. Dangerous. The ancient civilization of Mahabalipuram disappeared. If you noticed, none of the temples are finished."

Yes, I noticed. What do you think happened?

"When I lived there I studied its history quite a bit."

So, what do you think happened?

Something supernatural," the shopkeeper said.

"Something about harmony," she said right off. Malavika Sarukkai. Perhaps the most important Bharat Natyam dancer in India.
"My work is traditional, exploring tradition's possibilities. Grammar and freedom. Transcendence. In classical Bharat Natyam we have emotional dances and pure dances. I do not integrate them. And find it impossible to dance pure dance, classical Bharat Natyam, without classical emotional elements."

Her mother. "To write the Vedas, three thousand years ago, the writers searched in their minds with their hearts."

Malavika. "There is a book from the 2nd century BC that discusses the importance of improvisation in the structures of ancient Indian dance."

Malavika. "That is what I search for in my dance. That is what my audience comes to see, experience."

Her mother. (very excited). "India is such a wonderful place to live because we have everything here, an ancient culture and MTV, cows in the streets and limousines. Death on the streets and the gods everywhere."

Malavika reads Tarkovsky but has never seen his movies. Which confirms my belief that he is the greatest filmmaker of all time.

In the news: "Hand cut off for stealing. Jiddah: Saudi authorities have cut off an Afghan's right hand by sword for stealing at Islam's holiest site in Mecca, the Interior Ministry said on Sunday. It did not say what Mumtaz Driar Khawaja allegedly stole in the Kaaba mosque. Khawaja was punished for defiling the sanctity of the mosque, said the ministry statement."

Where you from, brother? To a young man from Sudan, a student, receiving a money order at the bank. At first I noticed his particular blackness, more gray. Then, the kink of his hair. Finally, the swagger, African, by way of modern Africa, by way of America. "The traffic, the food, the people, everything in India is bad," he says, feeling more at ease. Before this impassioned opinion he was extremely reticent to tell me where he was from.

In the news: "Chennai. Sept. 29. Strict adherence to certain rules prescribed in holy texts will make God himself visit devotees and fulfill their desires. Foremost among them is to speak the truth only. Under no circumstances, even if unpalatable or even should it incur the displeasure of others, should one utter falsehood. At times, a person may try to wiggle out of a piquant situation by telling a lie but later, he may find himself duped (There are very few exceptions to this golden rule)."

Fathers and mothers die all the time, I tell myself. He is Death, on whom all life depends.

Ah, but the music! Karnatic music. I diligently find a concert every night. This night, flute, violin, mridangam. Young men jamming. One is a law student living in LA. A good flutist. "I try to keep it up but it is difficult in the US."

The taxi driver is delighted, has been drinking. The day that I leave India we drive through a holiday. Dyudha Puoja. Weapon Worship. A celebration. Day, and then night and jasmine, marigold, banana leaves draped on buses and cars. Gold red kumbom powder splattered like Jackson Pollock on shop windows, doors and stairs. Green melons with the faces of demons.

I arrive three hours early to the airport, to discover that my ticket was booked for the day before, a mistake made by a travel agent in the US. The flight is completely booked and there is no chance of my boarding any other flight tonight. I book a flight for the next evening.

In the taxi parking lot of the airport there is, strangely, none of the active shifting and haggling of drivers. They are all asleep or drunk, passed out inside their open cars, spread on front seats, foreshortened figures, corpselike.
I wake a driver, momentarily. As we drive back to the hotel he nods off, swerving and then slowing down. It becomes a pattern. I place my hand on his shoulder the remainder of the ride, occasionally hitting his shoulder, head, to keep him awake.
When we arrive at the hotel he stumbles out of the car. He stands, wobbling, then moves to the back of the car, to the trunk, to help me with my bags, I suppose. His eyes are closed. I pull my bags from the trunk. Unleashing my demons letting them bounce.

Hotel Orient. Anna Salai, Chennai. Part 3.
In the lobby there is a well dressed man, disturbed, ranting at the receptionist, then me. "I was having some friends over for a going away party last night and around 12:00pm the receptionist called and asked if any of my guests were staying the night. Did you know that it is against the law for foreigners to have guests spend the night with them in a hotel? And these are the people that created the Kama Sutra! If they assume someone spent the night, a maid is sent to the room the next day to check the sheets for semen. If a single drop is found she is to report it to the management, who then reports it to the authorities. Heaven knows what happens then. But the law applies only to foreigners. I am Indian but live in Singapore. Whatever connection I had with this country has now been completely broken. I come here only for business anyway, so fuck it! Last night I sent all my friends home."

On my way out of the hotel, to the airport, the second time, a room service attendant stops me, "Please, I cannot afford to travel. Saving money is hard here, it is impossible. If I come to the US will I get a good job? I will need someone to help me, to house and feed me, while I try to get work, a visa. I know that you can help me. You are a very important man. A great man!"

Important, great? I try not to laugh.

"Because you can travel. Please do not forget me and my problems. I know that you can help me. Please."

Aiming at a sparrow with an unloaded rifle.

I preferred the North, and that it was difficult once.

If.......
then you play forever the role of a man without a shirt.

Chou wa. Harmony

The air, the order, the pace, the light, the tools, the brown eyes that I can barely see, the white wood, the bare space, the detail, the food, the priests, meikakuni.

"Noh, you should see it, no, experience it. Brings sleep."

Oh Japan

Akiyoshidai International Art Village, Yamaguchi Prefecture. A three week workshop begins in one week.

From my room I call the US. My father is having problems with infections. His body is screaming, has lost a large part of itself, is trying to find a new order, eventually, but before that it is shocked, spewing chaos and remorse.

Kiku. Listen

The phone to his hospital room rings, the thought of hearing his voice, finally, brings tears to my eyes.
I talk to my father. Hearing his voice is calming, refreshing. He is jocular. His mind is quicker than I remember. Perhaps from fear.
I am frightened. And find it difficult to contemplate his dying. Instead, I worry about what I will have to do if he dies. That I will struggle with guilt, his dying and my being here, or my being there and not fulfilling my obligations to a workshop, my travels. I have a week before the workshop begins and have plans to travel to Kyoto City, the only place I thought of when I thought of Japan. To look at temple gardens and see Noh. I should fly home and be with my father. Maybe I could return in time for the workshop. Then, I talk myself out of it, because it would be such a long trip, and, I have a large family chorus that tells me to stay where I am, that my father's condition does not seem that dire. Not sure what that means.

The rolling Akiyoshidai tablelands, the green fields, are dotted with curious rock spheres, and beneath the picturesque plateau are hundreds of limestone caverns.

My father says, "I know it is difficult for you. I would rather be where I am than where you are right now." Yes, father. That is how I feel.

Perplexed between the emotional paradox of being in a place where I have absolutely no challenge beyond the dilemma of looking at beauty. And my father is dying nine thousand miles away. An interesting problem.

My father is almost dying. I do not know from moment to moment how he is. So I suffer. So far Japan is firmament.

Riding a bike through rural Japanese farmland. The sun bright, soft. The air simple.

Not India. But people are people.
No, the Indians are not niggers, they are Indians.
Not China.
No, "The Japanese's truth is different."

If we do not see the cypress in our own garden how can we expect to see into our own true nature?

"You have a fax."

"You should call 404 349 5447 as soon as possible. Apparently they've put your father on a kidney dialysis because his kidneys are not doing well. Your sister has been trying to call you but can't get through. She has the same number that I have, that I called yesterday, she has your fax number too. Don't know why they haven't been able to get through. I'm sorry to send such a terse fax, and I wish this weren't happening to your dad.
Love, L."

Tombo, a dragon fly.

Oba Taido Roushi. 51 years old. Jiju Zen Zi. One thousand years old. (A neighborhood temple that serves this small community, mostly funerals, what most Japanese find useful about Buddhism).
Sitting with Roushi. A precision unlike anything I've seen in the US. A straightening of slippers and the spotting dry of water spills, a drop. An ease of immaculateness. The most natural act, acting. Our nature. Glorified. Dignity.

Oba Taido gives me a book that on the inside and outside appears to be useless. It is a gift.

The Buddhist Revolution. "Its opposition to Brahmanic thought must be regarded primarily as a reaction, a revolt, rather than an effort to present the "Buddhist" point of view." Zen was, is, not new. What was, is.

First. Kung-an
And then. Koan
Third. It does not imitate

Karada. Body

My father is unclean, not bathing, not digesting. No dignity. Only surviving. So, I shall have no dignity. And trust that I can be polite. If only polite.

I must pack. I must move.

If it is not a good horse how can it succeed.

He will be a new old man. He will eat better, more thoughtfully.

I arrive in Kyoto City. I walk the streets in a fever. I imagine my father, old, crying, remembering his childhood.
"Ralph, there was a moment when your father wanted to check out. I saw it in his eyes."
His sister travels down from Cincinnati to visit him. Maybe that is why he decided to stay alive. He becomes inspired, "You kids stick close to one another because you are all you have."

Me wo akeru. Open your eyes. Me wo tsuburu. Close your eyes.

Hello, L? It's me. Japan is beautiful. Yes, the tea, noodles and sleeping on the floor, tatamis. Great stuff.
You know, something is happening, I'm getting it. My father's dying over there, and I'm here and I'm getting it, us, what happened....
Anyway, can't talk long it's really expensive here, ridiculous, kinda funny.......I'm OK.

I like Kyoto because all the blond wood has turned black.
Tomorrow I will sit zazen in Myoshinji Temple, a three day session.

How is he today?
My sister says, "Ralph, dad doesn't look like dad, lying there with tubes all up in him. He looks so old, Ralph. But when he's able to talk, he's present, his mind has not forgotten."
Tell him not to go anywhere until I get there. She says, "OK. When will that be, again?"

Tanuki. A little fox.

Up at 4:00am, stretch, have tea, take a shower and call home. "Dad is stable, a little better, for the moment you can breathe." My mother will not tell the truth when the truth is not necessary. "What can he do way over there? The news will only make him worry," my sister confides. At 5:30am the moon is full to bursting.

Myoshinji Temple 6:00am. Other than me, there are no foreigners. All locals, ordinary, mostly middle aged men, one young man, three women. We sit for an hour and then a howa, talk, in Japanese, by the head priest. Outside the zazen do, a family of tanuki digs holes, snouts searching for something alive, edible under the garden surface. A monk walks out onto the keidai, porch and shoos them away. And then again.

The priest speaks for an hour. Afterwards, a young monk kindly asks, in English, if I understood any of what was said. I answer, No.

The rest of the day I walk and walk until my legs cramp.

Up again at 4:00am. Up before the alarm. Barely making out the hands of the clock. But know that it is near 4. There is no giant moon today. Another monk conducts the zazen ceremony, the chanting, before the quiet. In his zazen, stillness, he scratches, rubs his cheek, pulls at his left ear, looks at his watch, often. And what a chant, operatic.

Improved? "Yes, he just finished watching the ball game." Atlanta in the playoffs once again. The final morning of sessin. Another zazen, another howa.

He's better? Are you sure? How sure?

On being asked if a dog has the Buddha nature, Trieu Chau replies "yes" once, and "no" another time.

Two choices, one chance.

Gardens

Ryoan-ji Temple at 8:30am the best time to look, before all the school children and business tours. I wonder if the raked gravel, the precise lines, are laid out exactly like they were in the 15th century. Daitoku-ji Temple, five gardens of Ryogen-in. Daisen-in, two tits of sand. A monk trimming the hedges with an electric trimmer, the coil laid out functionally across the raked gravel. I think I also saw Kiyomizu-tera. Yes, it is the temple near Sannenzaku and Ninnen-zaku. I don't remember it. I remember the dragonflies, tombo. In the mountains behind the Nanzen-ji Temple found a goddess glen, "naturalist," before Shinto. A tree that is a god, that cannot be cut down. Pools and hishaku and bibs on stones, prayers. Simple ones like, "Please, I pray that my child grows up well and strong."

Noh

Not Zen, Noh. Some parts are sung inhaling. A hundred years ago they routinely brought sick people to Noh performances because of Noh's healing qualities. To sleep at a Noh performance is common, encouraged, because of the alpha waves that a good performance creates.

In a shop in the Teramachi Arcade, a saleswoman in a gray uniform comes up to me and asks if I need any help. I say, no and continue wandering, shopping a tea cup. A few minutes later she comes up to me again and asks where I'm from. I tell her. She says that she's a student of Noh and asks if I would like to know more about it. I say, sure, why not. A timely and curious invitation.

She tells me that there are no performances in Kyoto during the time I'm there but that if I'm interested she can arrange for me to attend a rehearsal with her Sensei.

I meet Yuko the next day, outside the city, outside of a recess-immersed elementary school. Hundreds of yellow capped children running a massive relay race to hybrid pop music played on four electric organs.

She leads me up a flight of stairs, to an empty classroom. She introduces me to Kazuyuki Inoue. A young man. A Noh soloist, not born into a Noh family, something extremely unusual. "I trained as a western actor but I prefer Noh because it makes me feel better."

I watch Kazuyuki practice shimai, the short dance excerpts from full-length Noh plays. Barely moving. A fan, prop, his only emotional outlet. I watch, slowly, forced to focus precisely on the sounds that he makes, that travel beyond his masked voice, bellowing, so then I can see more, the stitching in his costume, the dirt smudges on his tabi, his small white socked feet.

At the end of the rehearsal, Yuko invites me to a class that Kazuyuki is conducting at her home later in the evening. Intrigued, I accept.

Yuko lives with seven other people who study with the same Sensei, two of them children, a family. Yuko is thirty-four and single. The other women in the house are also single except for the wife of Nozumu. Nozumu and his wife own the house. Nozumu was born in Japan but moved to the US when he was eight, went to college there. Moved back to Japan fifteen years later. Discovered that his heart was in Japan. "Kazuyuki has stopped the rain with his Noh, I have seen it, a monsoon. He has also cured a patient with cancer, who came and watched a performance. Usually, people are just in tears."

Privately, Nozumu tells me that Yuko tells everyone who enters her shop, when it is appropriate, where she has to wear a gray uniform, that she is a student of Noh.

At the end of the class I say good-bye to Kazuyuki, Yuko, Nozumu and the rest of the family. Yuko asks if I would like to travel with them tomorrow to another town for another Noh workshop. I say that I can't, that I have more sightseeing to do. They all seem disappointed.

Back in the city I walk to an udon bar and gulp soup with other ravenous men, crowded around the counter. Others queued, waiting replacements, every five minutes or so.

In a ryokan, in my room, I eat half a persimmon, walk out into the hallway, down to the men's room. I toss the half eaten persimmon into the toilet bowl and piss on it. Pissed, feeling thwarted that I was not the only one Yuko singled out as a potential Noh novice. I had wanted to feel special, did for a moment.

"Ralph, they had your father sitting up today. And they've taken some of the tubes out of his mouth and nose. He's feeling much better. Last week, I thought he was ready to give up, but now he's watching ball games again."

"He's passing his urine but they're still finding too much albumin, still cleaning him out, so that's good, I guess." My mother places the phone down and calls out into her nest, my family, "What's that albumin stuff, y'all?" A sibling voice, one of my three sisters, gives a faraway, muddled and short description. My mother comes back to the phone.

Mom, I sure wish that I were home.

"I know you do, honey, I know you do."

Kyofu.

"What, honey?"

Shi no kyofu.

"Oh, you're learning a little Japanese? That's so good."

Yes, it is good. My father is feeling much better.

Now I can be in Japan.

On a ferry, down the Setonaikai, the inland Pacific, returning to Akiyoshidai. A ship equipped with large open, empty cabins. Carpeted. In each cabin there are enough blankets for thirty or more homemade beds. At 10:30pm they turn out the lights. Passing Shikoku. When you wake up it is day. Settling into Kyushu. There was no snoring, no one talking, no one making love. Only a baby crying, throughout the night, close and far away, as its mother walked it up and down the ship's passageway.

Akiyoshidai. Every morning, early, the farmers shoot their rifles into the air to scare away the karasu, crows. They fire at twenty minute intervals. The shooting lasts about forty-five minutes. On the weekends the shooting starts later in the morning. The karasu are patient, timely. I use the distant hollow popping as an alarm clock.

The workshop begins

The days seem full. Many ideas are explored, misconstrued. A diverse group of people who love to dance. Nine salient artists. Paz, Carlos, Cheng-Chieh, Robin, Paulo, Kakuya, Kenzo, Takiko, Mikuni. Five-hour classes. Slow, meticulous. And there are photographers and musicians in other studios, led by Nan Goldin and Dr. Fred Tillis. Every night parties and saké, and cigarettes. Twenty-seven artists in culture shock, fourteen Americans, twelve Japanese. One Japanese Brazilian. Two are gay.

A question of breadth

Roushi when you sit how do you breathe?

"I am not aware of my breathing. I am ordinary. No goal. I just sit."

I meditate every other morning with Oba Taido. We sit. Afterwards we have tea and omanju. He brings out small indigenous objects to show and tell. They are broken, dying, and perfect, cupped within his tiny hands.

One artist

Kakuya is from the butoh tradition. Wednesday is his day. This is what I remember: Butoh was born in 1959 in Japan when the modernism of the West was losing its value. (The translation that I remember). A return to the situation before modernism, based in the oriental philosophy of the body and mind as one. A going back to spirituality.

"Sleeping is very important to animals."

"Treasure the moments where you don't know what to do next. No animal thinks and then moves."

"Maintain time within a movement. How much time you spend in a movement controls the length of movement, the form."

I chose the life of a bear. Cheng-Chieh chose a pigeon, a city pigeon. Kenzo became a cricket. We also explored the physical textures of dust, rocks and glass.

Buyo

A young man, who works as a postal clerk in nearby Yamaguchi City, plus, five or six elderly ladies, obasan with fans and flowered hats, present a special performance of Traditional Japanese Dance.

Afterwards Mikuni provides some context

"Japanese people do not express their true feelings, it is complicated by their history with the fan. One thousand years ago the fan was an emotional modifier. Through the fan they expressed love, fear, disapproval, consent. Now there are fans only in traditional theater forms and dances. So, the Japanese people improvise with emotional disguise, making it up as they evolve in the broader world. And in the case of the young, being very foolish."

Winter soup

A friend who works in the administrative office invites me to a izakaya, a local restaurant, to eat traditional food. A cross between a pub and a restaurant. We eat Yone chan nabe, Yone, the owner's name, and her local version of winter soup.

We drink and drink. My friend says, "The young people in Japan don't care about tradition." But for her there is a dilemma. "My tradition is in the bottom of my being. But modernity is exciting. I want to follow."

In my bed, in sleep, I have a dream that my throat is exploding.

Weekend

Hiroshima. All Americans should go to Hiroshima. To learn of the responsibility of power.

Pearl Harbor? "No, there was very little, 'Banzai, Long Live Japan.' But plenty of, 'No, no, no, no. Mommy I don't want to die.' Some young men drank liters of soy sauce to turn their skin blue, so that they would not be inducted," I was told.

Home

This is a description of the proportions and contents of a young musician's Tokyo apartment: It is a building inhabited by other musicians. A studio apartment. A small room with a grand piano and a futon on the floor, under the one window. She has another piano, upright, in the notch that is a kitchen. She has a bathroom, one must squat to take a shower. Her rent is 70,000 yen a month. She cannot have male guests.

Theater

A not so old black performer. A not so young black performer.

I danced, improvised, while Dr. Fred Tillis played soprano saxophone. I wore a green lungi from India and a black hip knit shirt from Hong Kong. Dr. Tillis improvised with American gospel, and Japanese folk tunes.

A required informal performance, concluding the three week workshop, an evening of music, and dance and a gallery of photographs, for the Akiyoshidai community. Proof that we Americans, and our contemporary Japanese accomplices, were here.

Afterwards, an adolescent girl comes up to me shaking, sputtering sweetly in Japlish, almost crying, she asks for my autograph. Her mother stands behind her, nervous. There's a younger sister farther away, less interested.

I sign her program and hand it back to her, placing it into her shaking hands. She stands in place, not moving, and then squeals, "I love you, I love you, I love you". Six times. Her mother, in place behind her, nervous. The younger sister had walked away.

A night out in Yamaguchi City (a bunch of us)

I have heard the Japanese play jazz like black people. Not appropriation but honest to goodness soul. I'm serious.

There are gangs of Sumo wrestlers walking the streets like giant gorgeous fat-assed women, dressed in floral silk robes. There's a tournament.

"Most cannot wipe their asses, too much body to reach around. Wiping is administered by wives and or hired help. They cannot expose their penises during a match, or they are disqualified. After all, Sumo is ceremony."

We end up at Milky Way, Hot Space. A karaoke bar. A yellow pages of song titles, mostly black music. We spend twenty-four thousand yen and have no money left to take a taxi back to the village, which is going to cost another ten thousand yen. We assure the driver that once we're back at the village that we'll come up with the money. Back at the village we wake a lot of people up and come up with the money.

The next morning I ride a bike to the temple, hung-over, sit zazen hung-over. "God, last night was fun. More fun than I've had in ages." Roushi smiles and gives me a fan. In his calligraphic ink he writes on its folded paper, Storage-To the Limit-Nothing. My koan. After a few days I translate it as, A limitless storage of nothing.

Is that right?

"Ralph, you ask too many questions. If you don't seek anything, you can see everything."

Like Last Night Watching A Penetration Of The Mystery Of The Eleven Headed One Thousand Armed Avalokiteshvara Who Embodies Compassion And Reaches In All Directions.

Saké and karaoke for hours. They keep the place open for us, and we pay dearly for it, barely. And then steal a ride back to the village.

I sit falling asleep in the front as they begin. In the back seat of a taxi. then the hard surface of the parking lot, surrounding each other like large yielding cats.

Softly, "You gonna break me." Standing, she was still red faced, falling asleep and then waking.

Curiosity, now sheltered. A room, not discerned, safe. I continue watching. The rolling and smelling. Looking at the bones in each other's faces, the small and larger lips. He kisses her teeth. The neck is that of another animal. Looking again, for marks. Of what species? A taste.

Trying to smell each other under the skin, and finally tasting. To see their whole bodies is difficult. She smiles without hesitation. A voyeured happiness. Perhaps a happiness he has not seen in a long time.

Is this elemental bodied love, love? Before it grows up?

He imagines hair on her legs. The sour under her arms. The tart inside her ears, burns. And then she smiles again.

"How you know me so well?"

"Yes, I know you." (No, he doesn't know her. He is improvising.)

Hours pass.

I wonder when they will rest.

"No, no first we must have music."

She likes black music.

"It is important for making love. It is very popular in Tokyo, to have an African American boyfriend. Black African men in Japan lie and say that they are Americans, or from Canada or Jamaica."

"Is that why you are here?"

"No, you are not black and I am not Japanese. And anyway, to me you look like you from Nepal, Tibet."

Yeah, what is black music, anyway?

Hours pass.

"You have not come yet . . . actually, here it is opposite. They say, 'Iku, I am going.' Like going to the river, upstream."

It is morning

"Daite hoshii," she whispers, in perfect Japanese.

He understands and does, asking her many things. I barely hear.

The lightness of foreign language.

She said, "Sh," to be quiet, so that she can hear the dawn, brightening bird noise.

He stops talking and the birds stopped singing. Karma.

He's afraid to ask her age. The centuries.

"Everyone think that I am Chinese from Shanghai. Because of my eyes and the bones of my face. I love sex so much. What if I pregnant?"

"OK, I will be you. I leave in eleven days and I don't know if I will ever see you again."
And then she becomes him. "Your legs are like the roots of a tree. Maybe after a million kisses, we can talk about love."

Which one is the hero? I cannot tell. I stop watching and now just listen.
She playfully slaps his cheek, over and over, commanding that he tell her a story, a narrative to help her sleep. One he had stolen.
Verse
If you are thirsty, don't drink dirty water.
Food alone will not fill your stomach.
If a child licks the sugar off the knife
He may well cut his tongue.

The next afternoon they describe how they rode bikes to the temple, early, hung-over.
Past simple traffic, small precise farms and cypress trees.
She sat in the temple, crying. And later tells him, "I could hear the tears falling, splashing into my cupped hands. Did you hear them?"

Yes. I did.

I could stay, travel to Tokyo, not been there yet. See no reason to hurry home. Other than it is time to visit my father. Time to fly nine thousand miles, in two days, to kiss my father.

Once home I send Wen Hui and Wu Wenguang a letter along with the piece of paper with the names of the Yunnan farmer/musicians. Two sets of Chinese characters circled, the ones I had marked while in their village. The one who never said a word and just played a string instrument as though it were a body part, a scratch, that natural, and the handsome one who wouldn't sell me his small reed.

December

My father sits frail, sweatered, doesn't stand. His face and neck are so thin and his gray-less hair has been cut much shorter.

With his brown fleshy face, thin lips, white collars. His vaguely crossed eyes, the pupils and the irises that are brown but look black like looking into a reflective pool of dark petrol. Those of a deer. With his left ear which is lower than his right so that when wearing glasses which he sometimes wears, they rest on his nose slanting downward towards the right of his face, a long brown nose with an Irish bulb that supports two powerful animal-like burrows. Not overgrown but long thin hairs are always present. His bottom lip often hangs open, not from its size and weight, projecting a pout. On both sides of his family there is Cherokee blood and this I suppose accounts for his hairless face. All these things shake and become incandescent when his faith is challenged.

I acquiesce, bend over, kneeling, and kiss him ferociously.

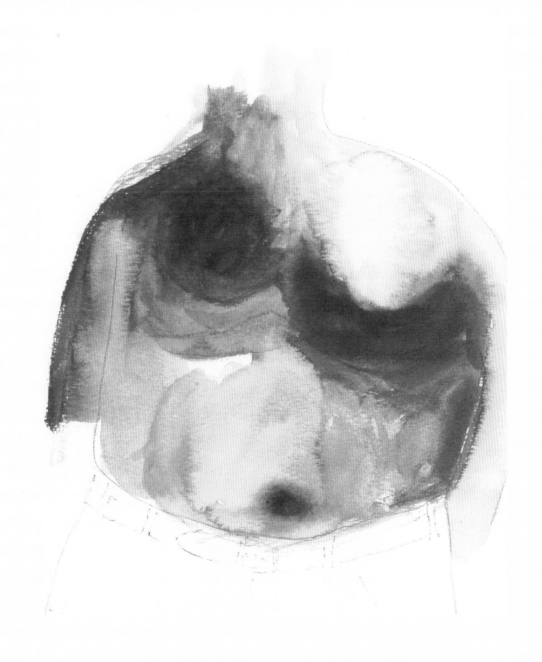

December 10, 1999
Dear Sir
Hello, how are you. I am fine here. I wish you a happy and properous new year. I got your letter. I really miss you my friend. I really remember trip with you you really cared me so much. I can never forget you. Well, if you or yours any relative plans to visit India, do write to me in advance so that I can make all arrangements Once again happy new year.
(A greeting card from Rajesh, written by his wife.)

Rajesh was alive. And instead of being relieved I felt guilty, that I hadn't contacted him, informing him that I was traveling back to India, the south this time, that maybe we could meet up.
I didn't hear from Rajesh again. Stopped writing.

Had hugged her ferociously. Another teacher passes instead.

Christmas eve.
Viola Farber did not believe in heaven. Jeff Slayton said that her passing was "easy."
"Easy," a word like "recovery," not sure what either means. More news that the year is
almost over and that this watershed year will end. The concept of timing is vastly
underestimated. That we will never be able to make sense out of seemingly connected
events. Randomness, as certain and predictable as nature. Maybe there is control in
death after all. It did snow on Christmas eve. Viola knew.

February 2, 1999
Dear Ralph,
I have written to Ann in your office the progress of passport. It's like the Long March.
I don't think I want to copy it for you. Keep quiet with you in your mind, in your
Geography. Anyway, it's been going ahead on step by step. Don't worry.
But I am thinking the way of manage the passport for two farmer/musicians, that is
been covered the Geography of yours. Let us imagine, two farmers who never leave
Yunnan, never take on plane, also never think about America before this time. But
right now, they are doing for it from the original step. Wen Bin brought with both
them with a small truck on the road in country for get the permit of "Xiang" govt. (The
lowest official) and went to the office of police in the country. Both was just follow
Wen like shadow.
All things is happened in a small town of China. It might has been a part of journey
of your Geography, and so on.
Love, Wu Wenguang

Love Letters from San Francisco

Tuesday

Dear L

Just re-read a letter you wrote on January 1, the dream and other events you mentioned are powerfully instructive, and familiar. I wonder what it all means? You're just going to have to get use to being noisy. Me? I'm wildly improvising. And feel very lively. Hurting myself and then recovering, daily, winter weather.

Wang Liliang and Li Wen Yi arrived. Culturally sexy, like seeing the Africans for the first time at the airport in 1997, out of place, and happy about it. Wen Hui said that the customs man was remarkably nice, joking the whole time, they felt very welcomed.

At the hotel, watching them negotiate the bedroom linen, the electric kitchen stove, the bathroom and light fixtures and the door locks, was theater enough. I captured their hotel examinations on video: Water faucets (how to get hot water/how to get cold water), electric stoves and door locks.

Giving them money, watching them count it, hide it in their underwear was very strange. At the village all their needs are cared for. Imagine them looking at, touching a fifty dollar bill versus a one dollar bill, no difference to the touch.

And then Chinatown. They had never been in a restaurant of this scale before and found the menu overwhelming, too many choices. But they "don't want to go home." Yet. Seem to be excited. Intrigued.

Mr. Wang is 50ish and seems to be the spokesperson. Mr. Li is quite mute, so quiet, doesn't talk, just looks at everything, intensely. Doesn't want to know how things work. I suppose Mr. Wang will care for him.

They play music all the time. And everywhere. Wen Hui said that at their layover in Tokyo they played in the airport and created quite a crowd and stir. A clapping audience.

Steve Cho, our translator, will be invaluable. He is Taiwanese. Helped a great deal today. I forgot that Wen Hui's spoken English is limited. The four of them together speak at least four different Chinese. Mandarin will be the connector. Mr. Wang and Mr. Li understand Mandarin, Mr. Wang speaks it a little, Mr. Li not at all. Wen Hui, Mr. Wang and Mr. Li all speak Yunnan dialect. And Mr. Wang and Mr. Li have a private language that they speak to each other, one that Wen Hui does not understand.

Wish I had gotten James Lo out here sooner. Oh well.

Love

R

Wednesday

Dear L

Djédjé arrived safe. The only one in the airport in a boubou, easily targeted, sparkling. All here but Carlos by time of writing, but I never worry about him. Planning a family meal tonight in the hotel, the Chinese are cooking.

Earlier Wen Hui, Mr. Wang Mr. Li and I went to a jazz concert, Regina Carter. At first Wang and Li wanted to bring their instruments assuming that music was music, everyone participating. Wen Hui had to explain American formality. I felt a little sad. They loved sitting and listening anyway.

Thank god I came a few days early. No one here was really prepared for the introductory handholding that this kind of work requires.

All for now

Love

R

Saturday

Dear L

Last night I visited Mr. Wang and Mr. Li. Mr. Wang made me stay exactly one hour. Patting the foot of his bed for me to sit and then describing one revolution on his new watch, bought in Chinatown. We sat and watched a Mexican soap opera. They played their music and intermittently laughed every time someone kissed someone, in Spanish. Mr. Wang brought out a notebook covered with practice Chinese characters and notated traditional songs from his village. On one page there was the English alphabet and the numbers 1 through 10. In the written alphabet the letter C was missing. I asked for a pen and wrote it in between the B and the D. He then wrote the whole alphabet over in lines below his original series. Then we re-did the numbers, maintaining a peculiar symmetry to the alphabet. On the cover of the notebook was his name in Chinese characters. I wrote it in English, vertically. He made me write it horizontally as well. He put the notebook away and picked up a small reed, joining Mr. Li. Mr. Li played the si xian, the four string instrument throughout, smiling, eyes fixed on the soap opera. After what felt like an hour, I got up off the bed and said goodbye. Mr. Wang again motioned to his watch that there were fifteen minutes left before an hour had passed. Mr Li motioned that I should go. I left. Mr. Wang smiled, conceded.

R

Sunday

Dear L

Worked on prayer forms yesterday. How bodies physicalize praying. Wanted to see some immediate dancing phrases. Didn't happen. Better yet, a lot of talking about what religion and prayer mean to seven very different people, cultures.

Djédjé talked for what seemed like hours about how he's not so certain that Africans pray, that of course they do, "but not like Buddhists." "Obviously, one prays for someone who has nightmares of people who have the heads and tails of dogs."

Or, burning leaves to "cleanse the unwanted ancestors from a house."

Carlos said he prays in the clubs, calling on appropriated ancestors of Africa. The club, "house," is his temple. "Spirituality and vibes."

Cheng-Chieh prays as she prepares food in the kitchen.

Wen Hui "prayed to Mao," with song and dance, borrowed from Tibet, "because the steps are simple and can be done by old people, everyone." Now her "heart is close to Buddhism," sort of.

The musicians don't remember the songs or dances to Mao. Maybe because Mr. Wang is from a wealthy family before the Cultural Revolution and was not allowed to sing to Mao, but he probably knew the words at one time. His father was publicly humiliated, and died soon after.

Today Mr. Li was afraid to go outside the rehearsal studio to take his break. Someone had told him that it was dangerous to walk around SF wearing his Yunnan clothing, a target. He stayed in the studio, alone, with me, looking at my watch, which I had left on the studio table.

R

Monday

Dear L

We have a Show and Tell on Wednesday. Should be quite different from the first showing of Geography workshop material at Yale two years ago. Nothing exciting or fancy. And only two weeks of questions, compared to the four weeks of that showing. Silly to even think about being sensational, affecting. (The beginning Africans certainly were that, more.) So, I won't try to sensationalize. And wonder what I will do.

Otherwise I am good. My body feels in shape, again. Took two weeks. Not bad after three months off. Late at night rehearsing to Bach for Viola's memorial on the 11th at 3:30 at the Joyce, something like that, to answer your question. Will have a live cellist, I am told. I'm improvising. Looking forward to sharing the stage with Trisha B, Merce C and Viola's original company. That stage will be a shallow lake of tears. Viola would love that part.

Love

R

Friday

Dear L

The showing went well, although well or not well are obviously inappropriate verdicts at this point in the looking. I discovered a few hidden moments, perhaps three or four seconds where my plans broke down. The prize. I'm sniffing like a dog. On the trail. But must find some more Africans or black people, with their hammers and chisels.

Yes, one day the entire group joined Mr. Wang and Mr. Li in a traditional Yi circle dance. We were all terrible except for Wen Hui, who knew the steps already, and Djédjé, who did not but did. Surprise, surprise.

Off to Bali in June/July to look at more intricate physical moving. I'll visit Wang and Li again in September.

My revelation was the discovery of "quiet," what will set this work apart from the "fucking noise" of the Africans, that Geography. Djédjé was astoundingly out of place, by design. No drums, imagine that. No African dancing, imagine that. In fact, Djédjé danced modern steps, via his body's translation of modern dance. A new impossible form, ugly and a glimmer of hope. And by the way, there are no arrows in my quiver. But there is the quiver, the container. Empty. I want to keep it that way.

R

Thank You Letter

Dear Mr. Lemon of the United States of American, and other comrades,
How are you all.

First, We give our sincere thanks for you have cured my whole heart. Thus I did not have illness while I was living in the United States. The life of service person, hygiene, and conversation are all very good. My great-grandfather, grandfather, and father have not seen the scientific project. But I have clearly seen many sciences and arts.

The land in the United States is a full of rice and rice field as far as one's eye can see. I have seen the scientific Golden Gate Bridge, I feel much closer to it than to a relative! Even though it is not a relative, but it is better than a relative. It represents the superiority of the country. This way could make our civilizations, as members of family relatives, stand in the frontline to offer drops of effort for the Four Constructions. There is no worry on our backs. We could work together with one heart and one mind, learning to fight the warfare. Our heart of thanks is really hard to express in reality. We must learn from you. To promote your kind of revolutionary spirit to reach each and every one of our work post. Lastly, for the purpose of rescuing and preserving and promoting the traditional cultures of the ethnic world, we wish all comrades working with cultures in advance: In order to have a pair of eyes to see beyond thousand miles, one must arrive to the next higher level in the building.

February 29 1999 Yun-nan Ethnic and Cultural Tradition and Learning Center
Yi Tribe members Wang Li-Liang and Li Wen-Yi

Geography 2 workshop 2 San Francisco February 16 1999

Wen Hui China
Wang Liliang China
Li Wen Yi China
Djédjé Djédjé Gervais Côte d'Ivoire
Minh Tran Vietnam/USA
Cheng-Chieh Yu Taiwan/USA
Carlos Funn USA
Ralph Lemon USA

From this point on the language of Geography becomes extraordinarily important. Eventually I don't want to give as much credence to the words "spirituality" and "Asia."

Monday

Disoriented? No, not exactly. The black language, if there is one, seems outplayed. The Chinese are quietly loud. The musicians, primarily. Wen Hui refers to them as "natural." Certainly more tradition than I have yet experienced in my art process. No choice but to respect. Fearful that I will have to fuck it up. To get what I want. In the meantime how do I allow Africa to have its volume? Perhaps it is simple. About softening. I have been without the drum for so long, centuries. And when I'm really scared I run to string quartets, Bach, Mozart, etc., old world, practised, pretty stuff.

This time I will try to dance more of my dance, conscious, the way it's changing. I have Chinese women to dance with me. Strange. Carlos and Djédjé are enigmas now, powerful, making the puzzle somewhat irrelevant.

But the musicians! They bring a bundle full of homemade string and flute instruments. To my ears, a playful non-linear music that's not of an identifiable folk tradition.

Tuesday

Ok, this is what I don't like: What the fuck do I do with Djédjé? His African-ness is overwhelmed by the modern aesthetic and by the Chinese army.

The musicians don't have a clue what they are doing here but seem ready to share in whatever it is we might be doing. Mr. Li plays music non-stop, a four stringed instrument called si xian, which translates, four string. Very traditional sounding, the one sound I most likely won't work with, unfortunately it is the instrument he likes to play, all the time.

Worked on a formal dance phrase Monday. Desperate but necessary. Djédjé followed along, terribly frustrated. Carlos fell asleep. Mr. Li played his si xian. Better get used to it. Everyone else inspired.

That about describes the day.

Wednesday

A better day. Yesterday. Giving into the impossibility of this. Even with all the confidence I gained from the survival of Geography 1, I still fear this uncontrollable process. Carlos was awake today, asking questions and dancing beautifully. Djédjé has really grown, has been thinking about this "new work," his "modern translation," his "tradition translation?" Its possibilities. A full useful voice.

The musicians are adaptable. They remain true to what they bring and keep the rest of the space grounded. Powerful reference points. They go where they are. Mr. Wang is energetically a young man with the information of a fifty something elder.

I direct their instrumentation and get inspired. More simplicity, less strumming. They arrived with a total of twelve instruments. I'm emotionally interested in the sounds of four: A tiny bamboo flute called cao gan, a three string instrument, which reminds me of a banjo, called san xian, three string, a hauntingly deep toned reed flute called ba wu, and small green Yunnan leaves that they blow that sound like toy trumpets.

There are huge questions about cultural balance. Cheng-Chieh is in awe of all the Chinese here. Energetically crying and sighing, between China, Taiwan and America, not sure where she belongs. I am intrigued and cautious, like Djédjé, like Carlos. We hear, feel, but don't know. It is not ours. Djédjé's physical politic in particular needs more representation, I think. Or more of Carlos, or more of me. A black woman would certainly help.

Thursday

Asako Takami, who is Japanese, an Odissi dancer, living in San Francisco, danced for us today, a guest to the workshop. Exact and specific, rhythmically clear. I assume, knowing little of the form other than my Nrityagram experience, which was limited and breathtaking, the dancing of those young women. Asako doesn't dance like that. Watching her dance I begin to tear.

For one of her 'songs' I ask if I can dance behind her, she says yes. Her body a profound clock, keeping my body interested. I want to do more.

She teaches the group some extremely basic Odissi. And everyone moves foolishly. Not a good idea. Better to watch. Enjoy. Or, dance my own thing in the background.

Friday

Six hours fly by. Many exercises, not much productivity. A great amount of information exchanged that has little to do with art. I grab ideas where I can. Truly survival tactics. And failed attempts. Blips of alive moments. That has to be enough. Slow......

Saw the film Windhorse at the Castro last night with Wen Hui and Cheng-Chieh. A political message movie about Chinese brutality in Tibet. Wen Hui thought it was terrible. "The Chinese have done very good things for Tibet." In China it is obviously more complicated. Mao is still a kind of god. Tibet was a barbarian land. I found the film not terrible. Wen Hui asked if I believed the film's propaganda, I said yes, of course, I live in America. Through our exceptionally cured communication system, I have heard no moderate voice from China. Only China's propaganda and or China's political prisoners wailing.

Sunday

A long conversation about trance. Djédjé suggests that maybe he would try a "controlled trance" in this environment. I asked when? He replied, not now.

Before, in 97, we had this conversation:

RL The physicality of possession is really interesting to me.

DD In the video (Maya Deren's Divine Horseman) the trance dancer is shown in slow motion, and the rhythm is added on top of that. The rhythm you hear is not the rhythm he's really dancing. If you watch the drummer in the background and see when the stick comes down, you'll see that the dancer is really dancing to the drummer's rhythm. It's a fake image of trance.

RL What I'm interested in is the freedom of letting go, not the image, but the physicality.

DD Ralph, have you ever seen people in trance?

RL Yes.

DD It's not a stage event, people are really possessed. It's very real, dangerous. I can simulate it if you want, but it'll look ridiculous.

RL No, no, that's OK, I must re-think this.

In the meantime, Mr. Wang speaks of Shamanism in China. About ghosts and healing. He lays on the floor and sings part of a song, occasionally tapping his hand to the floor, creating an unpredictable rhythm. I ask if he would teach the other Chinese members the form. He does, while the rest of us busily write down the translation, of a translation. Djédjé picks it up by simply listening, hearing it once, he took no notes. As we leave the studio, at the end of the day, Mr. Wang says that we must never sing the song, not ever, because it will "bring on the ghosts."

Tuesday

We explore Djédjé's impulse to dance, where he dances from. We improvise with Djédjé and Carlos's djembe pulse. Letting that drive, rhythm, create whatever mayhem. An interesting non-conclusion. Designed, personalized forms with a beat, interpreted somewhere inside. Wen Hui finds the rhythm nearly impossible to dance to but it creates a very useful stir. The farmer/musicians play along with their various instruments. Can't hear them until after the drums stop. They're able to play longer than Carlos and Djédjé.

Djédjé was told while in Africa that the Chinese do not have tail bones. That that is why the Chinese are so flexible, and why their backs never hurt.

Wednesday

Asako returns, with Manoranjan Pradhan, a master Odissi dancer from Orissa. They dance for us.

Asako dances Odissi subtle and mysterious. Manoranjan dances like a girl and powerful folk spirit, male. Perfect.

At this point I add another version to the growing list of Odissi definitions.

Version 7: A remarkable form that incorporates every dance component that interests me, that I am aware of. Movement invention, rhythm, improvisation, a commitment to tasks, spatial design, expression, and centuries of refinement.

I suggest a modern dance and Odissi collaboration, a simple excercise about these forms moving in the same space at the same time. My suggestion turns into an hours long discussion on the sacredness of Odissi. How it cannot be simplified. Must be respected. I already know all of this, but in my way I push until I hear no. Asako had said yes. Manoranjan says no, and I'm curiously inspired. He says that a collaboration must be done deeply if it is to be done. That I would have to master Odissi and he would have to master modern dance. Impossible. Ok, so what would be possible? He'll have to think about it, well, even a small exchange would have to be done deeply, he says. And what might that be?

Mano nods, and I have to think about whether or not I have the resources to continue this conversation deeply. I would like to. I tell Mano that I wish I had met him before I went to India, twice. He replies, that I can always return to India again, and again, that that part is easy.

Thursday

A process discussion about what is coded. Laws, rules, signals. How it can affect and instigate form.

Minh Tran, Cheng-Chieh and Wen Hui, improvise with the gestures of Traditional Chinese Opera movement. A form that they have all studied. It turns out to be another badly directed study. Cheng-Chieh, especially, is confused, with other bodies on stage, moving independently, without voice. And yet something very beautiful appears. A quiet visual asymmetry. A landscape of ice. The quiet is what I am looking for, what will set this work apart from the energy of African drums, and some of what these particular bodies represent. My embrace, need for the refinement of chaos, that harmony, versus the embrace of spirit chaos that is African dance, that harmony. But the African presence is here, exists. And yesterday Djédjé danced a phrase that originated from a part of his cultural code, a phrase that was then re-organized from a Western perspective and then offered back to him, that he then made new. More new than the Western interpretations. What shall we call this new thing? That is a big question.

Djédjé says there is a traditional opera in Africa but only in one clan that he knows of, in the whole of Africa.

Djédjé asks the Chinese if their Traditional Chinese Opera work was influenced by the West. The uprightness of it. The detail. An obvious coded language, like Odissi. There is not a sufficient answer. Throughout Africa tradition is rooted in the oral tradition. In the West (is Africa the West or East, or both?) in the West, the tradition of codes has been marked by written scriptures, laws and an oral remembrance for sustaining an equilibrium. Where are the discrepancies? Djédjé said that in Africa a dance step will be the same from village to village but completely different from dancer to dancer, because "the spirit circulates differently from person to person." A drastic and not so drastic phenomena, like a group of unison modern dance elbows placed exactly three centimeters below the shoulder. Impossible, because the spirit circulates differently from dancer to dancer.

The "East" of Odissi might be 3000 years old, might be 70 years old. Historically, and definitely, not of the West. Its code is immaculate and completely limited within itself and at the same time, when fully realized, it is enlightened, without boundaries, free. The boundaries in Djédjé's dance seem more obvious, the obviousness of no boundaries, free.

What is common here? Certainly, the forms that thrive from working at something every day. And a belief system, written or sung. Certainly there is more.

Friday

James Lo arrives, on his birthday. Works a little with the musicians. Discovers, so far, that they "know what they know." That they are not improvising. That maybe we cannot work beyond what they know, cannot have them isolate, or find new sounds. Their old is enough.

I'm beginning this phase with a lot of modern dance. And I feel fine. Know also, that I am retreating. But I just don't know where else to go. After the Geography of Africa went home I was left as me. My body had not learned that much.

Friday

We have a small showing, for a small audience, of some of the more audience friendly play, that transpired over the two and a half weeks. Afterwards, Wen Hui asks why I'm still working with modern dance phrases if I'm searching for something more "natural"? My answer: I don't know what "more natural" is. My excuse: My post-modern shtick, is my only language. I use this language to communicate to the others.

Now that the showing is over we have a few days left where I direct the group forward into theatrics of minutiae, something more natural, whatever that might be. How about, simple chores that take everyone out of their trained bodies, challenging them to survive in the research of unplanned tasks? Material that I could never show to an audience, right now. Too bad.

In one exercise Mr. Li and Mr. Wang are perfect and untranslatable as they resemble the forms that they see the others creating. With kneeling and glasses of water.

But basically, the direction and chores turn out a failure. Only Wen Hui seems capable of the theatricality I'm looking for. Her body has little fear. I can't recognize/define any of the other physical solutions. Muddled and awkward, uninteresting. Moments, possibly useful. The end.

The last night in SF I'm invited to a rehearsal of Gamelan Sekar Jaya, there I meet I Madé Sabundi, a gamelan master and Ida Ayu, a Legong doyenne, both from Bali. They invite me to Bali. A reminder. I had forgotten that it was part of my map.

Yes, I will come, but not to dance, I want to find out why the Buddha didn't stay in paradise. "Oh, but he did," Dayu smiles.

When Viola was the queen bee

March 14
Viola's memorial. A reunion of a period of time, the 70's and early 80's. A reminder.
Perspective on how we grow and evolve, dissolve, die. Old bodies with young spirits.
Her original company, moving in forgotten shapes and paths on the stage, together, as
strangers. A lot of laughing. A few take it very seriously.
Her sister sings a song that she and Viola "sang as children." Merce reads how much
he misses her, will miss her. Merce, surviving all of it. And then Jeff Slayton, crying,
trying to share the last words. Describing how he had heard she was found, lying in a
pile of leaves, arms raised to the sky.

Then I dance, like Viola was inside my soul, pushing and shoving me, and I hanging
on, and trying to give each yank a softness. Demanding that she see this kindness as
something alive. To let her know that it is all right. That her presence, influence, life
work, lives on.
Afterwards, I went crazy. In a bar, eyes out of focus, spewing insults. Vulnerable and
angry. Oh well. Here was the actual Shipwreck I had questioned for years, the dance
she taught me. Viola always knew all of it. Goodness and horror live in the same
world. That was my new dance. And again, like that first dance she offered me in
1977, she opened up my body to another position of moving, profound. Thank you V.
I loved her because she was certain of her pain. What she gave beautifully away.

Before the gates

There are only guards pacing. Undangerous. I call foreign friends wake them up. I have been up for days.

Twenty-five hours and then.....

"Two hours, I think." To Candidasa. East. The traffic is slower than that in Chennai. A customary greeting: "You are alone? Where is your girlfriend?"

Waking up to the ocean and an erection. Quiet slow, peaceful and Hindu. Doesn't make sense. *In Paradisum*

Tana wants to take me snorkeling, has a boat. Bagang wants to drive me around in his car. Tana has a motorbike but cannot drive a car, "It is too difficult, getting a license." Wayan got Wayan pregnant. Wayan's father screamed at Wayan, that if he didn't marry his daughter then he would kill him. Wayan said OK, "I will marry her. But you must loan me one million rupiah to pay for the wedding. I will borrow the rest from the bank. If you don't lend me the money then you can kill me." Wayan's father agreed to lend him the money. And Wayan married Wayan.

There are four castes: Brahmana, Ksatriya, Wesya and at the bottom Sudra, the common folks. All first borne Sudra are named Wayan, boy or girl. All second, third, fourth children also have corresponding names, Madé, Nyoman, Ketut. After the fourth child the names repeat from the beginning. Tana and Bagang are nicknames, perhaps describing some physical feature.

Wayan takes me to a cockfight, "blood sport." There are no other tourists. Knife blades, preciously held in a special case, are measured exact to the cock's claw. And then wrapped securely with bright colored string. Owners puff and preen their birds, preparing them to fight, to the absolute death. As the cocks fight it is hard to see what they annihilate, they always do. Usually one or the other of the claws is sliced off, disappears. Or the necks are opened wide red, easily. The birds are trained well and seem to take pleasure in the killing, at least know that they are killing. If death is not immediate the stricken cock backs down, retreats motionless in defeat. Both are then placed under a large bamboo cage back to back, no other space available, no escape. The killing is then certain. An old woman plucks the loser, after the feet and head are lopped off by the owner. But first the claw with the dagger is unstrung, taking more time than the actual fight. One cock is eaten, the other lives to fight another day. "Siwa likes blood, it wakes him up." There is of course screaming chants and gambling from the audience of mostly men. "After temple ceremony there is always a cockfight, sometimes during."

Who originally belongs here?

"We do," he softly replies. Tenganan. Before the Java invasion, the Majapahit arrival, whenever that was. A tourist village. And "very rich," he says, as I pay the shopkeeper a lot of money for a piece of old Ikat cloth. What is a rich village? Does that mean that you give the money that you make selling handicrafts back to the village, some kind of village pool? "No. We have a separate government. Six people lead. There is a chief. One wife. No divorce. Generally families have no more than three children. Physically impossible to have more." Something to do with the blood of the originals. They are darker than others, I perceive. "The ones who live in colder areas are more black," he says. The walled village of Tenganan is not in a colder area. It is remarkably neat.

I know this before I know it: they sweep their earth, elaborately polite. Dirt, temples prostrating.

Pura, Sanskrit, space surrounded by a wall. Pura Besakih, the mother temple. Mostly a vast stairway. And guides, liars, like the liars everywhere where there are tourists but more gentle as if the lie was not a natural resource of this geography. There are layers to the guides, after Wayan: the higher up you journey the more holy and off limits the prayer space and the younger the guides. At the very top are locked gates and three young boys who are sleeping through their jobs: barely conniving payment from tourists for a quick glimpse at the backside of the main temple's locked gates.

In Paradisum dogs are mongrels with mange and fleas, and sometimes wounds are so exposed that organs show.

Cripples are nicely dressed. Great deformities are draped in bright silk.

Diesel fuel blackens the air.

Wayan is starving the whole day.

What is your common food? Rice, vegetables, chicken, fish, pork?

"No. Rice and vegetables, Chicken is too expensive."

Because this place is Eden the young are desperate because there are tourists, and competition, and therefore not enough work, no jobs.

Yes, they lie. Responding to my lie.

No one is fat.

Men suck betel tobacco and are proud of their black red teeth.

Even the liars pray. And will not let their prayers be photographed even for money.

Rice terraces. Green rages. It almost rains.

Giant insects the size of my hand walk my walls, and smaller ones traffic the floor like the monsters in my grandfather's basement in Cincinnati.

A local rock band in the distance plays covers of Beatles' songs, examples of each period. And then McCartney vintage Wings. They know the music well. Precise imitations. The ocean roars outside of their performance.

In the morning the first voices you hear are those of women.

When does the attribute of deception become part of a culture? When there is poverty. And when does that happen?

What do you think of the Japanese?

Wayan says, "We like seeing the Japanese, and the Americans. We know the Japanese and Americans have lots of money. They make us happy."

And I become rude when aggressively approached by brown men wanting me to pay them for lying and a little information about their gods. Although I am certainly interested in their gods. I am rude. In the world, in their villages and temples. Their culture demands that they connive me and my rudeness is a hubris reflecting where I come from. If life were fair I would be a weeping disciple, as part of my travel visa. I am not. But I scream inside, instead and don't at all get that I can't come here and passively watch.

Wayan says, "So, you see my brother tomorrow, OK? Go snorkeling. No sharks." Wayan attempts to keep our artful discussion within his family business.

The Hindus just keep praying.

I did not know this before but I have come because it is an island of ritual, remarkable. Tourism subsumed, like the Buddha. The Veda consumes all, even honeymoons.

Euorpean men and women and the Australians come here to remind themselves of love. The Japanese come in groups and for other reasons, like opening businesses that cater to the tourist trade, like snorkeling.

I'm traveling to Ababi to study rice.

And I want to discover a quiet place where I can practice yoga. So far I only manage push-ups, 80 a day, after zazen. All cultures have always had a dominant spiritual practice. Indian temples, American gymnasiums. American spiritual muscle provided by wealth and heavy machinery.

Like India the men here have soft bodies, even softer.

At the SF Lesbian and Gay parade they cover themselves with glitter, it flies through the air. Here they adorn themselves with rice, neatly placed on foreheads and temples. In temples these Hindus whisper, sit and pray, wait in line under the sun patiently. Climbing miles of stairs to tops of mountains. Where other temples always appear.

A temple is guarded by the low flying of beetles the size of sparrows, slow retarded sonorous flying.

The sounds of cocks and cicadas and the human voiced brown yellow necked celalongan. At first. But actually the noise of a tiny celeck, gecko. And motorbikes.

I want to be a Buddhist but I have already killed a hundred and twenty-five ants, one large brindled spider, three mosquitoes and one insect of indeterminable species.

I want to be a Buddhist but I have stolen one bamboo latticed folder from my first hotel room, with stationery. And from the same hotel I agreed when the receptionist made a mistake by charging me for two days instead of the actual three days of my stay. She found me later, by motorbike, on another day, in another village, at another bungalow, a losmen, asking for payment for the third day. She said nothing of the bamboo latticed folder.

First walk. A barefoot boy comes out of nowhere. "This is rice of course. Our rice, tall rice, two harvests. Java rice is smaller, three harvests. Tapioca. Sweet potato. Red rambutan. Jack fruit. Mangga. Mangoestin. Cocoa. Silik, wrapped in baskets, a black fruit, orange inside."

"This house belong to a Germany man. That one there is from Sweden. Sometimes he helps the farmers plant rice, helps tend cattle. He is not married."

Three hours through a rice culture. More stairs, lustful terraces, only traveling down. The seed narrative. From lake to long grass to harvest and pounding on to rocks. Women, not singing but gossiping, that music. All women, all ages making a perfunctory love to grass. Some sitting in ranguans, huts for screaming, not musical, shaking fields of "ore-ore," screaming. Some fields strung out in glowing black, reconverted cassette tape, reflecting sunlight in a way that disconcerts the birds.

An old woman snatches my money without a thank you because I took photographs of her, many.

The women work hard.

"Yes, but so do the men."

Where are they?

"Out building houses. Carrying trees through the forests."

In Paradisum ownership is a male map, father to son, or nephew, distant cousin.

When planting rice one plants approximately three to four stalks at a time. "You must plant the stalks twenty centimeters apart, like this."

Everyone in the family kept giving me the thumbs up. Although I knew that my technique was too generous and too precise. My careful symmetry would cause me to starve if I were living in this place. "You cannot plant on a horizontal plane. Rows are always vertical, moving from up to down."

Mud knee deep. I wore boots. "It is better to be barefoot, more flexibility."

Yes, I know, but then I would have to clean up and I have no idea where I would do that. They laugh.

Everyone works until 10:00am. When the grandmother, mother, wife brings out lunch for everyone, wobbling on top of her head. "We do not eat breakfast, only coffee. We can only eat two meals a day, it is too expensive otherwise. The rice that we plant is what we eat."

They also eat jackfruit vegetable pindang (fish) urob (mixed vegetables) fried gerang (rice and fish) jackskin fruit/salak and of course nasi putih (white rice).

During the planting the men take many breaks, smoking, the women keep working. But eat as much as the men when food is served.

After lunch it is too hot to work but planting continues another hour or so anyway.

That was quite a day, I thought. Sitting on a hill. Drawing an overview sketch of a naturally remote farm temple. A temple where only its scenery, landscape seems to worship. Behind me a distant grunt, faint, continuous. I look around. A young girl with a kite, far away but not so far away to see perfectly. Her free hand in gesture, miming the hand of my own, drawing. I don't understand. I don't know what she wants.

I walk up the hill to meet her, she does not run away.

She cannot talk, the grunts are refined, the only sound that her bright happy face echoes.

She wants my pen, what I draw with. I have another and return to my bungalow searching for it. I find it and show her how it works. She already knows. Takes the pen and waves good-bye.

At this losmen a young man named Madé cleans my room, He has typhoid making it difficult to eat. I tell him that ginger might be good for his digestion. He tells me of a snow white ginger that he has seen but not tried. He says that he must be patient with his weak body.

He is patient with his pet. His is a broad beautiful white cock.

"I will train my cock for another year."

How do you do that?

"I hold it, shake it, preen its neck."

He demonstrates by rocking his empty hands forward and back.

Won't you be sad if it is killed?

"Oh, of course I will be sad but I will be happy if it wins."

Question:

Why the knife on the back of the claw, where another set of claws already extends?

"Because when the cock attacks it sends its front claws forward, up towards its own body, the back claws then come slicing down on whatever is in its path. God's creation, already. We have simply refined it, made it a more efficient machine."

The cocks are surprised at the efficiency. When defeated a cock will not move. All the bluster, fearlessness from before shuts down, when there is missing a right or left claw or a wide slice into its abdomen, and blood everywhere. And they do not whither in defeat. Just freeze. It is over. Their bodies know it. Surprised.

Madé is also patient with his best friend. Ketut is from a very poor family.

"My father was very stupid, refused to work when he was young. He got my mother pregnant. Had no money to marry her properly. Then he had to work, a little, and raise five children. Or, we raised ourselves and took care of our parents. Usually, the parents take care of the children but in my family it is different. I worry very much about my future because I have to take care of my parents. They are older now. No longer stupid, just old."

Now every morning a little girl, the sister of the girl without speech, holding her infant brother, stands a few feet away from my window, waiting for her gift. Not just a pen, but several. "Beaucoup, beaucoup." Yes, yes, I will, tomorrow.

There is also malaria. Broken backs and infant mortality. Buttered toast. Huge rains. Sounds that one is not sure are inside or out. Mouths of the elders are drenched in blood red "medicine" that keeps their teeth from falling out. Rich and poor. Gado-gado, mixed blood. But everyone prays at the same altars. Everyone walks up the same number of stairs to the temple. Some hire others to carry their offerings, banten. Orange Fanta soda.

Madé says, "My sister is also without speech."

Later he says, "I do not like white people. I think the people from India are the best. Their brown is the most beautiful. Not too white, not too black. I don't like the Chinese. They are colonialists. They don't belong in Indonesia. They are everywhere. You must be careful and keep an eye on them in America. Yes, they are also white people." He pauses. "I have a sixteen-year-old girlfriend from Germany. She was here for two months, with her mother." They had a two month romance completely chaperoned by the girl's mother. Mother and daughter traveled around the Island and sometimes Madé would meet up with them, whenever, however he could, acting as guide and culture. Now the girl sends letters from Germany. Madé can barely read them. But he can always be reached by telephone at the losmen.

Madé likes Shania Twain, Madonna and Guns and Roses.

From a small shop I buy pens and notebooks for the young girl. Present them to her. She asks me to write down an English lesson in one of the notebooks. In large letters I spell out, THIS IS AS GOOD AS IT GETS.

Every day I desecrate. Without thought. It is not easy.

What is your caste, Ketut?

"I am Sudra."

Outsider, the bottom, and ninety percent of the population. I have seen no Untouchables. In India they are ever present. I have heard that there are those who wash the clothes of the Untouchables called Unseeables. I have not seen them either.

"It is good to be the roots of the tree. Without the roots there is no tree."

There is more that the young girl wants. The pens and notebooks are not enough. She beckons me to come into her house. I decline. I am better at giving things away anonymously. No, this is not about sex, but something more tender.

In Paradisum there is no future. Here future is everlasting. A fixed placement, "made once and for all time by birth. Unchangeable law."

The Buddha considered himself Hindu, seeking reforms of unchangeable laws. And so the gods subsumed him, making him part of the Veda. The Hindus love the Buddha, to them he represents a quiet spirit. Nothing threatening about that.

There are no missionaries. Mormons, Jehovah Witnesses, Hare Krishnas are banned.

There are more temples than homes. Or they are the same existence. I tried to draw the Pura Puseh Arabi again today and instead of being surrounded by a dozen yapping, dying dogs I was covered with twenty small boys who would not go away no matter how inhospitable I was in their scared backyard.

So I take Ketut and Madé to lunch. We all ride huddled together on Ketut's vintage Honda, to The Good Krishna restaurant. They both order tuna grilled and I order saté tempe with greens.

"This is a boss meal." Madé smiles.

When was the last time you had a meal like this?

"Once, twice a year, maybe."

I flirt with the young waitress. She tells all of us that she does not like the native men. That she is looking for someone large, taller, who wears a mustache.

Madé also likes white girls. But doesn't think he would have much of a chance marrying one. "I am very poor, my family are farmers. We rent the land we farm, giving up half the crop we bring in. A white girl would want to work in an office, would want a hot shower. I also eat with my hands."

Sekala - Niskala
ruwe bineda
ruwe BiNEDA
yin   YANG
Two   worlds

my grand father Name
was PeKaK Tegeh he was
a Balian, he cured peoples
he was an indra Balian
wich has job to cured
people he has some thing
like magic to cured people.
and to fight the black
magic, some day when
he fight to a black magic

he was standing up at
the river side wich
his spirit fighting with
the black magic,
when he fight the sky
become cloudy and
much tunder the
situation is so scariing
and then my grand fathe
is found unconcius
the the villagers are
taking him to hospital
aweek after that he
passed away. after that
we have to do much
~~the~~ work, we made
sescjun that needed
for the ceremony —

to ngaben (burning dead
body) be for we do ngaben
we have to do wunch
Ceremony so that the
god accept his soul.
the ceremony like bathing
the dead body.
do you know when we
do the ceremony to
bathing my grand father
dead body the situation
is very dramatic
the wind belows up
the trees and the
flowers are falling down
to my grand father's
dead body.
                    Tobe .. continued .

People says that
my grand father's friend
who has been died first
coming to see him,
and they sprinkle flowers
to my grand father's
dead body for respect
him.

In Paradisum girls drop blood, then they grow up, boys drop their voices, then they buy their first motorbike.

The next morning I move on, to Lake Batur, the crater lake, missing Madé and Ketut and the little girl with no voice whose sister was so mysterious.

I want a room with some windows, a view. I subtly plead, to an attendant standing in the courtyard of Segara on the Lake, a hotel, after I had been shown one too many rooms without a ray of natural light.

"Sorry, but we have only this view," the attendant gestures up towards the luscious sky and the breathtaking mountain.

The room I choose is still dark.

The food I choose is a local fish, whole, greasy. And eat to a Bruce Lee movie whose VCR deck is having difficulties. Plays the same ten minute major fight scene over and over, five times, while I try to eat the fried, fried fish.

I have memorized the fight sequence and return to my dark room and fall asleep under a mosquito net. I awake the next morning staring at a mosquito also under the net. Frozen. Fat. Drunk. Inches from my groggy eyes. I smash it and fresh blood, red bright, puddles the sheet. My room is no longer dark. I check my body. It was not my blood.

Breakfast of tea and powdered milk. I sit in the sun. Arrange a boat to Kunban, the Trunyan village cemetery, really the only reason that I am here, where they don't bury their dead, "And it doesn't smell." The banyan tree, it is said. More bargaining.

I buy an old sarong for the journey from a young man at the hotel, he says that it belonged to his grandmother. I don't have to take off my shoes to visit temples. I love this part. An unrehearsed Hindu.

A motorboat down the "river of death."

Who originally belongs here?

"We do. Trunyan. We worship Bayu-wind. Wind God."

Mepasah. Corpses of the dead covered in white cloth are laid down in open pits side by side, seven or eight of them, perhaps twelve inches shallow into the earth, left to decompose in the open air. There is no smell because of the "fragrance of the holy banyan tree," which has no discernible fragrance, the only one of its kind that grows in the village, I'm told. The bodies are covered with simple bamboo roofs. When the remains have completely decomposed the bones are moved, thrown into the nearby forest, making room for the newly dead. The death and birth cycle in the village seems to fit this mere and profound system.

There are two other cemeteries in Trunyan. One for babies and young children, who are still god-like. And one for those that died in accidents or in some other violent death. Polluted deaths, whose karma is not happy.

There is still daylight, bouncing. I am wildly awake now and in a car leaving Batur with an older Madé. We pass a walking funeral procession. Happy faces carrying a coffin. Madé stops and gives money to the leader of the procession. "It is only a body, the spirit has already returned."

Madé also beeps his car horn whenever we pass a temple. "To say excuse me, I am here, thank you for letting me pass without harm."

"When I saw you I spoke to you in Indonesian but was then told that you were American."

Yes, I am African American.

"Yes, American Latin, I understand, brown like us."

I ask about his family. He has a six-month-old daughter. Birthdays are celebrated on the sixth month of one's birth. Two birthdays a year in the Western calendar. "There are two celebrations a year if one can afford them, if there is money." His wife is now pregnant again. Madé wants three children. And then no more, does not want to be burdened like his father who's now just having another new baby. "He will have to work hard until he dies." Madé wants two daughters and one son. Daughters, he says, are the best things a father can have. "They work hard, carrying great loads, cooking and massaging their father's heads. Boys are always away, busy."

It is somewhat similar where I come from.

North

At another breakfast I watch a white American family sitting at a table next to mine. A father, mother, daughter and what I assume is an adopted African American son. The son plays with his Indonesian noodles, the daughter reads a book, the mother and father talk.

I write by candle light.

5km up. Brahma Vihara Ashrama. The one and only Buddhist temple. Top of the hill. Built in 1965. Bhikkhu Girirakkhitu, an old priest. Calm. Sitting tired. "Excuse me while I eat but I must eat before 12:00. Once at 7am, sunrise and again at 11:00am, before the sun slides to the other side."

There are young monks here from Java, Lombok, Burma. A retreat. The monks have to perform their meditation in front of tourists with cameras, me and others. But I have also come here to sit. And to be watched, I discover.

They're building a new stupa, for the founding monk who died recently. I meet the engineer overseeing the construction, which seems to be actualized very very slowly, by two or three locals and their children. Later in his life the engineer wants to be a monk, he tells me. But for now he needs to make a living. He knows a lot about the dharma. He draws a map for me of the path of Buddhism as it traveled through Asia from India. That it theoretically journeyed through Indonesia before reaching China brings him a reasonable pride. Later, I color the drawing with the juice from flowers I pilfer from the monastery's gardens. And search for the engineer, intending to give the drawing back to him, adorned, but he has disappeared. Along with a brief spiritual entertainment.

I am not my audience. I am more lonely here than I have been in other places with similar air and color, light and dirt. I have not danced. Can't bring myself to ask, for permission.

At another dinner in the restaurant of another hotel in the north, I sit drinking Bintang beer. Waiting for a Joged dance to begin. I have heard. There is no one here. A white sparkling floor empty. The dancing is supposed to start soon. I eat. The food everywhere so far is always overcooked, like food in the southern United States, soul food. I eat quickly because I'm bored, the waiter tells me to slow down, he does not want me to finish, leave and miss the show.

Digression. For two days I have bathed in a warm sulphur pool, in eighty degree weather. I have had enough of cold morning showers listening to my own singing, howling, how I was able to fathom the temperature.

Digression. At the Buddhist monastery I had the best meal I have had so far. That day I had walked back to my hotel in sun rain barely. The homefolks covering up like it was raining fire and brimstone. It's only drizzle, I said.

"The dancer is here. She is changing," my waiter announces. I order more food. Entertain me.

Digression. I called my mother from the hotel's front desk phone. Her voice full of morning. "Son, what are you doing up so early?" Mother, it is night here. We spoke for five minutes. I just needed to know that no one was dying.

My father is full again. Walks with swollen ankles, no colon and twenty extra pounds, from his bedroom at 11:30 every morning, down the stairs, to the kitchen, to prepare his breakfast. He sits at the kitchen table and eats very slowly, eggs, grits, bacon and toast. Coffee is what he brings with him, as he walks to the recreation room to sit in a reupholstered chair, four feet from his 70 inch television screen. For the remainder of the day his posture is similar. After 5:00 p.m. there are variations, mostly to do with what he will eat for supper, how it must be prepared. At 1:00 a.m. he falls asleep deeply in his chair, and awakes two hours later to watch what's left of what he has missed on his giant TV. He cares little for time, but at 4:00 a.m. every morning, he turns off the television and softly steps up the stairs to his bedroom, to my mother and his sleep. Three times a week he walks out of the house, to his car, and drives to the Kingdom Hall, his religion and biblical community, where he is adored. Once every month he walks out of the house and into his yard and tool shed, to mount his riding lawn mower, where he will spend hours meditating on grass, sometimes wondering what would happen if the creek in the back of his property were to swell and rise due to rain, submerging the whole of his house. Diluvial awe.

By the way, now I'm ready, prepared to return home whenever I need to. Being a tourist in Japan was instructive for many reasons. I can relax. And can force it, by walking to the temple up the road, sit, for two days maybe three.

The trash on the ground that is not swept up is Garuda cracker wrappers and skin from the salak fruit.

There is yet no dancer.

My waiter makes sixty thousand rupiah a month, about ten US dollars. A young man. His father is also a "poor farmer." It seems that most young men I've talked to, the few I've talked to, have fathers who are poor farmers. And so the young men work long hours to support their families, their parents.

Digression. The student monks, "they study the self. The real life. Not the life of desire." I wonder what is real about my waiting......

Finally, the dancer danced. Three of them. Small boned immaculately made-up. A village dance. Improvisational. Not as specific as Legong (I know so little). In the village, the dancer will dance with someone from the village audience, mostly teenage boys. Here there is no village, there's me and a large table of Dutch tourists, a family. Seven of them, three generations. One is a teenaged girl, jet black, who looks African American and speaks fluent Dutch, like a daughter.

(I paused from the entertainment to think. First a brown African something boy at breakfast with a white American family and now a jet black African something girl at dinner with a Dutch family, both in the north. This must be a conspiracy, I think.)

The dancers pulled, seduced the tourists one by one from their table with a red scarf and then danced with them, musical, intricate, playful, the dancing tourists mostly skipping, the seated tourists clapping.

I was approached three times and each time I refused. I thought that maybe if I had been paid by the tourists or if I had been in an actual village I would have danced.

I sat in a corner with the brothers of the waiter, three of them , all smoking clove cigarettes, heavily. I was offered one. I smoked one.

After the dancing one of the brothers gave me a lecture late into the night, about Hinduism, Buddhism, Christianity, Islam. On a piece of paper he sketched how they all worked together.

Hindu represents the earth, the farmer.

Buddhism represents the wind, the breath.

Christianity represents fire, bright thinking.

Islam represents water, and or oil.

The Dutch have a long history here. This large Dutch family's presence is docile. The whole family smokes. Maybe the Dutch brought the cigarette here and this place refined it with the clove and boy children smoking long before they learn to ride motorbikes, some becoming cigarette salesmen. The next day, still skipping, with matching canes, the grandparents circle a small five foot circumference in the parking lot of the hotel. Thirty minutes of choreography, exercise, a walk. The rest of the family is bathing in the sulphur pool.

There is no guilt. Misunderstanding is valuable. How one can be killed. What is more important than meditation is the awareness of the results of one's actions. Without judgement.

The brother of the waiter who had shared so much about world religion invites me to see "real Joged." A flashlight is needed. A dark path leads to low flying bats, navigating playfully near the heads and faces of passersby.

A village. Same three dancers from the restaurant performance, plus more.

And many young men, boys acting out, shamming hormonal desire, sexy and beautiful. The dancers give them permission. The rest of the village, women, young and old, men and children sit, stand and joyously watch.

Do women ever join in, dance with the Joged dancers, these beautiful girls?

He did not understand the question.

I don't dance. Not even here. The cultural code seems too complex. And I do not want to be laughed at.

Bhikkhu, is it difficult for the monks to practice with so many tourists visiting, walking through the grounds, peering?

"No, I told them in the beginning to ignore all but the self. Especially the younger monks, with all the young foreign girls fascinated, yes, I told them already. You know, some of the younger monks are underage so it is very important that they concentrate on the self."

The younger monks have their eyes closed most of the time, nodding asleep, sitting.

I meditate for three hours today, sitting and standing. Red carpet. Bald, golden draped forms, passing in and out of my periphery. I wish my head were shaved. Sometimes it is, but not here.

There is a young girl practicing with the monks, the only one. She is overweight, full of light. Her own retreat. No golden robe. Wears a Nirvana T-shirt, Kurt Cobain, or so. My eyes are blurred by now.

The practice is in silence but I hear her laugh, only her, as the monk makes an obvious funny remark.

In Japan the Zen monks are comedians. Jokes are very important. But monks don't really laugh. Wee smiles are practiced.

On a bench with a monk in the sun.

Bhikkhu, when will the stupa be finished?

He laughs.

"We are short of builders, so it will take maybe a year, maybe longer."

He sits with a walking stick. Literally a stick. A three-foot weathered, one-inch plank. Attached to the top, with lots of tape, is the bottom half of a small plastic water bottle, his handle. I assume he made it himself.

I say good-bye. I want to give him a hug, to touch him. But then think that it wouldn't be appropriate. I put my hand out to shake his. He puts his palms together and says, "It is done like this, just this." Keeping it reverent.

On the way back I pick flowers from everywhere leading to the hotel. Later, painting temples I have seen and then remembered, with petal juice.

Orange kumbang or is it a kertis?

red pucuk

purple andang

yellow kuning

You cannot predict the color that a flower's petals will make by the color of the petals that sit under the sun. Sometimes pink becomes brown. Baby blue becomes ash. Red becomes purple. Green leaves are always a shade of green. Yellow begins yellow and becomes brown. All the unpredicted colors that appear fade overnight.

Sunday is like Wednesday or Thursday. Rice is planted. Shops are open. Boys and girls on motorbikes. Others lounging in bales, roadside shelters. The old seem to dress more apparent to Sundays, Sundays that I recognize.

2.5 million motorbikes, I bet.

At Brahma Vihara Ashrama a young monk was not feeling well. Sighs and belching through meditation practice. Later, loud farting. But he keeps sitting and walking. Thinking "only of himself," I imagine. After I finish my practice and am about to leave the hall he offers me an unopened bottle of water.

South

I call I Madé Subandi. He lives in Sukawati, near Denpasar, in a traditional compound with his wife, young son and extended family. His life consists of playing gamelan and going to ceremony, just like it did in San Francisco. His father is perhaps a more renowned musician than he is but his father does not attend as many ceremonies. And now seldom plays the gamelan. Hierarchy.

There are no hotels in Sukawati so I stay in nearby Sanur. Madé picks me up the next morning on his scooter. In time for ceremony.

Ceremony permeates all aspects of life. Like wristwatches and the English language to the rest of the world.

Madé dresses me.

Undeng/Destar-head wrap

Safari-jacket

Kamben-inner wrap sarong

Saput-outer wrap

Sentang-belt sash

Many comment that I look Indonesian, Muslim, East Timor, the curly hair. I begin to think that none of this matters.

Tirta Yatra. "Traveling to temples to clear our soul."

Mekiyis. Cleansing ceremony, the body, the world, bringing peace.

A seven hour temple ceremony. A 10km walk to the ocean and back in full religious regalia.

Gamelan sing along. In the blazing sun. The Barong line up, three of them, two lions and a boar. Different villages. Maybe 1000 people, maybe more.

Destination Pabian Desa. Black sand. At the ocean everyone plays, running through the sand, eating watermelon, littering the black sand with empty plastic containers. No one goes swimming or even wading.

At an exact moment, an hour and a half later, everyone stops. And walks the same ceremonial line in reverse, home. A few veer off taking shortcuts.

Week three. The food has gotten better.

Had a wonderful dinner at a small family restaurant near Madé's village. Grilled fish, giant prawns, squid, beer.

Eating with one's hands makes the food one is eating indistinguishable from the gestures,

*motion of eating. Hands and food become one. Taste all but disappears, becoming body, flesh.
My experience. Because, perhaps, I eat with two hands and not just the right. Too much of good
thing.*

Then I grow ill. Dehydrated. Too many days walking uphill in intense humid heat, not
knowing where I am going. Not drinking enough water.

I'm not on my back.

Yesterday I spent the day riding on the back of a rented motorbike. Found a field of
watermelons. I prefer taxis, less active participation. I was never in danger.

*I do not feel danger, even with all the evil spirits that temporarily wait in every nook and cranny,
confused by walls and banten.*

Daia-power of nature

Daya-power

Again Madé dresses me. The first time the saput was yellow. This time it is red.
Another ceremony. But we are late and miss the teenage girls dancing sacred temple
Legong. Do see them made up like goddesses, wafting incense into their breastless tor-
sos, hands delicate, girl awkward.

At the end only priests left, sprinkling water, chanting ancient Kawi, interpreting each
other, on the spot, in four part disharmony, into cordless microphones. The garbled
sound that comes from the temple's loudspeakers is unintelligible to me, not to the rest
of the village.

Priests wear white, only white, that too seems incomprehensible in all this color.

Like Madé, Wayan, a "cousin friend," seems always to be dressed for ceremony. A job-
less young man who shows me a magnificent wooden dragon he has made that took
two weeks to carve, 8 hours a day. He asks if I would like to buy it. I tell him that it is
beautiful, but no thanks.

Madé has arranged for Wayan to drive me to Ubud which is not far, after Wayan drops
his family off at ceremony.

I say goodbye to Madé and his family, knowing I will surely see them again. I give
Madé's father two new Jockey sleeveless T-shirts as a good-bye present, wrapped in
newspaper. He refuses to open it in my presence. But seems happy to receive a gift.
What it is is not so important, I can only assume.

It takes 2 hours for Wayan to pick up his family and then drop them off at a ceremony
about a km from where we start. Stuck in traffic in Sanur and Sukawati. Traffic jams
because of ceremonies. I know both sides of the line-ups, privileged in the ceremony,
powerless, pretending and practicing reverence in a stalled motored vehicle.

We reach Ubud. Some, and foreigners who write travel books, suggest that "one" has
not seen this place until you have seen Ubud. Ubud is not this place. Not quite.
Anyway, we find the bungalow suggested in the "Rough Guide." But before entering I
balk and beg my driver to take me back to Sanur. He does and then rushes off to
another ceremony, or maybe the same one.

I immediately find another driver, another Ketut, and head North, again, this time to Bedugul. Relieved.

Sometimes it is good to change direction. We stop at a checkpoint gate. Ketut gets out and goes inside a windowless shelter. Twenty minutes later he returns to the car with a form that he has filled out, which asks for:
THE NAME OF VISITOR
OCCUPATION/COMPANY
CAR NUMBER
ADDRESS
WISHES TO SPEAK TO:
SUBJECT
DATE
TIME OF ENTRY
TIME OF ARRIVAL
SIGNATURE OF VISITOR
SIGNATURE OF SECURITY
At the bottom of the form it asks, PLEASE RETURN THE ENTRY PASS TO THE SECU-RITY GUARD. THANK YOU.
The gate opens. We drive along a road uphill into the farm. A strawberry farm. At the top of the road we stop at a complex of single story windowless buildings. Three or four. Another guard appears and directs us into one of the buildings. Inside there is an empty room, basically, two chairs and a small refrigerator cooler in a corner. The guard/official gestures to us to sit, as he walks over to the cooler. He opens the cooler and lifts out one pint of strawberries. All that the cooler contains. He looks at it. He places the pint back into its empty space, closes the cooler and tells us to wait a moment. He leaves. One half hour later a woman enters carrying a large box of approximately twelve pints of strawberries. Now it gets complicated. All the containers are approximate pints of strawberries but depending on how large the berries are, within the pint, the prices vary. Larger berries are more expensive. Prices are determined by sight. I pick four pints and pay about $3 per pint. Ketut tells me later that the official gave us a discount. Some of the pints go for as much as $8 a pint.

Almost North
Bedugul. A four hour drive. A colder area. Yes, some of the people are darker, but none of them are "originals." There is a large Muslim enclave around the Bedugul Botanical Gardens. The Garden itself is breathtaking. 524 species of trees. 320 orchids. I make up a project: videotaping flowers, roses, in slow motion.
Then I find a place to stay. The owners of the homestay greet me completely covered in traditional Muslim dress. They discover that I am not Muslim, smile and quickly begin taking off their coverings, exposing contemporary pants and T-shirts.
Fadhillah and Nining. Two thirtyish women. They live together, business partners. No husbands, no children. Fadhillah is from Madras, India. Nining is from Java. They have an unusual beauty about them, how strangers look exceptional.

They both find me amusing. I'm always asking them to repair something that has gone wrong or is missing from my room, hot water, light bulbs, toilet paper. I think I get charged for the toilet paper. They make dinner for me each night and it is wonderful. The first evening I had asked for pork and they said, "No pork, just beef," giggling.

At 5:00 am the Koran is sung. A male voice far away. And then from part of the home-stay a female voice chants, briefly. By 6:30 it is quiet again.

By 7:00 I'm in the Gardens videotaping bamboo and shrubs, another project, the same one, hoping to beat the rush of tourists. Two empty tour buses enter and sit nearby, waiting with their motors running, the whole hour I spend with my camera, filming. When I'm finished the buses drive off. Then there is perfect quiet and I have run out of videotape. The rush of tourists begins.

By the fourth week I am no longer killing thousands of ants that inbreed every hotel bathing room.

In Paradisum poverty does a better job of discarding waste. Perhaps all that it does. Water falls are called 'air water.'

I read road signs, directions, on the way, all the way back to the East where there are no waterfalls.

East

Almost nothing but ocean. Watching the saltmakers. Amed.

Here are the niggers. Finally. Men, women, children, black not brown. But this is not a colder area and I am confused. Dirty field work. Literally groveling in dirt salt. So this is "salt of the earth." Maybe it means "almost slavery." For the first time I hear the word, sound, "niggra!" I'm called that once. From one of the field hands. An ancient pronunciation. One of them, they understand, the origin of being abhorrent and simultaneously obscure, that it comes from a life debased, impoverished and too hard work, work that gives nothing back.

They buck and wing in bowls of sand and sea water, stomping out the salt. That's what I call it, am reminded. Straw hats and clothes soiled the color of flesh oiled brown. Mid-day. Sun blazing. The perfect time to make salt. Intense glare air. Unfriendly terrain. No rain. But ocean wide sand, waiting for their sweat.

They do not smile like all the Madés I've met.

They shit in sand. Also. But don't cover it up. Yes, it is human shit because the skinny dogs can't possibly eat enough to shit turds this size. I accidently step in some. And lose another pair of boots. Here in the sand at the ocean. The other pair under the Buddha tree. I walk a while before discarding them, before I give way to the smell. I bury them. Wouldn't feel right giving them to a salt farmer, it would be an insult. No longer their shit. Plus they would have no use for them, even clean, no snow, no hiking.

At 5:00pm only the women remain, ladling up the salt from hollowed logs. Scooping it into baskets. White domed.

Across from them in the ocean an old man squats in the far end of a fishing boat while six young boys wearing goggles and snorkels swim around him occasionally climbing into the boat and then jumping back into the ocean seeing something in the water they want. Breathless swimming. They never emerge with fish. Every fifteen minutes or so the old man stops the boat and pulls in a net, holding nothing big enough to see from shore.

Underwater there are tables and chairs made of corral color bands that sparkle glow and also starfish throwing knives startling into the skin. It is not so quiet if you really had to listen and my face explodes eyes sedated. Floating is deceiving. Far seems not so far until it is a brand new suit is brown and growing nutrition becoming alive like everything inside of water. No smell of shit no smell of anything nostrils cannot work mouth pushes air slow motion. Fish are not as brilliant out of this light. There's no desire to eat any of this beauty

Another young man standing on the beach claps at specific intervals, giving some kind of signal, directing, perhaps..

On the beach, the slight strip between water and salt work, there are young men, like Mawi, who have long hair and live on the beaches playing out of tune guitars, always incomplete chords of American pop rock.

Bob Marley is very popular.

Mawi, do you like Bob Marley?

"No. I like Firehouse."

Who?

"Firehouse, American pop rock."

Why?

He has no answer.

He sings well. His guitar is more in tune than most. Actually, his guitar is tuned but the fifth string is almost completely frayed, fraying the sound.

"I like country."

Country?

"Of course. 'When I was a little biddy baby my mama use to rock me in the cradle in dem ole cotton fields back home.' Yes, I like it. Sounds like our folk music."

How about a cotton field, ever seen one of those?

He has no answer. But asks for my American address and phone number.

In Paradisum *children are waiting to become adults, when they can play with the toys of the adults, the ceremonies: kites, dance, music.*

When these children play with Lego toys they build cremation towers.

"My first job was selling cigarettes at cockfights, when I was a very little boy."

Now a beach bum. But industrious, without reciprocal power, hustling for work without a motorbike or car. Impossible. So guides tourists to those with travel vehicles, gets a small commission. Saving pennies to finish a year's course in hotel management at the University, like many young people here. "I want to be a bartender, waiter, receptionist." Where power is, where extraction of the privileged US dollar is possible.

I think of my privilege. I give away pencils, T-shirts but not my shit-smeared boots. I buy dinner for everyone. It is almost nothing.

Mawi joins me on my porch this morning. Obviously the management lets him have the run of the place, one system. I am not pleased. My privacy, the privilege that I cannot give away. His first words are something like, "I was not lucky last night." Why? He's not sure but maybe he got too drunk on the beach and anyway the point was that he had lost my address, his "godfather's phone number and address," someone he could write to in case he "needed help."

He asks me to write my address down again. He has no paper, nor pen. I ask, has he lost his entire wallet and contents therein? He answers, yes.

This time I write down my real US address and phone number, give him a few rupiah. And Mawi guides me to a travel vehicle, that will take me to Denpasar.

And South

Denpasar is at the bottom of the map, in the middle, the capital.

On the way I sit in the passenger's seat, crying the whole way, listening to the driver's cassettes of MTV's Fantastic Females and Modern Pop Love Songs. Happy to be on the road and crying. Not wanting the drive to end.

I have friends in Denpasar, which is not particularly tropical but there the indigenous outnumber the tourists. And one witnesses how courteous modernity, the velocity of the "new Asia," has been to this culture. Denpasar is not a frightening city. I call Ida Ayu.

My Denpasar family: Or, A Brahmana marries a Wesya.

Ida Ayu/wife

Gus Tut/husband

Gung Wah/son

Gung Gék/daughter

Citra/cousin

Ibu/grandmama

Agung Oka/grandfather

Brahmana women are named Ida Ayu, or Dayu for short. Men are named Ida Bagus.

In Dayu's kitchen there is the sound of loud frying in a pengtantokan, breakfast, from rice fields, snakes. Occasionally she bangs the wok like a gong.

She crushes belut into the pengtantokan squatting. Cutting onions. And then the peppers.

Dayu, what American food do you like?

"I like salads and spaghetti. I like burritos."

She thinks that hamburgers are European food. She likes hot dogs.

Dayu is a famous Legong dancer.

Gus Tut is a famous Gambuh dancer.

Agung Oka gives me beginning lessons on the kendang drum.

Later, much later, driving in the rain to Pura Luhur, the temple for "divine inspiration." Where artists go to pray. In a car that Gus Tut has borrowed. It is also sunset and on the way Dayu sights the priest on his motorbike, driving away from the temple direction. We stop him.

"We want to do ceremony."

"OK, but it's late, raining and cold. What's the gift?"

There are four temples on the grounds. A temple on each level extending upwards into the mountain.

1. Pura Petals
2. Pura Rsi
3. Pura Luhur
4. Pura Taksu

We climb direct to Pura Luhur and have ceremony in dim shadowed light. And then we climb to Taksu where it is now almost pitch. The path is small and uphill, mud steps.

A silhouette of a tree. A beringin tree, trees that are planted in temples, becoming sacred. "This tree is male and female, two trees together. The leaves are red and also white. And the roots are like tables and chairs. It is a very magical tree." A tree like this can grow faces in the trunk that are cut out and made into masks.

The priest treats us with dignity, speaking to Dayu in a high language because she is royalty caste. The priest laughs often, tells us he likes to make jokes, does not like to be too serious with his magic. Dayu quietly provides a sufficient gift, out of sight.

It is now completely dark. Black outlines of merus and the beringin tree, a priest in lightless white chanting, black flower shapes, not the red, green and white of daylight. Tonight Brahma, Wisnu and Siwa are all darkies. There is some light from incense. Holy water generously poured over heads and into palms. "Drink three times and then wash your face." I sit zazen, all I know. Listen. "Divine Inspiration." Hmmmm, that would be nice. On top of a mountain. I wish I could see this place. It must be beautiful.

"You are lucky Ralph, to be here," Dayu tells me. Yes, I'm lucky. In the dark, rain, divinely forced to drink water I know not from where it comes. Sitting on the damp ground, sarong drenched, wet holy hair, excited.

The path down completely disappears and is more mud.

On the drive back we stop at Dayu's mama's house. A full house. Eat and watch television with bodies sitting every which way, children and others rolling and laughing, house lights and sound blazing, blaring, like my mother's and grandmother's houses on any given holiday.

West

Plato spoke of creating the 'heavenly pattern' in society, in one's own heart. It is said that the Balinese imagine that heaven looks, smells and tastes like Bali.

Dear L

For a whole week I danced what I could remember of Bali. There is no one from Bali here but I have cassettes of gamelan and a rare gambuh recording. So I danced remembering, impressed, showing off my travel. My body, history, prejudice, moving as paradise mutates within my earnest, kinetic system research. Joyous and muted source material, is what I offered. What the hell was in that water, under that tree? The group laughed, impressed. So, I stopped, momentarily.

Love

R

Geography 2 workshop 3 New Haven August 12-28

David Thomson USA
Asako Takami Japan
Djédjé Djédjé Gervais Côte d'Ivoire
Jeanne Beatrice Pehoula Zerehoule Côte d'Ivoire
Carlos Funn USA
Cheng-Chieh Yu Taiwan/USA
Ralph Lemon USA
Goulei Tchepoho Côte d'Ivoire
Katherine Profeta USA

Week two. Continuing field research. I'm working with found information. Or information generated by a particular involvement with a place, people and time. From text to movement. Compiling it into a personal comprehensive logic. Sort of about "belief." Mostly, here in New Haven, what it represents, I think, is how to collaborate, corroborate, react, to the traditional definitions of linear theater, from the perspective of an arch formalist choreographer. My history reflects this: The more blurred a body, message, the better. The people part of Geography, the part about the world, is interesting language, but the people part exists already, unadulterated, with or without me. I already know that it is inscrutable. But I think that I have a suggestion (one of a canon of many) to what is perceived as stage relevant. This is most likely the heart of the experiment.

Monday

David's getting his legs back after a few years of not dancing. A little struggle. A fresh actor. Helping the narrative experiments immensely. We improvise. A perfect foil for my raw movement sensibilities. He is a beautiful dancer. I've known David for seventeen years, sort of.

Asako, Japanese and Odissi, is a gift of terrifically odd performance presence. Asako cannot improvise within my improvisational language. Says that she does not want to imitate what she sees others doing and so cannot move because she cannot think of anything else to do. She has no idea what it is she is doing here. Other than to offer the experiment of her Odissi dance, in this context. David is working with her privately, offering advice on what might be improvisation, in this context.

Djédjé arrived two days after the workshop began. Pehoula, his wife, arrived one day after the workshop began. Pehoula is a revelation, her dancing, the dancing of an African woman, after the years of seeing nothing but the energy of the African men of Geography 1.

The drummer Gouzouo may arrive next Monday, maybe not. Djédjé and Pehoula need an advance to send to Africa to pay for his flight. And we've run out of money.

Carlos and Cheng-Chieh arrive today. Disrupting our company of five.

Plan.
Welcome Carlos and Cheng-Chieh
Improvise and then...
Work text ideas:
1. Indian pilgrimage text/ Hardwar
2. Essays on the history of rice
3. E-mailed visa correspondence
4. Chinese jokes
5. Remington knife salesman interview

Tuesday
Carlos and Cheng-Chieh enter the working space without a hitch. Cheng-Chieh's dancing is always beautiful. Carlos has grown more muscle. David is taking care of everyone.

What worked what didn't? Improvising was dense and improvised.

Plan
Improvise. 30 minutes
Create tasks from lists:
Sink and water
Podium
Garden dirt and flowers
Rocks
Water
Boards and steel plate
Bicycle prayer wheels

Thursday

Last night a pot luck and Cleopatra Jones and the Temple of Gold. Great food and trash TV. Perhaps source material.

Today: More Carlos club dancing, translated to a floor phrase. He has a problem retrieving what he may have danced last night, in a club. He has no problem retrieving material from video, what I captured on stage the day before, his suggestion of what he might do that night.

More Asako mudrā work, beautiful. Pehoula creates a magnificent problem: She's completely foreign here and has no community to sway her sensibility. Her mudrā response to Asako becomes African and African only. Djédjé has more information, and is working with her privately, offering advice on what might be improvisation, in this context. They work well together.

The bicycle wheels, strapped to the back of moving bodies, are a stunning image. Whatever that dance is it should begin sitting.

More Odissi phrase work. Asako dances faster today. Today she remembered to bring music, which has destroyed the modern dance's relation to it. Start over.

Plan

Improvise: prayer

Water ritual experiment:

1. Two places on your body to cleanse (prayer)

2. Those two places are absolved, what happens??

2. Sink represents memory

3. The floor must stay dry or you fall under/ lose your body, what you are cleansing.

New image: Djédjé dressing in garden/dirt. Refers to Cheng-Chieh botanical text. Not done at same time, or is it??

Friday

Long long discussion about the water ritual excercise. That there is the exercise and then the meaning of the exercise, what it might believe. That belief and structure can be independent, my point. Djédjé could not comprehend belief without logic, or its opposite. I took my clothes off, he threw water, one formal, visual, the other emotional, felt. Both believed.

Plan

Improvise: the danger of ritual

Cue up video of Asako phrase

Pants for Djédjé today?

Text not finished

Saturday

Plan

Work parts that might be interesting later:

Man in garden bed, dressing

Woman dressing in kimono with microphone
Woman reading botanical love letter
Carlos and Cheng-Chieh floor phrase rolling off stage/change clothes to something formal??
Man sitting on edge of platform. Man rolling off edge of platform. Then on platform telling Hardwar story
Woman in kimono with toy gun telling Hardwar story
Man telling Samurai story/knife text to man from Hardwar story
Pehoula singing John Lennon's Across The Universe in Wobé, her West African language.

Sunday

I have made a number of skits. Short, interesting cultural juxtapositions.
Scattered. A series of one liners, text and movement studies. Much to do about nothing or I'm completely unproductively unfettered. The workshop questions I'm coming up with seem relevant but there seem to be too many. I've created my monster. Or is there a divine logic to this funhouse? I feel fluent and this is frightening. My propensity for boredom. After all, these different languages inspire difference. Cut and pasting these moments together will not be an easy task. Not like what happened in SF. Because here we are not just dancing. And there is a provision of circus props.

Tuesday

An exercise about a body burning. One body representing fire, the other representing a body being consumed. Many variations on the theme, all working. And then the surviving body talking into a microphone. And greater wonderful problems.
Watching David and Cheng-Chieh dance modern dance is an elixir. The few times I don't feel foolish. It's beautiful. It's also the most time consuming of all our work here, the repetition of knowing what is known.

Gouzouo never arrives. I invite the drummer Goulei, from Geo 1, who now lives in NYC, to join us for the time remaining.

Wednesday

Huge problems with too direct a juxtapostion of Carlos' club dancing form, Djédjé and Pehoula's African form, Asako's Odissi form, and my modern form. A bad idea. Improvisation does not hold together within this cyclone.

Plan
Improvise: ?
Continue Odissi and modern dance experiment. More movement. Last phrase does not work, needs to be longer.
David enter stage r at appropriate moments, 2/3 times. David enter on big jump. Cheng-Chieh enter on micro movements. Trade off on sitting.

Look at video of Cheng-Chieh's improv.

Look at mudrā phrase.

Djédjé and Cheng-Chieh, get water exercises from video.

Add Ralph and Pehoula (sitting) to men dance.

Hardwar monologue: Asako in garden. Carlos and Ralph take David down with wall.

Carlos dresses lying on back.

Men dance with Pehoula.

David begins David finishes.

New floor stuff for men.

Find where Asako can finish duet with Cheng-Chieh.

Video Djédjé's arm phrase.

Work rock toss dance with David, Ralph and Carlos.

Cheng-Chieh recover water ritual.

Cheng-Chieh polish mudrā with Pehoula and Asako.

Before break, run botanical text monologue. (David go back to beginning stance until Cheng-Chieh is finished).

Break

Look at visa text: Although, Stan W. hates it. Says it makes no sense to him and therefore he's not interested in listening to it. And we exercise it so poorly.

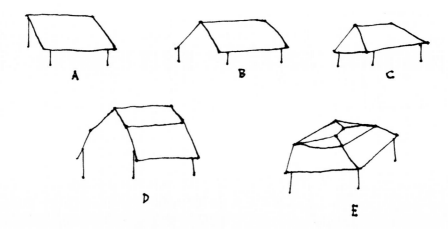

Thursday

Dear L

The past couple days have been garbage days. Days when all the exciting scraps become a heap. Moving too fast with too many ideas. Basically, there are five too many worlds in the space. No obvious link. Everyone brilliant when they have their own music, as we continue to work in silence. So I make architecture for five landscapes. And a community does not become a neighborhood, a house, a room.

Love

R

Not really. There is a room but it is shadowed, so are the lamps, the desk, the books, the chest of drawers, the night table, the bed, the windows, that look out onto, through the windows of the adjacent building, onto the third floor of an opulent stairway. Those walking the stairs cannot look back into the penumbrous space. For two hours a day there is the impression of daylight.

Solving The Mystery Of The Eleven Headed One Thousand Armed Avalokiteshvara Who Embodies Compassion And Reaches In All Directions

A towel laid on the night table drenched in the red blood and green tops of eaten strawberries, finished.
She had an odd look on her face, forehead burrowed, eyes squinting, smaller.
"So, you did not make a son."
"No, he is all over your sternum, melting."
She was awkward, history, doors locked, some open, squeaking. Not easy making love to someone divine. Gandharvas sweetheart. 4000 years of making love to gods. "That history takes care of my sensuality." Didn't seem to mind penetration. But hard to tell if she enjoyed it. "I like sex once a year," she said. "It is like fireworks for me, on a holiday. You wait, you watch and then it is over." And that there is a wild side to her, can become a spectator. She was silent when not gasping rhythmically. Basically, she does not trust and holds onto her body, dignity. Is ageless and does not want to make over the same common mistakes that are her fate. "I think that I will be alone or maybe with a woman. I'm not sure."
Enjoys sleeping, short deep intervals, lips buried into the cavity of an arm and its torso.

Each step scripted. "I saved the bath for you." Wearing only pants, no belt. Takes them off. Settles into the bathtub pressing his back carefully into the faucet, so that she could rest facing him, plain. He washed the ashes from her body, from toes to neck. And then kissed her face, salty. Resting, back to faucet. She placed his feet on her breasts. His long toes grasped, not like fingers. She smiled, closed her eyes, fell asleep. Wakes. They dried each other, sharing one towel, new rituals, pretending.
"Now, you can penetrate me again, but three times, no less."
She looks at his penis, holds it, guided. And then remembers. Shiva linga.
"Dark and unpredictable."
She speaks seven languages, three old ones. When intimidated, just one.
"When I was on top of Mt Himālaya I prayed to forget about you. Now something changed."

R. Galleria degli Uffizi   TIZIANO - La Flora   Who's the Hero Now?

151

Thursday

U

I have not written very much because I've been spending my mornings and nights making love to the girl who looks like Pārvatī, daughter of the mountain, Himālaya. Then trying to get her to leave my bed, my tired body, so that I can sleep for two extra hours.

I cannot send you this letter.

P

She continues to come to his room. Their bidding. They make love that is dangerous. And tell each other that they must stop. She opens more and more, losing safety.

He tells her, "You can contain me even when I don't want you to." He has lost all safety.

"What do you do?" she asks.

"For a living?"

"Yes."

"I throw knives. In tournaments."

"Oh, I want to try, it sounds so American."

"Maybe someday I can show you, but not now, the season is finished."

August. Kaliyuga

In the South. Ninety degrees, in the hills it is a hundred. There is an earthquake. He lies in bed listening, mostly to the rhythmic thumping. It sounds like his house host making violent love to someone he never saw. And then the house and his bed rolls. For thirty seconds and it stops. "It's a big one," his host shouts, alone from another room.

He moves to the beach. A hotel, a "medium located" room that cost $335 a night. Outside the window there is a photo session of a couple just married. The photographer vocally choreographing. "OK, this is the last one, let's make it a good one."

She meets him there. It has been six weeks. They have two days.

"Do you want to wear this?" She had brought along a brown paper bag full of single packaged condoms. He places the paper bag on the bed, the white white sheets, and photographs it.

There were many forms. But she was not comfortable with the falling, that form. They paused surprised. "We had spent the day talking and sometimes we were quiet. I was not ready to try something difficult, unusual." He apologizes. She stops talking. The phone rings. He backs away, breathless and tries to hold a conversation with the receptionist about his reservation plans for a car to the airport the following day.

The next morning. She wakes him and they make love one last time. She talks now, more awake than he, exhilarated, "This may be the last time, and anything is possible, anything."

Cowherd: "Home seems good. My body feels extremely odd. Wondering how much I am satisfied. Haven't yet looked at any and all the girls on the streets. Be careful what you wish for. My soul feels drugged. Satisfaction. Or exhaustion. And how does this affect the nature of how I perceive the purpose of getting out of bed and functioning at work? I think that I am more grounded. Making love in the morning and 'in the midnight,' I love how you say that. Certainly found erections and enough semen, except for that one time. No fear, No guilt. Discovered that there is a quality of time to sex that can help it move unpretentiously along, for hours, like watching television. That's a compliment."

Gopī: "Yes, it is in my blood. My mother was frustrated all her life, and I think she passed her unredeemed desire to my sister and I. My sister was first but is now a doting mother. I'm not sure I want to have kids. Making love is how I think of my world. I also play the piano. It is a simple life."

Yes, I have matrika qualities. I enjoy making tea. Sewing hems on the legs of pants. Tying laces, my lovers' shoes. Doing these things makes me think of others. Friends I've not seen for a while. "Oh, I must call this person." Good thoughts.

It can be a well lived life. Purposeful.

But she continues to leave lovers because she wants "to do what she wants to do." When she wants to. Smoking a delicate bone pipe, drinking *soma* from a water glass, making her large exhaustive embroidery, *padmas*, a quilt. A hymn for her lonely nights.

Her socks are black. Her T-shirts are brown. Nothing else is specific. Everything used and only clothes given to her, that fit, pants, dresses, shirts, aprons. She buys nothing. "If I were to shop at the GAP, buy something for myself, would that change me?"

Likes to have the stains, wet of lovemaking on her fabrics. Letting them dry, stiff spots. "I like it." So leaves her clothes on as long as possible. Always removing the black socks first.

As time goes by they become more and more familiar with each other's plans. An old repetition.

"Did that hurt?"
"Yes it was painful, but I liked it."
"Are you finished, want to sleep now?"
"Yes."
"I regret that there is no more time."
"When I wake up there will be more. I promise."
"OK, then I'm happy."

His delirious dream: Watching them run after, apprehend, slower running terrified bodies, he stands against a wall, peering around a corner, privately hiding.

A uniformed man rounds the corner, armed and hatless, and softly orders, "We've been looking for you. Time to go."

Immediately behind them, an older man, in plain clothes, breathing frantically, roughly drags her forward, this woman, and pleads to the uniformed official, "I want her. Is that OK?"

"No, no, he is my husband, I will go with him," she pleads. She looks at her lover, stunned. They look at each other for a long time. Beyond love, no settled emotions, as though there were small pins in their eyes.

"Yes, you can take her away," the armed official replies to the older man.

He stepped away and fell, was crippled. Could not walk. Crawling from bed to phone, or stove. Broken by desire, between his legs. Sleeping weeks at a time. His mind remembering fat goldfish. "I'll be fine tomorrow." He won't. Finally exhausted.

"I was supposed to have a good dream after a long talk
with you.
I woke up 3:30am with shaking body and shrinking
brain. It was very terrible feeling.
I thought I got over from the fever...103F..I took
ALEVE.
5:30am I fell sleep. I had very short dream (5 sec?) I
was kissing you from your back...my face was on your
right side shoulder. I was feeling your lips.
I haven't take bath for 5 days now."

He thought she might die.

Reading survivor stories from Hiroshima in bed. (The horror of Hiroshima is called Hiroshima, is not termed something larger than the city, unlike the Holocaust or Apartheid or Slavery.)

She held his penis. He read to himself and could only make it through one chapter. Two nights before he had read Ondaatje to her, Coming Through Slaughter, another myth about another shadowed force. She said that she tried to read Ondaatje once but found his writing style too dense.

Is love all that is not love? She was told that to love someone you must love every cell. She held his hand, looking closely, lying pale to his side. "I can make you feel guilty, it is my power. No, I do not enjoy it so much, it is life, how it works." There are never apologies.

"Like Purūravas and Urvaśī."

"Who?"

"We are like pieces of wood. Rubbed together our bodies make fire."

Fires warm and destroy. She brushed his hair, tying it differently, a bun, pillowed. Then wiped the powder (ash) from his face.

"You are one mellow chick," he said.

And then, "Let's smoke." Time passes. Of course. They survive.

Her Gandharvas, lover, god, shows up, shining, awesome, wearing a gown and crown of blue lotuses, granting a favor.

A decision.

Of course it leads to this. "I'm frustrated."

"Me too."

"We are so different. And I need you to be practical because I'm reacting beyond the pleasure. It is a dilemma."

"Yes, me too. But I enjoy the beauty right now."

There is still hot water and blood on white cloth linen and broken skin tissue. And drives his body wild, "a qi snatcher." And still making him disappear, soften. Ok, we'll meet for one night a year. Two millenniums left, a moment, poof. It's not about sex anymore.

She calls him from the airport. And as usual has little to say, instead feeling in every molecule of her body. They both mostly listen.

"Hello, are you still there? It is so quiet in the background. Are you sure you're at the airport?"

"Yes, there are so many people here."

Clear, cheerful, no limit. Now the sky is dull and weak.

But a lot of hope.......hope of spring, billions of cherry blossoms. I love this season..... waiting for the spring.

"P.S. Did I tell you on the way home I went gun shooting in L.A. It was fun to hear the sound, feel the shock and hit the target. I was so surprised that I felt so differently when I watched someone shooting and when I held the gun and shot. I was so scared when I watched but I wasn't when I shot, I enjoyed. Throwing a knife might be more beautiful."

SAMURAI: You got a lot of different categories of knives, you know. Some people usually buy knives because they like to go hunting. And some knives are usually made for hunting and some of them for fishing. It's like, for instance, This knife is made by Hawk, this by Buck. This is a skinning knife but it's mostly used for fishing, you know, like if you go deep sea fishing. Then we have a zipper with a gut hook, This is mostly for fishing and skinning deer, whatever you want to skin. Because the gut hook automatically -- you just plug it in, make a little hole, and then you skin it off. That is the hook there. Then we got different styles, varieties of knives. Mostly this is for fishing or skinning deer or whatever you want to skin, you know. The long ones are mostly for fishing. Filleting fish. Then we got the diving knives for coral reefs, you know, but it's illegal to... or to cut something real quick. You know, we have different varieties of knives. Like we got fishing, for skinning and what we got here, These are trophy masters deluxe. They got three different, um two different blades. One different blade is used to make the puncture hole right in the skin, and then he rips it real good and clean. And Then the bigger blade, you see where it is? That's mostly to finish skinning it off, nice and soft. There's a difference between skinning and gutting. Guzzing is taking out the entrails. Entrails are very quick. What you wanna make, like say you wanna, like if you have a fish you know, you don't have a knife to do what you wanna do, it's like with this one... let me show it to you. There's a difference between gutting a fish and gutting a deer. Gutting a deer is uh, is uh, the skin... The texture is very rough. So you use something like this for the skin, I mean for the deer, the material, the hard metal will automatically penetrate real quick and you will make the little hole and you just skin a little bit, a little bit. Then that's when you use the other one -- you start ripping it off. Like for this one, This mostly a lot of people use this for fishing because of the different hooks it has. And This one is just to get the guts out, real quick. You just open it up and clean it inside. But it is also a dangerous knife. Now there are for cutting. But people then use their hands. It's like when you're going to get a deer, you stab it, you gutted it out, and Then for like the internals, you know, you start cutting it off with your hands. You open and cut it off with the knife and you are using your hands at the same time. This big one? This is a Kaybar. It was issued in World War II. It's a Marine knife. It was issued in World War II for um, then after the services it was a gift of the _____, or you know a medal of honor... Like you won something or you got hurt they automatically gave you, you know it's the Kaybar. It's a, It's not the original, but it's an imitation of one because the originals they don't make them any more. They're hard to get. They're antiques. And if you have an original there you have a lot of money. They stopped making them. They starting, They started making those to stop it and they made a smaller one. It would look like something like this. Smaller blade to carry around with you. There's not many things about knives you need to learn. It's not like I'm going to buy a knife and then do this. You have to know what design and what to look for. These are hunting knives. Some hunting knives are used for like say fishing or for cutting wood. You can decide whatever you want to use the knife for. It's not always like, you know, I've got a knife so I'm gonna go kill somebody. A lot of people use a lot of different knives to do a lot of different things. Some people use them for sculptures, to finish the edge. This is the Stiff Kiss, This is mostly a carving knife, like for wood. You can use it for carving or anything you need. To cut nails, or whatever. The Bridgers is a hunting knife. It has a very nice edge, the knife is made in Spain. The blade is 4/40, it's a hard steel. What it will do is help you out if you want to cut or chop pieces of wood. A lot of people use it for carpentry. 4/40 is the thickness of the steel. The Thicker it is, the harder. You will get more stability using the knife to cut wood. You have 15 variety of metals. The lower the metal gets, The harder the steel gets. And the harder you get the edge. It goes from 5/50 and then goes down from there. 5/50, 4/40, 3/30, That kind of thing. We have 3 different styles of throwing knives. One is called the Blazing Arrow. It is a thick one and it's mostly to build your firearm and the ability to throw, to feel the aiming. Then you graduate to a different step. Then you go to an On Target, it's a 3-piece. It's very light. It's a very small knife and very light. It's for the balancing of your hands and the eye coordination with the throw. Then from there, you go to a 2-step, like a Gil Hiven Thrower. The metal is a little bit lighter in the bottom of the blade. The handle is heavier. So when you start aiming, it will travel farther. With the 3-piece Gil Hiven, The second two pieces are the ability to throw, to handle it. Very nice and mostly used for tournaments back in the 1800's. They would see how far they could throw, like a bow and arrow. It was just for tournaments, for fun. Then a lot of people made it into killing people, for throwing it. The martial arts come along, like the Chinese stars. The martial arts were throwing knives much longer than the 1800s, but they were for tournaments. It was not to kill. It was mostly American when everything started coming over, people started using different things. Like with the samurai swords, a lot of people think, "oh, it's a samurai sword. I want to have one." To graduate and become a samurai, you are supposed to be skilled in many details. To carry a samurai sword is to carry respect. It's not like "I'm a killer. Look at this, I'm a ninja." It's not that. A samurai sword meant respect. It was like the police. Have you heard of the movie Ronin? Well, the title Ronin was mostly known in the 1600s. There was a King that had a couple samurai soldiers. He sent them to do a job, but they couldn't protect the king. They were like the musketeers, but everybody died. So they hired outside samurais, other state's samurais, they were known just to kill. So that is where you get the word Ronin. They just came out of state to do a job. It's just like a professional. Like an Italian mob getting someone just to do the job. That's why they are called Ronins. But people think, "oh, he's a killer." But he's a Ronin, it's a different word. We have regular samurai swords, and we have the Tachi. The Blactachi is mostly known for when you retire. When you are old and you are giving up everything, they used a ceremonial sword that they gave you. But also, the thing about the samurai swords: the samurai soldiers, as they were walking, if somebody else touched the sword, they automatically had to break it because it was something for them to have, not for somebody else to touch. If you touched it you were disrespecting it. So automatically you had to break the sword and they had to rebuild a new one, sharpen it. It took years just to make a sword. The market for selling samurai swords is pretty good, really. A lot of people come, they just buy it to collect. Mostly Americans. You got a lot of people who just want to have something that looks good in this blade. There are a lot of people who say, "Oh, I went to Japan and got this." But they just got it in the States. If you get a samurai from Japan, it's an original samurai. And it's hard to get and illegal to bring it from Japan to the United States because it is considered a weapon. These are made in Spain, some are made here in the United States. Samurai swords are illegal to bring from Japan, so the only person who can carry back a sword to the States is an antique dealer. They have the right licensing. But knives are also weapons. Before guns it was knives. That was the street weapon in the States. You've got the Blacks and you've got the Latinos and the knife was purposeful choice. The knife is a delicate weapon. Once inserted, you can do a lot of damage. It's not like a bullet. A bullet you shoot it it comes in and that's it. What a bullet does is burn your skin and it hits major arteries and you die. But a knife can do a lot of harm with it. If you cut a vein with a knife, forget it. You don't have time to sew it. With a bullet, it comes in and it comes out. A knife is a deadlier weapon, but it depends on how you use the knife. There are skilled persons that know how to use the knife and know how to kill. There are some people that use a knife and they don't know what they are doing. They cut themselves. Knives are silent. They are small and easier to hide. In New York, I remember about that girl, that model, who was slashed in the face. It's dangerous, you know. You can do a lot of scars. It's very painful. Like when you get a paper cut, a little paper cut, you are screaming, "Oh my god." Imagine a big knife just cutting your skin open. I've been cut a couple times. You know, it hurts. The guy just pulled it out of nowhere. It was a fist to fist fight and he just pulled a knife out. When I got cut, I was like, "wait a minute." I didn't know what he had cut me with. I thought it was a broken glass or bottle. But it wasn't. It was a blade in a switch blade and he just pulled it out of nowhere. I was beating the guy up big time just with my fist, so with his background, he just pulled a switch blade and I just didn't see it. Like I said, it's a very concealable weapon. You can pull it out and nobody will know. I was on the floor with him and he just pulled it out. That was when he stabbed me, I was like, "what in the world?" And then I see a big gush of blood and that was it. I looked at the knife and I was like, "whoa, that's it." Then I backed off, and I was like, "you're the man. That's it, it's over, you're the man. You're the man." So, he stopped. Yeah, that was his statement.

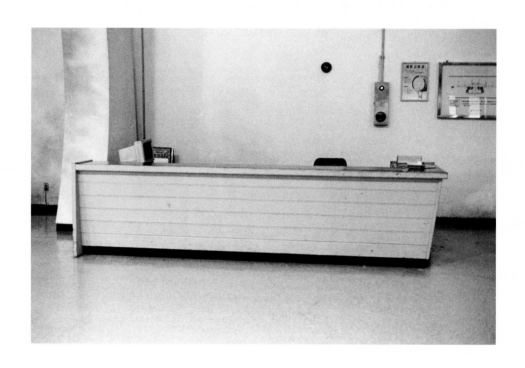

He calls from the airport.

I'm on the ground at 2:30 in the morning. For all I know of the eyes I see, distinguish, I could be anywhere west of the Pacific, anywhere.

On the ground again, inside, a woman walks up to where I am sitting and pulls on the cart I use to hold my bags. She wants it because I have two small bags resting on it and she has four or five large bags that are resting on the floor, that she needs to move. I take my bags off the cart, awkwardly.

I notice a young man named Jiro watching me at all the lay-overs. In Seoul he comes up to me. In broken English he says, "The Chinese are strong." Jiro is Japanese and has just spent three months in Brooklyn visiting his girlfriend. He tells me that he is in love with black American culture, that he studies it back in Hiroshima. He's no longer a student at a University in Hiroshima but studies on his own. He tells me that black children are the most beautiful children, they wear the best clothes. And black American children are his favorite. He asks me why there are so many police in New York, in cars, on bikes, horses, walking? In Hiroshima he says he never sees police, not so much. I ask him about the Barakumin, the Japanese minority, that look like all the other Japanese but are treated differently. Spelled the word for him in my notebook. He doesn't recognize it and says he has never heard the sound before, the way I pronounce it. He tries to explain to me how the Japanese and Chinese written language characters are different. I don't get it. He says that most Japanese have lots of money but he doesn't. He's young and unemployed. Jiro says his grandmother remembers the bomb, but will never talk about it.

I meet this other interesting guy named Choon-kon Kim, who's "almost unemployed" but flies business class because his company Samsung pays for his travels and his apartments in Seoul and Beijing, where his wife and two kids live. He works and lives most of the time in Seoul. He works on commission. Sales are down so he's "barely making any money." He sees his family in Beijing five times a year, two to three days at a time. Prefers the school system in China to that of Korea, where he thinks there is too much pressure on young school children, "like in Japan." When he was in school he studied Chinese Communism. Now he sells electronic equipment worldwide. But has not sold much lately. He thinks that for foreigners, living in China is good. But expensive. He tries to explain to me how the Chinese and Korean written language characters are different. I barely understand.

The impression of daylight, when rooms can be discerned.

September 10 1999
I hang up the phone. And again, feel that this is the first time that I've been separated. It is not, in fact, it is the third or fourth time. *What is missing is that liberating element: emptiness. Nothing is more important than absence.* There is the impression of daylight, I can discern where I am, it is not an empty place.

I begin wandering through the apartment, trying to figure out how appliances work, how to get hot water to turn on.

There is no teapot. I make three cups of tea simultaneously. By the time I get to the third cup temperature is not really an issue.

Over time I create other systems. Whenever I take a shower I also fill a red plastic water bucket. Then I don't have to fill it in the kitchen sink every time I need to flush the toilet.

The air conditioner has a recorded child's voice that goes off at times I cannot discern, possibly telling the temperature. I've left it off and opened all the windows throughout each room and the door to the screened balcony. There is a dead potted jade plant on the balcony, I water it daily, curious.

I wipe away layers of dust from window ledges, bed sheets, plates, bowls, silverware, tea, my eyes. The current sky. As dusty as I remember from the year before.

Before I go to bed I unplug the television to plug in the adapter charge to my video camera, in the one available outlet.

At 6:45 every morning the ballad "When I Fall In Love" is mysteriously broadcast through the neighborhood. Sounding an alarm. And then the construction work across the street begins. I get out of bed.

On Monday, Tuesday and Thursday mornings I unplug the adapter charge to my video camera and plug in the television. The television has cable. There are two half hour moments, one in the afternoon, one at night, when I can watch an English news program.

Mostly there is CCTV. I have seen women's basketball, badminton tournaments, a professional sport that looks like an American schoolyard dodge ball game, Chinese checker tournaments, bowling, adolescents in a Latin ballroom dance competition, women's softball, kick boxing, ping pong tournaments, a sport that looks like kung fu volleyball, where they don't use their hands and can only kick the ball over what looks like a standard volleyball net. High school girls dancing hip hop.

Sunday 26. 2:30 p.m. 900 FM China Radio International Beijing has for its theme song the title orchestration from Gone with the Wind. The station's program changes, mostly from Chinese, to Spanish to English to Hebrew to German to French to Japanese. Hour to hour. Day to Day.

But mostly I'm watching a lot of television.

Late one night I watched a documentary on a boxing sport in some indescribable town, city in China. A standard sized boxing ring was set up in the town square. And the audience was invited to fight and take on other challengers, onlookers from the town. The winner of the most fights received a live black goat. The matches seem to last one round, maybe five or ten minutes. There seemed to be judges outside the ring determining the winner, although they were never shown. All the fighters entering the ring wore street clothes, what they happened to be wearing that day. All barefoot, it was summer. Boxing gloves were provided. I watched a young woman fighting a young man, she won. A pair of men fighting each other and an old woman fighting a boy, the boy won.

But most programs prelude the upcoming 50th anniversary of the PRC. Sentimental documentaries abound. Mao Zedong as an old man, physically shorter than before.

Six days before the first of October Beijing is adorned, flowers by day and competitive high-rise lighting at night. A great glare, showcasing all the many new office buildings that have sprung up recently. At night the main street of Chang Aang Jie is lit like a vast football stadium.

By some American estimates the Chinese government has spent 10 billion US dollars to spruce up Beijing, Shanghai, Shenzen, and other major cities of commerce, to celebrate the anniversary.

Five days before the first of October factories were shut down and large freight trucks were banned from highways. Remarkably, the sky over Beijing turned blue.

"The fifty year anniversary celebration is actually a marriage ceremony for President Jiang Zemin. His bride is China," Wu Wenguang jests, over the phone.

I haven't seen Wu Wenguang for a little over a year. We set up a time to meet and then another time to have another phone conversation, one where my translator, Liu Tran, can be present, so that Wenguang can give his apartment address, in Chinese, to Liu Tran, who will then write it down for me in Chinese, so that I can direct any taxi driver in Beijing to Wenguang's apartment.

Wenguang and I meet on Sunday and talk from 2:30 p.m. till 3:00 a.m. the following morning, his work, my work, China, America, Lesbians.

"In China if one does not get official permission to work, corroborate with the government, one is considered *Kong bai*, a blank in society." Wu Wenguang is considered blank. And that's often what his work's about.

His latest project is a documentary on the Lesbian community in Beijing. At a recent party he interviewed a pair of lovers, two generations, one in their thirties from Shanghai, the other in their teens from Beijing. The younger couple considered themselves husband and wife, and couldn't fathom how the older couple, who considered themselves simply lovers, made love.

"Who's on top, who's on the bottom?" they asked, suspicious.

"We do both," was the reply.

"There is not a gay rights movement to speak of. To ask for 'rights' would be the end of the community. There can be no protest, no marches, no demonstrations. Simply to 'come out' is a revolutionary movement, enough for now."

Wu Wenguang then asks if I like men or women. I tell him I like women, a lot. He says that many of the Chinese I met last fall assumed that I liked men. I tell him, that yes, many of the Americans that I've met also think that I'm gay.

There are four gay bars in Beijing at present, one of them for Lesbians. Ten years ago there were only two privately owned bars in all of Beijing, before the city closed them down. Wenguang is not sure why. Then the government opened Bar Street, a street lined with many bars and a few prostitutes.

One evening Wen Hui, Wu Wenguang and I sit in smoky Half and Half, a popular gay bar. We watch a small group of white men, loudly surrounding the bar, drinking, smoking, dancing, embracing each other and then large groups of Chinese men sitting at large round tables, drinking, smoking and talking quietly. Everyone dressed stylishly, black and denim, relaxed, understanding the fashion of this remarkableness.

Wen Hui and I think the cross-dressed hostess is beautiful.

Wu Wenguang says, "Beautiful, what? He is ugly."

Wu Wenguang is not able to film, too many self-conscious individuals enjoying their privacy. And sits with his camera on his lap.

Outside the bar, young, handsome Chinese men stand, lined-up, for sale.

Before the gay bars opened, gay men met in parks or in the two main public toilets of the Forbidden City. The east and west public toilets became "The East and West Palaces." To merely be with each other, before or after sex, to talk, they walked the streets of Beijing all night.

I ask Wenguang if there is gay bashing in China. He doesn't understand the question. "Why would they beat up a gay?" he asks. "In China most people just consider gays strange, that's all."

Wu Wenguang tells me that many of his generation grew up being told by their parents that they were found in the street, in rubbish, any dirty place other than their mother's bodies. "Sex could not be discussed."

Wu Wenguang and Wen Hui have been together for twenty years. They are not married.

At Dinner with Wen Hui and Wu Wenguang. Wu Wenguang always cooks. He's invited his twenty-five-year-old niece, who has recently moved from Kunming to Beijing. A product of the one couple one child policy. After dinner I sit and watch Wen Hui instruct her neice in the art of washing dishes. This lack of experience is a big problem with the recent "only child" culture. One child, one sacred protected being that is not taught how to organize a basic life. Wen Hui and Wu Wenguang have arranged for her a long term course in how to clean their apartment.

I've been invited to Beijing to conduct workshops with the Beijing Dance Academy and the Beijing Modern Dance Company. I originally accepted the invitation because I'd been asked to work with students from ethnic minority nationalities enrolled at the Academy, young dancers from places like Yunnan and Tibet. An anticipated exchange. That plan was canceled. Those students suddenly became unavailable due to the PRC 50th anniversary celebrations. I'm disappointed. And instead will share my particular modern movement information with Chinese modern dancers and choreography students learning the heroic poses of Classical Chinese Dance. A collaboratively layered and disconcerting venture. But this schedule also provides an opportunity to rehearse with Wen Hui in Beijing on Geography 2. And the even more valuable adventure of traveling again to Kunming and HongHe county to visit Wang Liliang and Li Wen Yi, Mr. Wang and Mr. Li.

It takes an hour to taxi to the Beijing Modern Dance Company workshop and an hour to taxi back to my apartment. Two hours a day to observe the voracity of Beijing's most recent skyline. And car culture: A long caravan of perhaps 20 new black Audis, with red balloons hanging out of closed windows tinted deep black, led by a single black Mercedes covered with bouquets of red flowers and bride and groom dolls, strapped onto the front hood emblem, ravaged by the wind. The Mercedes also carried the bride and groom.

In traffic, on the way to the first day of the first workshop, the director of the Beijing Modern Dance Company told a story about one of the dancers that I would not be working with. "She got pregnant by a young man in the company. They are not married. It is illegal. They do not want to get married. She must either get married or have an abortion. She practices Qigong, part of a sect, maybe Falun Gong, not sure. She refuses to have an abortion, wants to live her own life. It is illegal and our company will be at fault if we support her. No one knows where she is now. It is too bad because she is a beautiful dancer, has a strong body. The boy, I do not care about losing, he can go."

They both were fired. I remember the boy, the young man, from my first trip to Beijing. He was a beautiful dancer then, had a strong body, I recall.

The Beijing Modern Dance Company has an intensely dutiful and collective working method, focus, that would seem to go along with a long tradition of tenacious dignity and little money, large dim studios and cultural maltreatment. Attentive exhaustion, well trained, maintaining an anatomic and choreographic legibility. Passionate and sad.

My classes were attempts at physically surprising them. Five women, four men. Sometimes I did, sometimes I didn't. They were confused, amused that little of what I shared with them seemed energetically organic. Consequently, I think they found it hard to find the "duty" in the work. Still, they came to class on time, every day. All along I hoped the pregnant girl would show up.

She never did.

Liu Tran helps me negotiate. An ex-student from the Dance Academy. He tells me to call him "Spring."

Spring's mother was a dancer. Ballet, Russian training. "The Mao ballets, of course! You could not make a mistake. They were very precise. But the intent, drama was pure. The dancers knew what they were dancing, had intense passion for the revolution." Now he's not so sure why dancers dance.

The Beijing Modern Dance Company has official government permission to exist as an institution. The company gets very little financial support from the government, if any. The Beijing Dance Academy, on the other hand, is part of the government. "The most dance studios in one building in the world." Seven floors and forty one studios and right next door to my apartment building. This proximity is a good thing. I teach at 8 a.m., Wednesdays and Fridays, students of Classical Chinese Dance Choreography, the arguably many things that that is.

The first Wednesday, at 7 a.m., Spring calls to inform me that I can do what it is that I do for the first half of the workshop. He continues, "The second part will be a question answer session." And before the workshop, I'm informed, I will meet with the director of the Classical Chinese Dance Choreography Department, briefly.

The meeting is weird. I sit in the director's office and am served tea while the director literally shuffles papers. Spring joins me but has nothing to translate. Not a word is exchanged. I study China's version of the map of the world. From the top to bottom center of the map, sits East Siberia, then Papua New Guinea and then Brisbane Australia.

Ten minutes later, taking the director's lead, we all stand, exit the office and walk up a flight of stairs.

I felt this. The students studied my presence as if it were a curious mechanical system they were instructed to take apart. This ergonomic-like examination was oddly helpful since I could do very little translated talking about what my body was doing in any particular point in an exercise or movement experiment. Spring could not keep up. Our results were interesting, friendly. I'm not sure what I shared and they were keenly observant, if awkward, impersonators.

The director joined us for the first part of the workshop, videotaping my warm-up and play with movement. He left during the Q and A. Leaving the students, Spring and I standing in a thick circle in the middle of the studio.

The questions from the students sounded strangely prepared and surprisingly familiar.

Are dancers respected in the US?

Not really.

What are the traditional dances in the US?

I imitated a tap dance.

Do dancers work other jobs to support themselves?

Of course.

What is the difference between a workshop and a class?

That's a good question.

After class Spring and I have an argument about the plié. He suggests that the plié is abstract, as physical language. He didn't elaborate and I disagreed. The plié came to China by way of Russia, perhaps gaining another interesting complicated layer in translation. But a plié is a plié. Maybe at one point it was abstract, and maybe abstract globally, but certainly not anymore.

I ponder that, basically, a modern dance workshop or class, is the same everywhere in the world. Highly thought of, energetic and anatomical improvisations are offered, and foreign participating bodies are always extremely curious, wondering why someone would move like that. (Papua, New Guinea is perhaps one of the "everywhere" exceptions to this theory).

In China the modern dancing body is perhaps more sophisticated and ready to take in new information and act on that information more essentially than most other cultural body/movement politics. My theory has something to do with the long historical placement of Tai-chi and various Qigong practices in China. Direct resources to harnessing and refining vital life energy in the body, expanding a movement outside of the body. A freedom, both wildly soft and aesthetically dangerous.

There was a male student in that first Traditional Chinese Dance Choreography workshop who was a breathtaking mover, energy as clear fluid form, transparent. He had no questions during the Q and A. I later heard that he was a Modern Dance student, covertly crashing the workshop. I was not officially scheduled to teach any Modern Dance students at the Academy, a department only a few years old. I wondered why? Spring answered, "One must always wait until the last moment because things will inevitably change. It is the culture."

I study this essential non-principle for a couple more weeks, until I lose my concentration.

Not a moment too soon. I conduct a final workshop and or teach a final class to the Beijing Modern Dance Company. I'm exploding from mistranslation, mine, theirs. Create an impossible phrase, punishment, because I'm maniacal and want to drive everyone around me crazy. They dance it well.

I've become passive to information around me. An interesting problem.

Creating attractive dance phrases that have no meaning to anything besides themselves. With all the new other information in my mind and body, this seems like a retreat to familiarity. Not enough purpose.

Later, I rehearse with Wen Hui. Working out an idea about remembering. How we each recall Indonesians moving, our profound and naive experiences in different places. We tell each other, that somehow, our bodies changed there, just by looking. She, Java (where exist some of the greatest pliés in the world), the men, slower than she can dance. Me, Bali, women and men, a faster, bone initiated energy. Simple stuff, our improvising, in narrow channels, from upstage to down stage. Vastly different but complementary. Wen Hui loves to smoke and holds a lit cigarette, but doesn't smoke it, dancing. The cigarette disappears in the fake mudrās, while the smoke stays present. Beautiful, I think. It ends with my bringing her an imagined ashtray for the sublimely gathered ashes reaching delicately out from her colorfully manicured hand. My hand collects the ashes.

Throughout the rehearsal I translate the words "intent," "task," "represent," "appropriate," and "inspire," for Wen Hui. The daily work of explaining what we are trying to accomplish, in English. Our bodies understand but there are times when it is useful to talk, to catalog, analyze, misunderstand, continue. After a few hours we stop, and rush off to buy plane tickets to Kunming, before the travel agency closes.

Saturday June 12 1999

Hi Ralph,

This is an itinerary of our journey to Mr. Wang's home:

1) From KunMing to HongHe county by bus, about 11 hours (pass through city, from KunMing, YuXi, Tonghai, ShiPin, HongHe county.

This intinerary not completeness ensure. Because my brother take night bus, sometime he sleeped. I do not have map of YunNan with me now.)

2) Fron HongHe county to A-Za village take bus, about 4 hours.

3) From A-Za village take walking to Mr. Wang's home about 2 hours.

4) from Mr. Wang to Mr. Li's home take walking about 30 min.

I call Mr. Wang today. He said no bus from A-Za village to he's home. Otherwise we have to rent car from A-Za village to he's home.

Mr. Tien not back.

I do not think our journey is adventure. But of course is very very very trial on the way, you cannot imagine it. So if we arrive to Mr. Wang's and Li's without fail very very very beautiful. Something we cannot anticipation.

Love

Wen Hui

Wednesday September 29, 1999

Driving through Kunming out into the country, Wen Hui continues not to recognize her hometown. Out into the country, to the village of Yunnan Minority Nationalities Institute Cultures in China, for a meeting with Mr. Tien, the director.

When we arrive Mr. Wang and Mr. Li are waiting for us at the top of the road. Grinning, faces red brown from the summer months.

Mr. Li is wearing his traditional Yi blue, jacket and pants. Mr. Wang is wearing a gray double breasted suit jacket, the one he bought at a Salvation Army in San Francisco, a pair of soiled, light colored pants and what looks to be, well-worn Red Wing work boots. He also carries an umbrella. The sky is clear blue. We hug, mutely grunt and walk the road back to the village.

We arrive inside the village square to three or four more musicians, also waiting, playing their instruments and singing. A performance, I realize later, auditioning for a possible trip to America. One man I remember. I had sat and shared tea with him, sipped out of a jar, a year before. I smiled, bowed and passed.

We are led to Mr. Tien's tiny room, home, privately situated in the back of the village, overlooking the village farm. We spend a few hours talking about my project. I described what it is I'm attempting with the mix of foreign performers, how the Yi musicians fit. I tried to explain the word "funky," that their music sounds like the free jazz of the sixties, that I don't really know what jazz is, how significant I feel it would be to offer this music to a Western audience and that Wang and Li represent a collaboration that I cannot drastically manipulate.

In Beijing, before leaving for Kunming, Wu Wenguang had suggested that when negotiating with Mr. Tien, to make sure and mention how much money Mr. Wang and Li are to be paid over the whole Geography 2 working period, quoting a lump sum rather than a weekly salary. It seems to work, Mr. Tien all but signs a contract to let them go, these very grown men.

While in Beijing, Wu Wenguang and Wen Hui had descirbed how difficult it was helping Wang and Li get to San Francisco. And once they were there how Mr. Wang considered not returning to China. Wanting to become a street musician. He was told by someone in San Francisco's Chinatown that he could make a lot of money in the US playing his music on the street. Mr. Li and Wen Hui convinced him otherwise. "Maybe for one week it would be OK. But then after that who would care? You would be nobody."

I don't know how long Wang thought about staying in the US, I do know that shortly before returning to China, he bought a Panasonic tape player in Chinatown, a small boom box, he was thrilled.

Mr. Li and members of the village make dinner for us. Mr. Wang oversees the preparations. A table is set up outside, in the square and we eat with Mr. Tien and his Managing Director, "Teacher Zhang." Wang and Li eat in the small dining area of the kitchen building, with the other artists. Don't see them again until we have finished eating.

We discuss a trip to the south, HongHe county. Discover that Wang's and Li's villages are too difficult to reach in this season. "Too much bad road and mud,very dangerous." So we rearrange a trip to another village, Potou, near Jianshui, Nani nationality, not Yi. "Now there's no reason for Wang and Li to go," Mr. Tien says. He offers us the use of the village van and the village driver. Mr. Li is very disappointed that we won't be able to travel to his home. "To see how he lives," Wen Hui translates. Wang sits, bright faced, smoking. I too am disappointed and suggest, that if possible, Wang and Li should come along on our newly rearranged trip, to give a general commentary, Wen Hui mentions this to Mr. Tien who doesn't like the idea, "Why would they go to a village that is not their own? Plus, Mr. Li does not like to talk and so would be useless."

Later, after the fact, Wen Hui describes to me how difficult the public bus trip to Hong He would have been. "It's a night bus with a crowd packed beyond the bus's insides, the noise and smell is indescribable."

We'll leave on October 2. I'm partly relieved that we have a private vehicle and won't have to travel so far.

We decide that once we return, Wang and Li will meet up with us in Kunming. Mr. Wang will bring along photographs of his home and family.

October 1.

I had seen the Air Force jets rehearsing from the balcony of my fifth floor apartment. I had seen students from the Beijing Dance Academy rehearsing in costumes of the People's Liberation Army.

One hundred thousand people, vagrants, the homeless, were removed from Beijing, the capital.

At the Kunming Hilton Hotel, on CNN, at ten o'clock am, the performance begins. Leaders parading tanks and missiles. Down the fat and giant Chang Aang Jie.

There is no live audience in this parade. It is made for television. Most Chinese are home watching on CCTV. There are a few people in the Green Lake Park, in Kunming, it's not much of a party. And only the Army line Chang Aang Jie in Beijing. A few selected guests are invited, placed to watch the ceremony. A large round black man in a Chinese military uniform stands out, says the camera.

"Hello comrades, thank you for your hard work," Jiang Zemin standing out of the roof of the black sedan, he has no lips. All the soldiers are the same height. And only handsome. Remarkable uniformity. Mass expression of loyalty. Marching Squares. Choreographed by a choreographer from The Beijing Dance Academy. Leaders look on frozen from the Hall Of Heavenly Peace.

Wen Hui's first English lesson was, "Long live Chairman Mao." Taught by a teacher returning to China, who had just been kicked out of Indonesia in the early seventies, maybe 1969. "There are Chinese soldiers who are too short and some who are too tall," Wen Hui explains, "but they are elsewhere." There are also many wedding ceremonies today, these are also choreographed and part of the parade.

Mr. Tien calls the next day and says that Mr. Wang can join us on our trip south, but not Li. Wen Hui also translates that Mr. Tien does not understand, self-servingly, as director of the village, why I haven't picked other musicians to bring to America. That Mr. Wang and Mr. Li are not the best musicians he can provide. His real point? Wang and Li are creating a rift in the village. Why them and not others, why not the whole village?

South Yunnan is remarkable. Rich farmland, some red earth like that in the southern US, even more red. Goliath terraces. And remnants of fanaticism. Most villages are surrounded by the emotionally devastating high square buildings that so enamored Mao. Concrete ideology weaving in and out of magnificent terrain. Most villages but not all. All the China I've seen seems remote.

There are moments in the drive when I can't decipher where I am, India, Bali, Africa. But then I wake up to the quiet noise of cultural conformity, Mr. Wang sitting beside me listening to his Panasonic tape player, enjoying his own music.

We stop and walk through Li Hou Zhai. A village with a few remarkable old women in their seventies and eighties with feet in tiny embroidered shoes teetering through small streets on their heels. Their knees do not quite function. No rolling through the ball of the foot to toes. So walking becomes exquisite balancing from side to side, what certain families did to their daughters, keeping them inside the home. But now the old women with tiny feet are seen walking through the villages carrying twice their weight, baskets filled with straw.

Every family whose darkened entrance we pass invites us to dinner, their way of saying hello, making sense of our being strangers. It is 4:30 p.m. They eat quickly and return to the fields, to farm, before sunset, it's harvest time.

We arrive in Jianshui at 7:00pm.

We find a hotel and unload the van. I have a great need to take a walk, alone. The town seems vital, congested and familiar. Wen Hui comes along, taking over the walk, guiding me to a temple that she knows of, but first a park, foyeresque, leading to the temple grounds.

It is dusk. Light fading, the temple grounds are closing soon. We turn a corner and I lose my breath.

Minneapolis 1974, 75. I was 23, 24. I was in college studying English Literature. When not studying Wallace Stevens I would read Krishnamurti.

In a Minneapolis neighborhood there was a place that provided "Isolation Tank Therapy." A yellow, one level suburban home, where one could go and be submerged, float in a small tank, a foot of water, sealed up, no light, no sound. For contemplation. It cost $65 for an hour.

"Astro projection," is what my experience was called. It began with my delight at being alone in a solid black anechoic environment. Relaxed. Deeper, stages from flesh sensations, to internal organs pulsing, to only my breathing, disappearing.

And suddenly, without calculation, I was floating down a picturesque lake or canal, lying in the hulk of a narrow boat, towards pagodas, a temple, Asian. I could see that, and my embroidered dress, satin shoes pointing towards the prow of the ancient wooden vessel. The surrounding colors were brilliant, golds, greens, startling blue sky, birds singing. Slowly moving. Astonishing quiet, as history. Forward, forward. When the boat reached the wall of the grounds I stopped being there and as quickly came back to my body, all of it, bumping the sides of the tank, soundlessness and black.

"Jianshui Wenmiao Temple, or Kong Miao or 'Before Mao Temple.' A temple built in 1285, to Kong Zi, 551-479. The most important spiritual leader in Chinese history." I want more information, Wen Hui cannot not give it, not in English. We walk the rest of the grounds, as light continues to fade, too dark to see. I don't mention any of my 1975 experience to Wen Hui. Not a word.

Early the next morning I return, alone, taking photographs. I think, This is the place, this must be the place. If it's not this place than maybe it's in Vietnam. That's what my intuition tells me.

Much later I translate Kong Zi, he is Confucius. Wen Hui had never heard of Confucius.

Mr. Wang and I were roommates for the night. He promised to bathe before bed, a hand signal. I hadn't asked. Earlier, the first thing that he did when he entered our room was wash his face in the bathroom sink. He somehow flooded the floor, and thought nothing of it. I suggested he find a mop and he did.
"I am a member of the Communist Party. There is no doubt that I will return to China." Mr. Wang blurted out, a bit drunk, at dinner.
At dinner Mr. Wang either drinks the strong cheap rice alcohol, er guo tou, or he eats a lot of rice with the rest of the many dishes that are served. But never both rice and er guo tou at the same meal.
Back in our room Wang took a bath, I thought. This is what I heard, behind the closed bathroom door: Water barely runs enough, in time, to fill a quarter of the tub. Then I heard him splashing in water for half an hour, an exertion of effort, that's what it sounded like.
Mr. Wang has a son at the University in this small town. Wang has a phone number to reach him but when he calls no one answers. He tries throughout the evening. Wang then decides he will rise early the next morning, hire a taxi and go to the University to find his son.

Before I turned out the light I watched Mr. Wang lay in his small bed. Eyes closed, smoking a cigarette, meditating, wearing a red sleeveless Chicago Bulls T-shirt and red long underwear with a single white stripe down each leg.
I watched later in the dark, as he slept rustling like someone simply sleeping, freely, maybe dreams, maybe not. Sounds throughout, loud sighs and uncaring breathing.
Wang woke at 6:30am turning on the light in the dark, in our early morning room and dressed quickly. He made a clear hand signal to me that he would be back by 8:00. I got out of bed.

I walk the path slowly, recovering what might be here, tracing time, approaching, musically, along the lake, the colors and sound are more muted now than then, that live dream, but I take photographs anyway of Jianshui Wenmiao Temple, until I run out of film. And then I walk back to the hotel.

At precisely 8:00 I meet Mr. Wang in the street in front of the hotel. His son is not at the University, has gone back to HongHe, Mr. Wang's village. Wang does not seem particularly sad or upset.

Rocks grow out of grass hills. We also drive through green mountains and
around lots of black, smoky twol la jis, tractors, the Chinese farmer vehicle of choice, or "small farming vehicle to loosen the soil."
Mr. Wang plays his Panasonic tape player throughout the trip. Music from his village, music of the Yi. I tell him the tape player is a Japanese product made in China. He mimics some disappointment but lets the music play.

We reach our final destination, the village of Potou. We park the van and walk about a half mile, through mountain countryside and find the village, empty, everyone out in the fields working, except for young boys having their haircuts.
"It's free. When I'm not working I like to donate my time and skill to help the people," the barber says, the only grown-up man present. There are also a few young mothers with new babies and three older women without bound feet. An old woman, sitting next to one of the waist height rock walls, that partition the many stacked, cavernous homes, places her small hand out. "Please, do you have some medicine for my headache, did you bring some?" Wen Hui gives her money, five rmb.

One of the young boys, head freshly trimmed, guides us through the maze of empty hilltop dwellings. Pitch dark rooms, empty kitchens. Wang comments on the architecture, his village is more modern, sophisticated, stronger walls.

A twol la ji ran into our parked van. We walk onto the scene as the twol la ji is trying to undo itself, its small front bumper locked to our larger rear bumper. Our driver screams at the driver of the small makeshift tractor, he screams back, as does his wife, brother, and a few others, who were obviously packed into the trailer of the vehicle. They actively bargain for an hour. While Mr. Wang and I sit and have tea in a shop across the street. Our driver walks away with 70 yuan/$8, for an extra large scratch on the van's rear wheel fender. The driver of the twol la ji wanted to give her 50 yuan, but conceded.

Every day of the trip we eat precisely at 9:30, 12:30 and 7:30. This has been a big challenge for me and my fragile stomach. The food is always remarkable.
On the final evening drive back to Kunming, I ask if we can go straight to my hotel, if I can be dropped off at the Hilton, in need of a hot shower and CNN. But our driver insists that she needs to eat. We are only a mile from the Hilton but it's 7:30. We eat again, the food again is wonderful.
Chill out, I carefully pronounce from the back seat of the van.
"Chill out, " Wen Hui repeats. "Chill out."
Yes, that's good. Chill Out.
"Chill out, Ralph."

Although changed, Kunming, by Wen Hui's rendering, is still quiet, less ambitious and not as complicated as other large evolving Chinese cities. She especially likes that there is still barbecue on the streets late at night, every night.

Wen Hui and I meet Mr. Wang and Mr. Li at Green Lake Park for tea and a meeting about Geography 2, their upcoming second trip to the US.

I tell them I hope to make something new with this collaboration. Mr. Li asks what is "new"? I give him an example of a marriage: That if he were to marry a black American woman their child would be something unusual, that's what I would like to achieve in Geography 2. Mr. Li does not understand. Why would he marry an American woman? Mr. Wang partially understands and smiles, blurting, "Yes, yes I want to marry an American woman, of course."

November 5, 1999

Jeanne Beatrice Pehoula Zerehoule

Dear Pehoula,

Bonjour. I assume that you and Djédjé received my last fax. I wanted to write you a personal letter attempting to explain the complex situation that led up to the contents of that fax, that I would not be able to invite you to participate in Geography 2. I write this letter with a great deal of remorse.

This decision was extremely unfortunate for me. Primarily, I had to base my decision on not having enough funds to work with as many people as I would like. But the decision was also based on the crucial balance that needs to be in place amongst those performers that I can afford to work with. Your work during the Yale workshop was fresh and inspiring. That said, I did sense that there would be a problem with our newly shared process language. Language, in how we communicate to each other with our foreign, physical and performance vernacular. Your presence in this research, as an African woman, is a very important and powerful element in my thinking. But given the extreme diversity of Geography 2, its foreign Asian focus, and the condensed schedule of developing the work, I did not feel that there would be enough time and space to work with you as individually, as thoroughly, as respectfully as I would like, to find a common ground to communicate, as would be deserved.

Why Djédjé and not you, you may ask? Djédjé and you share a common dance language, yes, but Djédjé and I have worked together before, intensely. We have come to separate but equal terms in our continuing and cryptic collaboration, in our understanding of one another. You and I start from an awesome beginning, one that deserves more care than this beginning research environment can provide.

Again, this unfortunate reality saddens me tremendously. I felt a strong connection to your presence at Yale. I respect your talent and process of working immensely. Hopefully, there will be the possibility of working with you in the future. I look forward to that opportunity.

Love
Ralph

ON THE WAY BACK HOME
I SPENT A COUPLE WEEKS IN
L.A., A RESIDENCY AT CAL ARTS,
WHERE I MET YEKO LADZEKPO-COLE,
A BEAUTIFUL MODERN DANCER, OF
GHANAIAN DESCENT, WHO'S MARRIED
TO A VOLKSWAGEN SALESMAN. ONE OF
YEKO'S FAVORITE DANCE FORMS IS
BALINESE.

A ~~PERFECT~~ HUMAN BEING.
PROMISING

I feel guilty.

Oh? Really, why?

Didn't mean to run away, for you to run away.

That's OK. You and me, we're like the weather, wait long enough and it becomes something else, was and is also something else.

Not sure I told you this but my travel itinerary was also the Buddha's map. Did I tell you that? A theory. But I reconfigured it a bit by starting in China because I have really good friends there. I took a side trip to Hong Kong to visit some other friends, then I traveled back to India, then to Japan, where Buddhism of course was already Zen. Much later I traveled to Indonesia, or shall I say Bali, which theoretically should have been my first stop after that first trip to India. Bali had maybe all of five Buddhists living there. Anyway, I certainly needed the vacation, by then. Before calling it quits, I returned to China because I have really good friends there and I love the food. Two years later I feel no more capable of sitting like my father, deeply, watching ball game after ball game, than I did before.

I do feel caught up.

I'm home. And have no desire to get on another airplane, be in another rice patty and feel inadequate, eat out of another unwashed bowl and pretend I'm satiated, speed down another road into head on traffic and not be able to manage one single invocation. Done with this particular field research. A year and a half of dire vacation. I've lost some old purpose. What I've prayed for. What I pray for.

Now home and working on logistical problems related to a performance. Trying to pocket equilibrium. What is this? What is that? This discomfort is familiar. Joyful, if prone. Seems to me that living in this glee of falling apart is greatly rhythmic, jazz. Understanding Charlie Parker and the rest of them better, those closer to home. Surviving is a next question. I imagine that I would like to stay healthy throughout all of this. At the moment I treat the many culturally disparate life forms roiling through my digestive tract, my scars, so that I don't forget where I've been.

Hmmm. I don't think it's at all possible to understand Charlie Parker.

THEN
I CALL MANO IN INDIA AND
ASK IF HE HAS THOUGHT ABOUT
WORKING WITH ME, MAYBE NOT
SO "DEEPLY." HE TELLS ME
THAT HE HAS TO CHECK WITH
HIS GURUJI. THEN HE ASKS HOW
MUCH HE'LL BE PAID. ~~AND THEN~~
~~WE BOTH LAUGH.~~ HE DISAPPEARS FOR
A FEW MONTHS.

NEW DELHI, India (AP. Nov. 5) - As devastating as India's latest cyclone has been, the destruction could have been much worse.

So while it took decades for the eastern Indian state of Orissa to recover from a 1971 cyclone that killed 9,665 people, officials expect to repair the damage from last week's super cyclone within six years.

Given the scope of destruction, this is no small achievement. Rice fields were water-logged, telephone and electricity poles were washed away, and flooded factories, poisoned wells and breached roads all need repair.

"New structures are built, new lessons are learned and it doesn't take that much time." The lessons have been painful.

In the southern Indian state of Andhra Pradesh, which adjoins Orissa, a cyclone in 1977 left 10,000 people dead. By the time a much more powerful storm hit the state in 1996, disaster preparedness councils had been set up and an early warning system was in place.

Nearly 200,000 people were evacuated before the cyclone arrived, and the death toll was kept to 3,000, well below that of the 1977 storm.

Orissa benefited from similar preparation last week. Although thousands are believed dead, Gupta said that two-story circular concrete shelters built on stilts had saved an estimated 30,000 lives.

Constructed since 1994, each of the 20 shelters used during the storm "has a capacity of 1,500 people, if they are packed, standing up, like fish in a box, which was the case," Gupta said.

Most of the victims are poor, which actually will speed up the recovery, Gupta said.

"Since these people do not have many belongings, putting their lives back again takes a lot of effort by them, but not much time," said Gupta.

Once the waters recede, they can gather wood and mud for huts, obtain special seeds from the government or relief agencies to plant rice in the sea-salted soil and use grant money or a loan for a cow.

November 4
Modern dance, I don't understand why it exists.
Maybe, I should make a dance about that.

November 5
Cheng-Chieh was in Taiwan during the massive earthquake there. She and her family are OK.
Maybe, I should make a dance about that.
Mano, the Odissi dancer, lives in Orissa, where there was recently a major cyclone that has killed thousands of Indians. I have no idea how he or his family are faring. Trying to find out.
Maybe, I should make a dance about that.

Cyclone = sky comes down to earth. Earthquake = underworld opens up to ground level.
In Minnesota, even in a mild winter, it's ice that takes over every surface. How beautiful the trees are then.

November 15
Still no word from Mano.

November 19
On a train, to a production meeting at Yale, Nari Ward and I conjure "a tree made of aluminum, with branches of bicycle spokes and wheels," falling into the theater space. Rolled off stage and lifted back to its original position and then falling again.
I tell Nari about a Gambuh ceremony I saw in Bali, an opera, dance ceremony, ancient poem, Malat. I describe the use of ceremony curtains, curtains that hang outdoors, from trees, announcing what character is in and what character is exiting a ritual space. I ask how he might translate this element. He takes notes.
He asks what I see as the skeleton of this work, process. I answer that I think, basically, the reason for all of these disparate lives on stage is to have a conversation.
I think he and I are beginning to converge. At least we have a basic design to house the upcoming process, a wall of warehouse pallets, windowed with burned sugar-stained Plexiglas, that shifts at a specific moment in time, slowly and mechanically falling to a 20" platform surface. A new floor. His translation of a temple.
Maybe, I should make a dance about that.

November 20
Watching videotapes from past workshops I'm disgusted with my choreographic sloppiness. Making a dance, theater, is not traveling, is not being a tourist.
Then I watch Asako walk, from a past workshop, just walk, and how it is there, precision and unprepared truth.

I call Asako and ask if she would think about going to Orissa to find Mano. I'd pay her expenses, of course. She says she'll think about it.

November 22
Asako gets through by phone to Mano in Orissa, he is well, his family is well. But Mano says that many people died. And that there are no more trees.

Ralph: So the cyclone stopped in the morning?

Mano: No not really stop whole day continue. Slowly the wind come down but the rain is also whole day. I had motorbike that time. I just bought it two months back. I start to go to Puri to see what happened. There is still the wind and there also feel like the tree will drop at anytime. Then from Bhuvaneswar, Puri is 60 km. We start to go to village to Puri and from Puri my village is 35 km. Thus all total is 100 km. I have three places where I have my family, myself in Bhuvaneswar, Puri is 60 km, where is my wife, my mother, my nephew, my niece and my brother, my brother-in-law and other family members stay. Then I start at 2pm to go to village. Also at time our roof was up and down and sometime some rock is falling and hit me and when I saw from the roof I still can't imagine this is Bhuvaneswar, all is like ocean. Also I saw so many buildings fall down. So many houses moving one place to another place. Then at 2pm it was a little less. Then we start, me, my nephew, other persons, start to go to Puri. From Bhuvaneswar on the way to Puri there is what is called Dhan damek unthupur. When we reach there we start by bike but after 100 m we have to take the bike and five, six person hold the bike and...

Ralph: Lift it over the trees.

Mano: And that is like 17km.

Ralph: 17 km?

Mano: It took us from 1 or 2pm to 10pm in the night.

Ralph: 2pm — 10pm for 17 km, took like forever.

Mano: We never ride the bike.

Ralph : Lifting the whole time.

Mano : Because whole road was ... and sometimes we go around the big tree fallen down on the road.

Ralph : How many people were with you?

Mano : We are six people.

Ralph : Six people and 1 motorbike?

Mano : Three motor bikes. When we reach there we are so cold by the rain, by the wind, we were so cold. I thought I will die or somebody will die from us. Because there was also dark, no light. There is some small cottage, we go and sit in there whole night. All of us were wet. And no dry clothes with us.

Ralph : Soaking wet.

Mano : Yeah ... then next morning again we start to go to Puri and road was a little more easy because of the day light. We reach Puri by 1 pm.

Ralph : And you hadn't eaten anything for two days Right?

Mano : Just we had in that village, somebody give some biscuits and water. For 60 km on the motorbike took us 24 hours. Then again I start to go to my village. Then I reach next day morning. Village everywhere was water. But everyone is OK. Really pathetic, I never forget in my life. Sometime after that other news about other places of Orissa really saw so many people died. Like 10,000 people died and house like no people there. With the house the people die. It is really big really really. I hope I will not see like that. From that day if I hear that there will be cyclone the things always reminds me.

Many years ago the gouvernement decided to construct a dam to bring electricity to the villages in center of Côte d'Ivoire. According to the officials, the construction wouldn't pose any problems for the surrounding villages. But, as it was later confirmed, the engineers who were in charge of the construction made an error in their calculations, and the creation of the dam caused irreparable damages and mourning for many families. An entire village woke up one morning underneath the water, everyone drowned. The luckiest among them, who had been off hunting, did not receive their usual welcome from the women and children who would normally greet them when they returned. Rather they were met by an expanse of water which had devoured the whole village. These survivors moved away, leaving behind them the bodies of their ancestors, in their songs and their origins, in order to set up their lives elsewhere, in the midst of other peoples, and start everything all over again.

Written by DjéDjé DjéDjé Gervais

I waa sitting in the room. I waa on the
~~floor~~ sitting in the /square ~~square~~ which sun light from
the window makes. /warm

my mother waa cooking in the kitchen.
TV waa on.
I ~~remember~~ a cow in a circle on the TV screen
remember
telling "it's "one o'clock noon" with ~~the~~ sound
of cow's ~~m~~ meowing. a soap company
commercial.

Next thing I saw was stairs.
going down fast. like animal. My mother grabbed me
and hold/ with her right arm on her weist.
/my body

I ~~don't~~ remember ~~the~~ whole world waa shaking ~~that time~~
but don't
I remember my hands and legs were ~~dangling~~
(dangling
This is my memory of
the big earthqu~~ake~~ in my home town when I waa four ~~years~~ old.
My father ~~thought~~ everything will submerged.
be coverd with water
when he walk back (wading water)
home to make sure we are OK.
~~that night we~~ the
~~slept~~ ~~outside~~ ~~on the~~ ground
and water was keep coming out from ~~the~~ splet of
my father told me
For many daya we had no water, electlicity or gas. ~~te~~
that without water and toilet waa the most difficult ~~that~~ time.
We slept in the outside ~~for~~ a while.
Many of buildings in our town got lean or sink after
the earthquaske. Our apartment building~~got~~ also slightly lean. ~~te~~.
Watching chopsticks tumbling on ~~the~~ table became
me and my sister's entertainment for our dinner time.

Written by Asako Takami

189

November 24
Reading the list of Lost Works of Art, et," from the great earthquake of 1926 in Japan. And the Abridged Modified Mercali Intensity Scale/Intensity Value and Description Lists.

How similar are the words "feel" and "fell," how I often exchange them, feeling and falling.

Ka, by Roberto Calasso, has been a gold mine.
I've been drawing most of the weekend, temples, more temples. Another repercussion of paradise, Bali and then India, China, Japan. Trying to remember. The practice of letting something else guide my hand. This "something else," a remembering of research, has a much harder time guiding the hands, legs, arms, feet and voices of hired performers.

November 28
Shift. Last night I made images of lotus flowers, perhaps the temple drawings are exhausted, but I don't think so. More of my wild finger painting, soft rigorous remembering. Earlier in the day I had seen the Passages exhibition at the Studio Museum in Harlem. Harlem artists work with art making like the Chinese, Chinese like African Americans. We cannot escape that we do not have complete societal freedom, not really. Images, materials are fundamentally grounded in hope, despair, dreams, screaming. Impossible to make work simply about color, shape and intelligence. But yes, simplicity also exists, that which is imagined. Maybe, I should make a dance about that.

Cheng-Chieh is back in the US. We plan a rehearsal period for December and January. We talk about Beijing, where she was recently teaching, how complex the dancing is there. We don't talk about the Taiwan earthquake and the 2400 people who died.

November 30
Another meeting at Yale, with Nari, Rich Gold, Kraig Blythe and Nari's appointed assistant Takeshi Kata.
Of course there is a reality check, of tonnage, touring problems and realistic wall movement capabilities, etc. This production dialogue continues to be eventful and challenging in the limits it sets up for me. For instance: Once the pallet glass wall is down, I most likely will have to limit how much of the new Plexiglas platform I inhabit. Thick Plexiglas, covering the whole platform is too expensive and too heavy for our budget. This limitation creates an interesting challenge in how and where I place a moving body. A forced option would be to create a phrase in three 8' by 8' areas, precise places on the new floor which could support a single body weight, where three bodies would enact this phrase in unison. An idea of literal symmetry, which is too literal a choice, but it could work. My point: whatever I end up with I'll try to make more difficult. (And of course, Nari will have another reaction criteria, which contin-

ues to keep my settling tendencies off the ground.).

Speaking of reaction criteria, at the end of the meeting, Nari shares his translation of the Balinese ceremony curtain. Clear plastic curtain strips, the ones you see outside of meat market establishments and NYC Korean delis, in the winter time.

We'll meet again at Yale on December 18. We'll have models by then and the opportunity to see how our ideas fly and or fall.

I called Anita Yavich (costume designer) this evening and formally invited her into the project.

Fucking exciting, feeling myself scramble through unknowns awkwardly and not fucking it up, yet. Staying upright. Energy is good. I need a root canal and I've resorted to taking a hair dryer to my stomach for three minutes each morning. It helps.

December

I've started drawing temples again. On postcards from India. Marring over bronze and granite photographed temple statues.

December 4
Q. What do you get if you cross a Jehovah's Witness with an Atheist?

A. Someone who knocks on your door for no reason.

Q. What do you get if you cross a Jehovah's Witness with a Zen Buddhist?

A. The sound of one hand knocking at no door.

December 8
Rehearsing with Cheng-Chieh and David Thomson this week and next. Rehearsals with Cheng-Chieh are revelatory. One on one with her and modern dance makes sense, again. David in another part of the space, working by himself, facing a monitor. Doesn't need me. That makes sense.

December 19
A good end of the week with Cheng-Chieh and David. The Cheng-Chieh phrase (titled December) is a good study/skeleton of a possible pathway into how I imagine myself dancing Odissi or Gambuh or Legong. No, not really. But rather the transmitted concept of trying to master a form. How mastering something can eliminate form while honoring it. I improvise in the studio, but Cheng-Chieh, the messenger, needs a different structured work and dialogue to accomplish what I ultimately hope of the phrase. She's game. We'll see.
David is extracting a phrase from videotape. A memory dance I improvised in China, about Bali, with Wen Hui. Physically impossible to teach for that reason. He's having a wonderfully convoluted experience with limited dimensionality. The talk, about what he is seeing, trying to capture, how it becomes his body, should become his body, is treasure.
Extremely interesting how potentially lifeless is the phrase, taught in parts, from my body to Cheng-Chieh's, compared to the perceived, unlimited possibilities of David's translation of my improvisation, where I was not thinking art, translation, taught, untaught. A problem, how to find more heart humanness in not being too personal?
We'll continue in January on a floor phrase. Some sort of empirical prostration.
Mr. Lo will come in at that time and compose to the December and January phrases. Should give him something to chew on while I move on to not thinking about a score.

The final meeting at Yale was useful. We're now arriving to the point(s) of design elimination, and discover that there's no technical solution for the falling bicycle wheel tree. There's a budget problem and the design team cannot figure out how to structure it to fall, repetitively, without it breaking over time.

Stan W. was there. Made an impassioned (Wojewodskian) speech about the "sweet spot," center center stage. Nari and I continue to consider the stage a visual art environment and not a theater. More on that later. Anita Yavich is a very inquisitive addition.

December 11

Ralph—

Your question "how to find more heart, hunamess in not being to personal??" set me thinking. but then I wondered – isn't the way the question is phrased a bit of a red herring? i mean, as long as you are conceptualizing it as "I'm not being too personal" isn't that very thought going to keep you from the heart of it? It seems that therre must be a very personal relationship developed even with outwardly "non-personal" material. the danger you're trying to avoid is sentimentality or over-indulgence, but that's not the same thing as being personal ...

Katherine

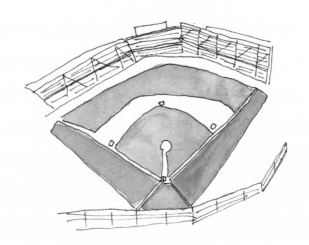

When Jackie Robinson played at Crosley Field (Cincinnati) in the summer of 1947 Black people came from places as far as Kentucky, West Virginia, Tennessee and Indiana, bringing lunch boxes of chicken and chocolate cake. The whites shouted, "Where is he, where is he?"

This doesn't seem like traveling at all, this train, and she, this stranger, sitting next to me, wearing all red, red coat even, she sits without removing the outer garment, brings her tray down, placed, opens a McDonald's bag, stares inside it momentarily, pulls out the smaller one, begins eating french fries. She places the french fries next to the larger bag, stares inside the larger bag again, reaches in again and pulls out a wrapped hamburger, shaking the smaller bag every few seconds, rhythmic, music, holds her umbrella with the other hand the whole time. Must have been raining in DC.

In Atlanta, over Christmas, my father tells me, that many black baseball fans of "the glory days" thought that Babe Ruth was part negro, or all negro. His nose and lips a giveaway.

January 20
Saw the Witness show at the Roth Horowitz Gallery, lynching photography. The gentleman who put it together happened to be there explaining some of the photographs to a radio interviewer. A very intense show. The stories behind them are even more upsetting, especially the stories of young men being burned alive and the crowds cheering with accomplishment. I was also struck by the image of bodies hanging/falling in space, not up, not down, or, falling up and down, from bridges and street lights and trees. There are lots of trees. The photographs seem extremely religious, to me, the way the bodies are suspended, and these horrific spectacles seemed to be religious events to the hoards of white town folk witnessing, rejoicing with ferocious joy these mini armageddons. Most lynchings were, of course, ritualized and the photographs show how important these elaborate set-ups were to the executioners, their symbolic association. Killing "the monster" in ritual procession. (To borrow from James Baldwin.)

Note to Katherine: Research religious acts of suspension. Vedic Sādhus fire-sacrifices. Native Americans spiritually altering themselves, suspended bodies, roped from trees, stakes torn through their skin, sometimes on fire, austere.
At what point does it become insane?

In the new biblical translation of the Watchtower Bible and Tract Society, Christ was impaled on a torture stake not a cross.

January 22
At a recording session, James Lo says that he wants to work with text as sound because he doesn't like any of the ways that I've been using text in my workshop experiments.
I decide that I would like to accomplish some beautiful modern dance within this other stuff that I don't understand.

There is a tree, the Tree of Transgression (to go beyond), the Aśvattha tree everlasting. Its roots are above in the highest, and its branches are here below. Its leaves are sacred songs, and he who knows them knows the Vedas. The Bhagavad Gītā

Preliminary script

Three primary elements/themes:
These elements interact throughout the rhythmic arc of the constructive process and into the performance.

1. Structure/ choreography. Instinctive, formal. Working with elements of bodies, dancing as composition and how these bodies inhabit the designed environment. How the designed environment encourages choreography. And how these compositions relate to silence, text, composed sound. And time.
a. An important physical element explored will be that of the body falling. An act of passing from one specified space into another, the velocity and freedom of that act. And a metaphor for the simultaneous existence of firmament and earth.

2. Entertainment, as ceremony, what that might be. Via different cultures.
a. How we dance/move together (all of us). What useful information is there in this juxtaposition?
b. Narrator. Who's telling the story and why.
c. Talking as performance language. Another productively confrontational element. A *theatricalisation* of a dance. The source of this language is "found" and re-arranged scientific text, discussing the natural and forceful elements of sand, rice, earthquakes and cyclones. A selection of natural forces and elements of the earth that act and react without sentiment, objectively creating earth balance. An important metaphor for the human environment I hope to create.

3. Actual mythological *poems* rendered into references of race and sex/sexuality: Shiva, Pārvatī Ganesh, Krishna and Rādhā/Gopīs. Not sure of order of appearance. Major source references are the Bhagavad Gītā, Upanishads, Gitāgovinda and Ka by Roberto Calasso...
a. Shiva. In some narratives he's a destroyer, in others he's auspicious. Of course he is both, all perhaps, Âtman, Tao, Dharma. In Ka he's forever practicing *tapas*, incubating, making heat, brooding, Hindu nirvana? I see him as power unknowable and sexually desirous. Incongruously, he destroys desire, *kama*, while physicalizing passion. He also burned his lover Sātī. I like that he reads to Pārvatī, recites the Veda. Shiva is depicted as black or covered with ashes.
b. It interests me that Krishna and Radha might represent illegitimate love. Krishna, the "endearing cowherd engaging the milkmaids in playful banter." Sex. Radha and Krishna are also "common," and also possibly pre- Bhraman and Vishnu/ Indo-Aryan, although Krishna is son of Vishnu. Krishna's color is always blue or black.
Ka speaks of the gopīs and cowherds as representing the sovereignty of illegitimate

love. That it is incandescent, because it cannot be possessed. (The concept of gopīs and cowherds could also be racial.)

c. Ganesh is prime remover of obstacles, clears the path to success. But more important here is his representation of forging unity between the Aryan and non-Aryan races in India (along with Shiva and Hanuman, the monkey king): Shiva is the sire of both Ganesh and Hanuman, he is described as "homeless," "scantily dressed" "and his body is smeared with ashes." The negative made light. Ganesh, Hanuman and Shiva were basically non-Aryan gods, already adored by the tribes of the land when the Indo-Aryans reached India. I'm intrigued that Ganesh has an elephant's head and is also a scribe and that Hanumān is literally a "monkey."

The use of *Myth* as lost mythology (Indian): (Indian mythology because it is so elaborate, elaboration to the point of chaos.) Partly inscrutable references, that have no crucial hold on my choreographic plans. There but not completely understood. A faint reminder of what might have been important.

From Ka: Books that make up the Mahābhārata are called *knots*.

"Narration presupposes the loss of the reality narrated-it makes no sense to tell a story to someone who has witnessed-but when the real has slipped away in space and time-all that is left is a dark room where words ring in the ear."

Cast:

Chinese woman/woman with cigarette -Wen Hui. China
Talking man/Master of ceremonies? -David Thomson. USA
Woman at sink -Cheng-Chieh Yu. Taiwan/USA
Force/fire -Ralph Lemon. USA
Force/water -Carlos Funn. USA
African man/poet/conscience -Djédjé Djédjé Gervais. Côte d'Ivoire
African woman, as hybrid/force -Yeko Ladzekpo-Cole. Ghana/USA
Silence -Asako Takami. Japan
Farmer/musician -Wang Liliang. Yunnan, China
Farmer/musician -Li Wen Yi. Yunnan, China
Rhythm/Indian musician -Guru Bijaya Barik. India
What is sacred/*HeShe* -Guru Manoranjan Pradhan. India

Set/Installation sequence, creates outline and clock/ritual for human insides. Represents sacred space and nature, indoors and out. Cathedral Plexiglas wall. Plastic strips. Set pieces: Scaffold platform, shopping cart vehicles, harnesses, bike wheels (chorus), benches, microphones, etc. are marks in space, and represent momentary forces of nature. Possible repetitive occurrence in the use of certain set pieces.

Text sources: Lists and scientific descriptions of events. The performers approach to the text will be to fulfill specific tasks.

Rice/excerpts from an Indian publication on rice-CC

Hurricane pilot text/ from the publication "Thunderstorms, Hurricanes, Tornadoes and Lightning"/RL
Earthquake/loss of art text/ from Bureau of Social Affairs Home Office Japan, 1926/AT
Abridged Modified Mercali Earthquake Intensity Scale/dt/replacing Hardwar?
List of Notable World Earthquakes and Seismicity from 856-1977/DT
Classification List of Low Pressure Systems/ from "Monsoons, Cyclones, and Floods in India", 1992.
Sand text/recorded from Indian televison program on desert sand composition.

Questions:
Why particular first, second, third acts?
Why particular text?
How are Chinese, Japanese, Indian, Côte d'Ivoire artists' languages translated? What are possible devices?
Why Wen Hui harnessed without apparent help?
Mr Wang, Li in blackface, why?
Is there a part one, intermission and part two? why? (Part one: an introduction of the more basic experiment of talking and dancing and who we are. Part two: ceremony, ritual, the myth. We become equipoise, if that is possible.)
How are plastic deli curtains brought into space.
When best for platforms for falling man (DD) and flying up girl (WH)
Why does Cathedral wall shift, what change in physical narration?
Wall comes down slowly, revealing anything?

Notes for Nari Ward:
How many chariot/shopping carts?
What is the image of garden?

Notes for Stephen Strawbridge:
A half lit stage
Whenever plastic is in place the rest of stage disappears?
Figures detaching themselves from shadows?

Notes for David Budries and James Lo:
Ka: "The Mahābhārata was an attempt to impose a silence in which the dialogue between two birds perched on opposite branches of that unique tree composed of an aśvattha (ficus) and a sami (acacia) might once again be heard." Again, the relationship of sound to silence is extremely important to this work's landscape.

Notes for Anita Yavich:
Image: bodies wrapped in cloth
What of jewelry, beads bracelets, bells, elaborate face paint (Odissi tradition)?
What of harnesses?
Meditation straps?

Tree

February 2000

Mano and Bijaya have brought all the volumes of the Mahābhārata in Sanskrit, wondering why I want it, in Sanskrit. "Ralph, you must never let them touch the ground." Both wear gray double breasted suits. It took them 48 hours to get to Austin.
Wang and Li spend their third day in the US still traveling, at the moment, resting in Houston.

Austin. StudioPlus/Deluxe Studios. On a highway, with a swimming pool.
In America Mr. Wang now wears mostly sportswear, striped running pants and soccer shirts, always red and white. Mr. Li wears his traditional blue pants and jacket.
On their second day in Austin, Mano and Bijaya wear matching Indian long shirts, kurtas, and white pants.
On the third day they wear matching gray and brown western dress pants and long sleeve dress shirts, pastel colored.
Wang and Li wear the same clothes every day.
Fourth day. Mostly, we ride in two mini vans, one silver, the other red, shopping Austin, for supermarkets and specialty food stores, for hours and hours.

Mano is in room 317. I'm in 217. He dances, practicing, pounding the floor throughout the night and morning. A jet-lagged schedule I suppose. No sound of drums. In the rehearsal space he mostly sits invisibly and waits for my odd sounding suggestions.
He's not pleased with the Oriyan translator. She translates much more than he or I say. This method is extremely informational for me.

Cathedral light
In a beautiful gymnasium from the thirties, on the University of Texas campus, Mano shows me a dance. I ask if I can I edit it. He says yes, but reminds me that it is complete as is, about a tree that grows full branched, a "Pallavi." Later, after thinking about it, he tells me that he will edit it, not me, and asks if that will be OK? For a moment I'm off the hook.
Yesterday Mr. Li got sick and threw up after an exercise about rolling on the floor. A similar exercise to the one that gave him a headache a year ago in San Francisco. He crawled on all fours into a corner. At first I thought it was an extremely creative response to the exercise.
Basically, pretty exciting stuff. Getting used to closing my eyes and picking objects I've never held before out of the air. A mess. Little of what I ask is understood. But not a single individual feeling stupid, I imagine. All of us finding meaning in what we need from being foreigners, I imagine.

Into the hill country of Texas on a day off

A friend's "ranchette," because it's only 20 acres. A chandelier in the middle of a trail hanging from a fat oak limb. A river, the Perdernales.

Drinking really shitty Texas wine. And then better moonshine. Rocks and 40 kinds of cactus, red hyacinth in the dark, yes, by the way, it was dark this whole time. A full moon. One firework, only, cause it scares the dog. Gorgeous smelling cedar trees. A not even half built house. And an RV, where the owner actually sleeps, a big one, tan, dark brown strips.

Wang puts out the fire made from gorgeous smelling dead cedar trees, expertly. Li doesn't want to go back to his apartment, wants to sleep here, outside, in the Texas hill country. A string of lights light the path back to the car, otherwise you'd be "a lost ass."

How to show something

There was a time when I would give instructions to a dance company, and everyone would understand and remember. And when an idea sprung from the performance of those instructions, it was relatively intact as it became physicalized on stage, in another performance.

Here, we have a showing of some of our research, and instructions are given and mostly not understood. So I sit out calling beginnings and endings for the group. The in between stuff is out of my control and therefore interesting to not know. Instructive. "Ideas" are subsumed by wonderment. I will have to get used to this.

Vacating an apartment

In the shower, soap in my hair, I hear a banging on my door. The door is unlocked. Mr. Wang enters and demands that I join him and Li for dinner. They intend to cook all the meat that they have left over in their fridge. I have eaten already and was preparing for bed, for an early morning pick up, to the airport, replacing Austin with New Haven.

Wang sits on my couch singing until I dry off, dress and follow him to his room. It's very late. I eat begrudgingly but politely, watching the Honeymooners, with no sound. I finish a serving, barely. They want me to eat more, Li jumps up and fills my plate again. I smile and look at the clock on their night stand and predict how many more bites I can fathom, finishing the hour I've given myself to be polite. I eat. Ralph Cramden is silent and so are we, using a chopstick sign language to communicate how much we're enjoying ourselves, or subtly not. When I leave there's still quite a bit of food left. They're disappointed. And unpacked for the 5:00 a.m. airport pick up time. Back in my room I don't sleep. Too much sautéed pork, beef, special Chinese vegetables and steamed rice. And a bowl of coke, that they kept filling.

At 5:00 they are the first of the group waiting in the lobby.

Dear Mr. Lo

Back for a blink. As I mentioned, I won't have a videotape for you till early next week (I have to transfer from mini digital to vhs). The material is not necessarily relevant to what it will become. I'm still getting to know folks. As you know, with my stuff, this beginning research gives only an inkling of its potential (there's quite a bit of manipulation which will follow).

Anyway, I'll send material for you to peruse.

About text: After trying out a few possibilities I'm not sure how the text will finally be incorporated. I need to understand its purpose/use in the whole, as it might stand, before your manipulation (which in itself is a good idea). I know I don't want to make too large statement with any talking, and when it does appear it's engaging and clear. That's about all I can say at the moment.

Obviously our major conflict will be how to match things, given our working methods: I like processing as long as I can before nailing a narrative. You need a narrative to begin composing.

Time of course is short. I do think I'm ready to begin building a beginning. We should start from there. Or if you have another suggestion? I can send tapes of relevant material once a week this month.

I can also predict that I will be putting together a series of parts, ultimately making a whole (some you've seen). Not sure if these parts are good for you to see/hear without knowing their connection to what's come before and after?

R

March 2000

New Haven. Eldorado Apartments. I have a room on the third floor, one not facing the street. The dim light of a monk's cell. Depressing if one doesn't have purpose to exclude what's left of winter light.

Djédjé and Carlos join us here, disrupting what's disrupted. No pretending postures. Don't know the environment, again.

But I remain calm. The religion of this work feels close to the comfort of home. God as a less complex person.

I get mad, bite my lip, feel the texture and pressure of the biting and am fascinated and curious.

Sunday 1

Mano and Bijaya spend the day and evening in their apartment, drinking scotch, lonely, missing their wives and India. Mano's wife is pregnant and due mid-May. He'll be in the US then, not there, his arrangement. "My wife understands that I must work, do what I love to do."

Friday Mr. Wang said he feels isolated. Mr. Li always says he feels like Mr. Wang.

I spend the day looking at videotapes from last week's experiments. Then watch the Lakers beat Miami. Now watching Oprah and Beloved on TV. "Twenty eight days of freedom," I wonder what that felt like?

Yale, New Haven for the last time, for three months. This time no African prayers, blessing of space, or group warm-ups. I have not the energy to coordinate any comraderie beyond the building work.

Wen Hui phones me quite late and suggests that we need to open the process up to more experimentation, complaining that the rehearsals have gotten too "structured," portentious. I agree to a point. Need to bring Bijaya, Mano, Wang, Li, Carlos, more into the primary material. We have time.

One week with everyone and it feels like a month has passed.

Freedom

After a year of useful thinking about Nari's set as a pallet wall, that then becomes a danceable plexi-surfaced floor, we now have a drastic set design shift due to budget and compositional constraints. Instead of the wall coming completely down to a platform surface it will now just shift like the semi-collapsing of a building, from a mild earthquake. Creating a ceiling/roof hovering over about three fourths of the space. A new visual tension. And I will have the full floor to work with.

Dear L

Everyone is being usefully bad. All is awkward and slow and misunderstood. So I'm in a kind of heaven. Laughing a lot, enjoying this family.

David is my doppleganger. Cheng-Chieh is a goddess. Yeko, exactly half African half American, is perfect. Carlos has grown too many muscles. Can't keep my eyes off Wen Hui. Asako is so slow. Mano is Ganesh, Bijaya is his human and man side. Mr. Wang is a 50 year old child. Mr. Li is finding his independence from Mr. Wang. Djédjé is dancing modern dance better than Carlos. Everyone here is taking care of me. Mostly the Asian women and David. Group dinners about twice a week. Great food.

R

More small parts

Excerpts. How this community builds. The only way.

Struggling with post post modernism, its obviousness and letting it really fall apart. Trying to move like Mr. Wang and Li or Djédjé, who's getting better at whatever modernism it is I suggest.

I've been physically improvising with Mr. Li. His body feels like a sack of rocks. He moves like a wide tree that bends freely and never snaps.

Then I put Mr. Wang and Li in blackface

And Mr. Wang immediately runs next to David, black, black David, put his arm around David's shoulder and gleefully announces, "Now I'm an American."

A little of how I feel about their music. I interpret it and can dance to it, so I must be Chinese. Or, and I've said this, "Their music sounds like the blues." A music I barely understand and can only mythologize as an original music of the Mississippi Delta, the blues, words soulful and incoherent, black lips. So I exaggerate my thinking and make it shameful because I don't really know China or the Mississippi Delta. Never have, how it/they have changed, making what they were forever unknown. I show Mr. Wang a few research photographs of blackface performers from the turn of the last century. He finds them very funny, seems to understand the photographed performers antics, how he understands performance, delighting an audience. For him it's not about race.

Wang, Li, Asako, Mano, Bijaya, Djédjé take a tea break, while Cheng-Chieh, Katherine, Wen Hui, Carlos, David and Anita corner and force me to explain what it is I'm trying to say with the blackface abstraction. Six variations of friendly outrage. I tell them that I could maybe answer their questions in 30 days. In the meantime, I'll dance, while Wang and Li wear blackface, while Li plays the san xian, which all of us now call the banjo. I'll dance a modern dance, that attempts to be a buck dance. I will wear no make-up. And I'll think about my grandfathers while I'm dancing.

Then we have a party, back in my room. We drink eight bottles of red wine, that some of us have provided, and a quart of Maker's Mark whiskey, that David has provided. Eat a lot of food that everyone's provided. For the first time in this process there's no accuracy, or inaccuracy, only liberated play, until Djédjé blurts out, "Sons can be forgotten but daughters can cause unimaginable pain." And then three completely failed translations are attempted.

Dear Mr. Lo
The latest tape is on the way. I'll try to be more clear with
answers to questions from week 1 tapes:

Lotus Dance
Yes, it is developing. It'll be about four to five minutes long. Represents how we all might be involved with the stage space and simple (translatable) movement, at the same time. It also represents a lotus flower unfolding, or petals blowing in the wind. An important dance, obviously, but simple simple looking. (And a bitch to choreograph).
Go where you will with it.

Memory Dance
About remnants of memory, what we see, don't see, what we remember, wish we had remembered, make up, how memory changes. I initially feel silence is right, pushing the slow, quiet, potentially boring part, as its nature. In one run-through there was music playing far away, from another place in the building, and that was interesting. Any ideas?
Sound designer, David Budries suggested the turning of newspaper pages, demonstrated it live, it sounded lovely. He made a CD for me to try, not so interesting. Obviously, this section depends on surrounding activity, sound before and after.

I'm also sending another example of the Memory dance, called Partial Memory. Not sure which would come first. (It incorporates some of the physical material of Memory plus the Cheng-Chieh solo you witnessed at the rehearsal in January.) Same world. These parts would not be presented back to back.

The Memory Dance with Rice Text was an accident. Interesting but I'm doubtful of it relating to anything else.

"Piano in the background"? What piano? Our rehearsal space has no piano, but is ambiently noisy. So I'll make sure to let you know if I'm playing with some recording. The live music will be obvious.

Pallavi Dance

Yes, Pallavi will have live drums, exactly as you hear. Not sure how much we can manipulate. This Odissi form and these performers are quite protective about their belongings. Sharing a compositional and theatrical stage with them has been a great work. That said, they are warming up to the process so there should be possibilities. We just have to do it respectfully, involve them into the ideas as much as possible. But some manipulation would be useful.

Pallavi Dance is a keeper and developing. It represents my attempt at collision. The obvious compelling power of tradition versus the potential irreverence of American modern dance, and then add the theatrical duet btw David and Wen Hui, housed far stage left, perhaps a comment on a relationship, somewhat cinematic (Wen Hui's sexual and theatrical sensibility, by way of China. And David's similar sensibility by way of being an older seasoned American performer)? The dance is a melange.

Carlos's floor phrase, style of it, will be scattered throughout. Won't be done as a solo. All "floor" information represents body architecture and gravity. Bringing the human element to level ground.

Thought you were sending me something to listen to??

Stay Tuned
R

Mano has problems with the design of his costume. "Nothing of India, why?"
Then he tells me not to worry, that it's between him and the designer. Anita calls me late, says that she can't sleep. Up worrying. I tell her that Mano and I go through this sparring daily and welcome to the debate.

Some of the foreigners are homesick
Wang asking, "When do we begin performances?" Had dinner with him and Li last night. We arranged it for six o'clock. I've learned that once a time is set I must meet them exactly to the minute. The door was open. They had waited three minutes, watching the Nature Channel, both lying on Mr. Wang's bed. I walked in and both rushed me into the kitchen. We ate. Twenty minutes later David arrived and they

cooked up a fresh batch for him. He brought along a pint of Wild Turkey. They filled their glasses and smiled, turned beet red. After dinner they played music, of course. Mr. Wang showed us the many second-hand polyester shirts that he brought from China and has not worn.

On Saturday
Mr. Wang spends the morning choreographing on the bodies of Li and Bijaya, making ants, marching, innocently ignoring my morning plan. Later he came up to me and through translation explained that he had a better idea for the Translation section, how to make the talking interruptions work better. A very complex suggestion that was way over my head.

Dear L
Mano has problems with the design of his costume. Nothing of India. What goes? I asked if he wanted to talk about it. He said that I shouldn't worry. Anita called me late, said that she couldn't sleep. Up worrying because Mano was so upset, sure it has something to do with her being a woman. I told her that Mano and I go through this sparring daily. Part of the cultural debate. She happens to be a woman in the debate, yes and Asian.
Here Mano cooks for himself and Bijaya everyday, but "never" in India, he says. Asako who has lived and worked with Mano in India, spends a lot of her free time visiting Mano and Bijaya in their apartment. Sometimes, Mano will call out for "chai," and Asako will make tea, enjoys it, intellectually, she says. She also has the freedom to make tea and then afterwards go to her own home, room.
Did I tell you all this already?

All of them are homesick. Wang asking "When do we begin performances?"
Had dinner with Wang and Li last night. We arranged it for six o clock. I've learned that once a time is set I must meet them exact. I arrived three minutes after six. Their door was open. They were waiting, both on Mr. Wang's bed, watching the Nature Channel, a program about zebras. I walked in and they both rushed me into the kitchen. Food was hot and waiting, and it looked nibbled on. We ate. Tofu soup, scallioned beef, rice and a strange mixture of lots of things green, with red neck bones. I enjoyed the food, except for the extremely salted egg dish. Twenty minutes later David arrived and they cooked a fresh batch for him. He brought along a pint of Wild Turkey. They filled their glasses and smiled, turned beet red. After dinner they played music, of course. Mr. Wang showed us his many second-hand, long sleeved shirts.

Four to five weeks to go. More walls to break down. And then three weeks of performances.

Love
R

Yellow rice, Chinese greens and dal

There is an order. One enters and eats a sweet temple prasad, from Orissa. Then you wash your hands. Sit and talk. Next Bijaya serves beer and explains how toasting, hearing the glasses clink, completes the five senses engaged in drinking an alcoholic beverage.

Mano serves deep fried floured fish eggs. And displays his many collected international performance program brochures. Identifying particular gurus, one his brother.

Early Dinner with Mano, Bijaya, Asako and David. We eat curried bitter melon, bitter melon bought at the local Chinese specialty store, curried fish, boiled egg curry and dal, lentil soup. After dinner Asako makes tea. Bijaya plays the many drums that he has brought to America, which I'd asked him to bring, most of which I'm not enlisting. (Along with the Mahābhārata. They smile and watch as my romance continues to crumble.)

Mano tells me that his final costume fitting went well. That there's no problem with Anita's original design. A moment to assert concern, that was all it was. And then leaving it in my care, testing my concern.

I tell him that I'm relieved that the problem has been solved and thank him for dinner and then rush out with David, in hand, to Yeko's apartment, where her mama, Dzidzogbe "Beatrice" Lawluvi-Ladzekpo, is visiting and has quietly invited all the black men in the cast to a traditional Ghanaian dinner, Carlos, Djédjé, David and me. Yellow rice, greens and roasted chicken. Carlos, excited by the food and exclusivity of the gathering, yells, "I want to eat like an African king." Mrs. Lawluvi-Ladzekpo yells back, "African kings eat alone."

I thank Yeko and Mrs. Lawluvi-Ldzekpo profusely, after this second dinner, which was supposed to be my first (I had originally arranged a late second dinner with Wang and Li, not knowing there was going to be a first dinner with Mano and Bijaya, which happened to be completely spontaneous). I say goodbye to Yeko and her mother, Djédjé, Carlos and David, and lumber off to a final dinner, which is actually a dinner meeting, to broach the subject of blackface and discrimination, which Wang and Li, as yet, don't quite translate. I'd asked Wen Hui and Cheng-Chieh to join us. Everyone eats, I nibble, sautéed pork, beef, special Chinese vegetables and steamed rice. Twenty minutes later Katherine arrives and they cook up a fresh batch for her. There are the requisite bowls of MSG and Coke, that Mr. Li keeps filling.

Near the end of dinner I describe a little of what it was like for my grandparents, my parents and myself to grow up in America. I mention the discrimination of early Chinese immigrants in America and how little I know of what it's like for Chinese Americans now. Wang deeply studies the translation from Cheng-Chieh, and then responds, with a description of different Chinese tribes. How the darker skinned Wa tribe is darker because they live in the mountains close to the sun, and that they build huts with no light, which also helps to make them dark. "Bad design," he says.

He says that there is no problem between his tribe, the Yi and the majority Han. That the Yi have a life and the Han have a life, they leave each other alone.

Sunday April 2

Ralph—

some assorted notes from the last few days — some small, some larger:

—at the point when Yeko "does" Asako, will we have already heard her normal voice? Obviously, the fact of transformation comes across much stronger if we've had a hint of what Yeko really sounds like.

—what are you thinking about the having-Bijaya-visible issue? I tend to agree with the comment that it's distracting NOT to be able to see him.

—A general comment: I was thinking the other day about a particular aesthetic sensation I get from certain moments of your work — a pattern wherein you have me look at something, then you have me look at it with a new element added, and then you take that new element away and I look at the thing as before. I take this as a very quiet, almost Zen-like statement: it's telling me that change happens, certain events are evanescent, and other conditions endure regardless of those changes.

I get this feeling in moments like: Asako's brief appearance and disappearance alongside the circle in moments of Lotus, or with the use of the gongs during Memory (now it's silent, now they're here and very loud, next moment they're completely gone, silent again).

I love this aesthetic, and at the same time I also recognize that it's anti-dramatic — the principle in drama being that a new event occurs and catalyzes the whole, spinning it into a new direction, thus the stage can never be the same again. In a dramatic structure we can't go back to A after having seen B. So maybe it would be interesting or helpful to talk about the structure of the piece in terms of these two competing kinds of structure — and ask, when do you want to use this Zen-like structure, and when do you want to use the principles of dramatic build? For instance, in DT's translation task with DD and WH, if you're interested in using the humor and having a section which pulls the audience into his dilemma, then we're talking about attention to dramatic build. I'm sure you're already familiar with these thoughts, but perhaps putting it into common terms can spur a good conversation...

—Watching the Lotus section on videotape, I felt strongly its importance, and its importance as a beginning. Lotus is sort of the "sleeper hit" of all the sections! It gives a sense of community, but what's more, it lets you read slight differences on people's bodies without yet knowing what those differences indicate... you're seeing something subtly that will be expanded later on. (You watch Mano, for instance, and know he's got a different approach to movement, but you haven't yet seen him do Odissi so you don't know exactly what that difference represents).

–The material from the end of David's story until Memory is all slow-ish in energy, and so I still have that concern we talked about before – is this the best context to watch Memory in? Memory is exquisite, and yet I think it may be done a disservice if the audience isn't in a mood to be patient with it, and really let it unfold.

–working on translation with DT, DD and WH – perhaps you could tell I was a little frustrated last time. Granted everyone was tired, too. But we should talk a little more about it *before* working with David, because if we seem to disagree too much in front of him he just gets confused. My basic disagreement was I thought we were working in a way that went against creating the tension between them that's necessary to the larger structure. I think David absolutely has to disagree with Wen Hui, and I suspect he has to do it from the outset – he doesn't get that nice, easy introductory question he wants from her first, because there's not enough time for it, it has to build from the get go.

I understand your basic concern that the relationship be subtle enough, and that he shouldn't seem to be blowing her off completely – that's not interesting, because there's no tension there either. But I think the subtlety you want is to be found on the other side of letting him disagree with her, by exploring disagreement – not to be found in telling him to stop short of completely disagreeing. He should disagree BUT he should also have the pressure not to dismiss her, to respect her at the same time. It all goes back to how Stan summed it up: the tension between them is the tension she presents as a threat to his story. Because of her, his story might not be told properly. And yet, she is excited, she is sure she has good information, she just wants to help.

Whew, that's the last note I think.

Katherine

For a moment last week Wen Hui, a Han, got really pissed off at Wang, a Yi. Wang refused to sing a song that they had earlier agreed to sing together. A Yi wedding song, traditionally sung between mother and daughter. Wang agreed to experiment with the mother part and would sing it if I were sitting in on the song's rehearsal. If it were just he and Wen Hui rehearsing, then he wouldn't. Wen Hui complained about his particular bull headedness. "He reminds me of my father," she says. A generation of men of the Cultural Revolution. When there was no discrimination.

I tried to explain to Wen Hui who Huey P. Newton, Bobby Seale and Eldridge Cleaver were and why they carried around Mao's little red book. She seemed mildly curious.

How to show something else

A breakthrough for structure. Forced to connect my ideas in front of an audience, an audience of collaborators, minus James Lo. It seems to be strong material. The black-face moment is welcomed. A "failure" by Stan W. standards. Which is a compliment, in how it is not about blackface but about something else. The inclusion of a non-plussed China compounding the issue.

So, yet another session on racism with the group. Again, for the Asians it goes no where. It is clear that they don't have the cultural experience to understand and deeply care. They just look at me curiously, flat. I feel embarrassed and foolish, for bringing this issue to the process. But I'll do it again, and again. My American exaggeration. Because I live in America. My vengeance.

After the showing, someone remarked on how kind everyone seemed in spirit, except for Djédjé, that he seemed more serious, burdened. His indignation, I posit.

"In America," Wen Hui says, "people always want to talk to me about politics."

Asako says that she confuses Americans because she often smiles when reacting to a statement, instead of replying in language. Men get the wrong idea. "A projected Geisha image still exists here," she says.

Our French translator, Marguerite, who's Haitian, tells me that Djédjé smiles when he doesn't want to because he thinks he has to, fakes it often, here, in an American context.

Wang and Li are complaining that the blackface paint, and or, the Handiwipes that they use to remove the blackface, makes their faces itch.

April 5

Dear L

Day before yesterday Djédjé practiced falling from 16 feet in the air, from a scaffold, bungee harnessed. My idea of sharing an essential physical energy with an audience, a body falling. And then, SAFELY, not colliding into the earth. Our crew seemed fairly well prepared for this action. Well, Djédjé rolled off the platform, for the first time, falling from 16 feet, and the bungee harness stretched a foot more than anyone had calculated. Djédjé's body slightly contacted the 2 foot thick mat positioned at the bottom of the scaffold. Enough to send shivers through the room. I've been planning this act with experts for over a year and never once did I consciously consider the danger. Now I'm terrified.

There's more. The following day we worked on a section of choreography that involves rock throwing. Mano, Asako and Djédjé dancing variations on an assignment. Carlos and Cheng-Chieh on the sidelines, tossing rocks back and forth to one another. A rock thrown by Cheng-Chieh accidentally hit Djédjé in the head, knocked him out. He had to go to the hospital. Five stitches. He's fine, ultimately a minor abrasion. Cheng-Chieh was inconsolable the rest of the day, and night.

Later in the evening Djédjé and I talked. He spoke of the "blood he had shed." Yes, there was blood on the stage. Significant. He cautioned me on my work. Not that we should not take risks, throw rocks, fall from scaffolds, but that I must be careful with the "energy" I'm swirling. He called it "displaced." Because it is dangerous, powerful, hard to know and control. That I must understand it better, know its dark side. He asked me about Shiva, a name, an idea I've been speaking of, naively, for months. I told him, that in directing this work, I relate to what Shiva represents, destroyer and restorer. But I relate to Shiva as a benign artist, no more, and there perhaps is the danger.

These past couple days have been very upsetting, a warning. I don't want anyone to get hurt.

I've gone very far in my desire of art, as creation and destruction of form. Been encouraged in this thinking all my life. The coliseum. Form, like dance, is a word.

Perhaps now I need to think of something that embodies more than form and its all too important possibilities. Perhaps it's now time to stop dancing out of my body, and heal, perform that?

Nevertheless, the velocity of the fall is breathtaking, beyond what I had imagined. And the rocks add an element to the choreography that is terribly exciting.

Hope you're swimming well. Give the cat a hug for me.

Love
R

That's the way it goes

Mano politely asks why Carlos and Cheng-Chieh throw rocks during his dancing? In his opinion when someone throws rocks at his dancing it means that they don't like what he's doing and want him to leave the stage. I tell him that the rocks add a tension and a danger, giving another layer of life to his dancing. Mano is not at all convinced, but he has asserted his concern, leaving it in my care. Djédjé is fine now, dodging the rocks, quietly. Earlier he did say that my "love for making dances is sadomasochistic," at least that's how it was translated from the French. The day after the accident I asked if he would bless the space, here, for the first time, as we did weekly in Geography. We made a circle held hands and only half the circle understood the instructions.

April 7

Dear Mr. Lo

We had another very eventful showing. New connections and of course new problems to solve. Feedback was extremely helpful. Very clear how much we NEED YOU in the work. HELP.

We'll send tape tomorrow and you'll see for yourself. All your notes sound exciting. Though still attached to Memory in silence w/ live gongs in beginning minute but I'm open to your convincing me otherwise.

Wall is up. And plastic curtains hang down. Promising. Two more weeks to go.

R

The work is rolling along

Modular. Re-ordering sections. Interesting how the parts are interchangeable, creating tremendous concern about connections.

We talk as a group of themes and arcs and human elements like race, sex and natural disasters. But ultimately this is a dance, a composition, unlike I

know, but surviving structurally, somewhat known.

This is how it all ends

I put on a recording of Robert Johnson, to warm-up to. Mr. Li and I were the only ones there. Suddenly, Mr. Li sang along to Robert Johnson. To my ears, howling, naturally, like it was music from Yunnan. Later, when I tried to make it theater, he said that it was too difficult, imitating the CD. That he couldn't understand the lyrics. And why would he sing this to an audience when he has so many songs from the Yi that he would rather sing?

A good question

Carlos corners me in the laundry room and asks why black men do all the falling in the process, Djédjé from the scaffold, Carlos from the stage lip and David from a 6" platform. Why them, and not others, who happen not to be black? I have no answer for him.

He then asks why he and Yeko perform a duet, that for all intents and purposes is a "fight," of sorts. Why he and Yeko and not any Asian couples?

"You and Yeko made the duet, not me," I remind him. The violent material of the duet was his solution to a simple question posed to the group: Create a physical conversation with someone in the group. We all began as strangers. And continue to be.

Carlos wants more finger pointing at white and black material and audiences. His is a specific voice chosen for this process. In that way he is brilliant.

Carlos continues

Why, since I honor ambivalence so, "the need not to be direct?" Why not use "being direct" as a material challenge? Why not call racism racism? "Black is black white is white." I have no answers.

After the incident with Djédjé

Cheng-Chieh finds it impossible to toss rocks in the rock dance. I ask David to replace her. During his first time tossing he hits Djédjé on the foot. Then he hits Asako on the ankle. But we go on with the work. Violence, danger, sinking in. The scene shop tries to relieve the obvious tension and makes these amazingly realistic looking wooden rocks. But they don't have the sound or weight of real rocks and so won't work.

Tech week

Yale begins the "lock down" phase. A knee jerk reaction to the gods of production. Oh well. I'm almost done, sort of, the beginning.

Watching the wall fall is an enormous experience. Kraig, our production point man, has been valiant.

And then the motor stalls, or something.

Like dancer's bodies, machines also break in the act of stress, with bare notice, schizophrenic.

At least this time I have an ending to fall back on. Mr. Li singing along to Robert Johnson. Sums it all up. The whole work in that three minute moment.

Not sure what the other hour and forty-two minutes says. Really not sure. At peace.

And I have a terrible cold.

botanical excerpts

The leaves are borne at an angle, and each leaf comprises of a leafblade and a leafsheath. The sheath envelops the internode to varying degree. The swollen sheath is the 'pulvinus'. The supermost leaf is called flag-leaf, which presents itself at varying angles. The leaves have parallel veins with midrib prominent on the lower surface. The bulging veins contain the vascular bundles which are continuous throughout the stem.

On either side of the base of the blade are small, paired, ear-like appendages known as 'auricles'. Just above the auricle is a papery, triangular structure called 'ligule'. Plants have either or both auricles and ligule while a common grassy weed found in most fields normally has neither auricules nor ligule. This characteristic is helpful in differentiating between the plants and weeds especially when in juvenile condition, which is agriculturally important.

Spikelets bear two outer glumes in which the floret is located.The floret contains a lemma and palea with 3 and 5 nerves respectively. There are two transparent lodicules at the base of the flower. Pollination usually takes place before noon. Under warm conditions it commences at 8 am and after 10 am under cool conditions. The lodicules become turgid and push lemma and palea apart to cause flower opening. This process is accompanied by rupturing of anthers which shed pollen grains. The glumes close after a while (3 to 6 minutes depending upon variety and weather conditions). The transfer of pollen of stigma completes the process.

I ASKED CHENG-CHIEH
TO RECITE THIS AS IF
SHE WERE READING A
LOVE LETTER.

Opening

April 26
Dear L
What a party! The show was also good.
Thank you for the flowers, they were beautiful. I'm still very much lost in it and every day still working out my own issues. I truly don't have an opinion beyond talking about it, the elements are way too big. As though I'm supposed to be finished or something. Yale gave a great push to the outside materials. Necessary and a bit overwhelming. We'll get over it and start developing inside now.
Hope to spend more time talking to the performers about what it is we might be doing in the hour and forty-five minutes we're on stage together. From now until November. Anyway, keep your fingers crossed as we try to keep our bodies together. NO ONE CAN BE REPLACED!
Love
R

P.S. At the party, James said that he would like some kind of clock displayed, after the wall falls, to count off how many more minutes are left for the audience to endure.

April 28
Yale University Theatre. The work has been officially open for three days. The changes now come fast and delirious. Still battling with the ending and audiences' expectations for a conclusion. And my expectations for continuing the process. I would like at least two weeks to re-write the final 7 to 10 minutes of choreography. To try a few variations. But will have to settle for choreographing in the wings, taking notes, the moments I'm not on stage dancing.

April 29
A new variation. Carlos went out club dancing on Thursday night after a good show. The next morning he couldn't stand, a seriously strained groin muscle, his balls shoved upward, something like that. Dancing without underwear!
So... I now have a modified piece, after such a lovely opening, introduction.
The Dalai Lama says that diamonds can be found in adversity, always. I haven't found one yet, but there's some tiny reflective specks sparkling in the dirt.
I'm embarrassed. That I absolutely cannot be finished with this project is breathtaking.

Dear Mr Lo
Wow, what a weekend! Carlos is suddenly out with some weird groin injury. He went club dancing and somehow shoved his balls up into his throat. Whatever.
Anyway, we've been performing without him since Friday. Odd. I think the work still hangs together. He's mostly missed in the Girlfight section. He'll try to attend a rehearsal today. We'll see what happens.
Been wrestling with the challenged ending. Nipping and tucking here and there.

Nothing is quite working so I keep elaborating the choreography. The biggest problem all along is what to do once the wall comes crashing down, with the expectations that this is the end. This is the one and only moment in the work where I'm actually choreographing to your music.

I've two major questions (countdown clock aside):

1. Is this the right ending to the work, the choreography. What's needed prior to the Robert Johnson song?

2. Is this the right score for the conclusion (as wonderful as the music is)?

Also, oddly, I never listened closely to the Robert Johnson lyrics until a couple days ago and find them extremely morbid. Maybe not so appropriate to what I think I'm saying. All that talk about the devil and a spurned lover murdering his sweetheart. Yikes. Thinking about finding another one of his masterpieces.

See ya Friday

R

May 3

I continue to make changes. Struggling mostly with the conception of time. My slower sense of time and an appropriate audience need for concisio, to get it over with. This work could easily be 3 hours. For me it is ritual, and ritual takes as long as it takes, until it is finished. Outside there is the knocking, ticking of time, passing, expensive.

May 7

Mr Li moves away, in inches, nightly, from the microphone placed far stage left, near his playing, walking more and more onstage. Finally, he tells Wen Hui that he doesn't want to have his music distorted by James' audio manipulation, which is dependent on what Li plays into the microphone.

Mano wants a new shirt for the fall tour. He hates the fabric.

Tuesday night Mr Wang wanted to wear his blue Yi village pants instead of his slim fitted suit pants, costume. I said no.

Djédjé's back has been hurting for two months. He doesn't want a massage nor accupuncture, but does want to see a Western medical physician, who will tell him "to either rest or to stop dancing."

Carlos is back dancing, limitedly, safely, I think.

Yeko is not sleeping. There's a mouse that crawls under her door at 2am every night to eat at her garbage pail. Lately, she sleeps in Asako's room.

May 11

The doctor gave Djédjé Tylenol and he says he feels better.

Wang has taken to imitating Carlos, waving his arms and screaming in Chinese, something that translates like, "I'm a pimp!"

Li has scotch tape wrapped around his four string instrument.

Yeko went shopping in the city, NYC. Came in a little late to rehearsal wearing dark glasses and carrying an orange summer bag, delightfully glamourous.

David says he will never do work like this again.

Cheng-Chieh rushes back to her apartment after most of her stunning performances. To be alone. Working on her body. The solace and uncertainty of brilliance.

May 12
The noise level backstage has grown. The men's dressing rooms resound with boom box house music. The men singing along in their various musical translations. The women lock their doors and scream in high pitched voices for silence, playful. Demystifying "Asian quiet."
Rather, it is the noise of human openness and community. No borders, no private spaces, that noise.
Actually, it is only Carlos with the boom box, successfully proselytizing hip hop culture. The other men enter and exit his loud space every so often, curious.

May 13
I had a dream where I had a terrific discussion with Bruce Nauman. He was actually lecturing me on globalism and the destructive qualities of primitivism in art. But it was Bruce Nauman in a short stocky body, wearing a fancy salesmanlike suit.
Later in the same dream, I met with Phil Jackson in LA, on the court, the Staples Center Arena, we discussed the theater of being fouled, via the technique of Kobe Bryant.
.

Dreamed of Kobe Bryant again. I rubbed his wooly head and told him about the dream I had the night before. I've been taller in these dreams.

Performance 22
End of the Yale run. Interesting, the need to affect, or not. The levels of volume. What those communicate. And then, when does this important kind of process become important work for an audience to witness?
This is the productive problem of Tree, of course.

Aftermath 1

Rushing out of the theater, someone rushes up to me, shoving a microphone towards my face. There's a camera crew, lights, makeup, the whole shebang.

"Ralph, How long is Tree? And Another thing, Buddhism:
1. Do you consider yourself a Buddhist? Or is it more accurate to
say you have an abiding interest in it?
2. When did you begin to explore Buddhism? Who/what turned you on to it?
3. How successful have you been at letting Buddhism guide you? (From your journal entries, I got the sense that you still struggle, in a healthy way, with wanting to be able to control things.) So, uh, are you now, or have you ever been, a neurotic control freak like the rest of us unenlightened New Yorkers?
4. Can you describe the Pallavi scene briefly, relating the three
duets to each other and describing the kind of movement they each do?
(my memory is fading ...)
You don't have to touch that last question if you don't want."

Well, Tree is 1 hour and thirty minutes. It would be longer if left up to me, but my cast is keeping it crisp, won't let me indulge, which I so like to do. "Crisp," of course is relative, considering that it is an hour and a half work, in American time and there's no intermission.

I am not a Buddhist."Abiding interest," perfect. Perhaps more, I'm still and probably always will be a "small dharma" person. I like meditation. Certainly has changed the way I walk and dance. I like the sound of the words, compassion, silence and formlessness. And whenever I get too lulled inside a quiet I've created, I look for some kind of loud noise to wake me up.
I started "sitting" in 1990. Boulder, Colorado, with Barbara Dilley (Cunningham, Judson and then Naropa) and Kobun Chino Roshi (Japanese Zen). My most recent teacher lives in Yamaguchi, Japan. His name is Oba Taido Roshi (Zen). Yes, one always needs a teacher, one that won't answer any of your questions, any of the important ones, no matter how many times you ask.
Near the end of July I'll travel to Colorado to sit with Barbara Dilley again. Important preparation for the "loud noise" of the Tree tour.
I think Zen/Buddhism is all about control, ultimate control, where one tries to let go of everything, and by that practice acquires everything. Which is nothing.
OK, back to earth: I'm a huge fan of hyper controlling most things in my life, if not all. I really enjoy meditation. That's all I can really say.

Describing Pallavi..Hmmm....

There are five obvious levels to looking at Pallavi, which in the Odissi tradition means 'elaboration.' An elaboration to the dance, and to the music that accompanies it.

1. There are three duets.

2. The central point in the work is the duet btw Mano and Asako. Theirs is an excerpt from a longer traditional Pallavi, that we edited and spatially manipulated together. Within the duet there is the remarkable dance itself, its relationship to Bijaya's mardala (drum) and the wildly different sensibilities that Mano and Asako each bring to this form. (Asako and Yeko represent a hybridity that astounds me. The way their bodies have extracted extra-cultural material, without losing any of what came before.)

3. Cheng-Chieh and Yeko dance what we call PM. Post modern material. An obvious play on the elusiveness of that dance language. (I think it's fair to generalize it.) An important objective of this dance is to enter and exit the same stage space that the Pallavi dance claims. Respectfully. Changing the traditional Pallavi composition to one that's obviously more abstract and less "frontal."

4. David and Wen Hui have a specific corridor, stage left of the center stage space of Mano and Asako. They enact a duet, that continues to be an experiment with a couple, evolving within a very passionate circumstance. We edited away most of the original dancing, paring it down to something more pedestrian, purely theatrical (perhaps). They have a score, a time structure and words like "secret," "contact," "separate," etc., that follows the build of the traditional Pallavi choreography and music. But there's enough space directed into their score that allows them to find integrity from night to night, wherever their instructions and games take them.

5. After Mano and Asako finish their dancing the stage becomes mostly PM, "pretty and boring." David and Wen Hui becoming subsumed into that sensibility. Then Mano and Asako, joined by Djédjé and Carlos enter into the distilled PM space of Yeko and Cheng-Chieh, changing it yet again.

I wanted to place three separate dances on stage at the same time and discover what an audience, and I, would choose to watch from performance to performance.

I'm also trying to find compositional moments when they are all connected. Looking for what those connections might mean beyond symmetry.

There's much more to be said but this is as far as I wish to go tonight.

What's this interview for, by the way? I ask.

"Oh, we're just serious fans," says the guy with the microphone.

Did you like the show?

"Saw it several times. Can't say I liked it. But it's a very thought provoking production."

How bout the rest of you guys?

"We agree," the crew choruses.

May 20

Wen Hui calls. "Hello, Ralph, This is Wen Hui. I'm in Hawaii, bored, studying Hawaiian hula."

She tells me that Mr. Li returned to Yunnan, cashed in his US dollars at the airport and counted the exchanged Chinese RNB/money on the airport floor, thousands of dollars. He would not be encouraged otherwise.

I wonder how Wang and Li will greet their wives? Before he left, Wang explained that in their village, you never kiss your wife on the lips, if you did she could retaliate by stabbing you with a knife. But he said that it's OK to kiss a man on the lips.

June 16

Dear: Ralph

Aloha!

I'm in home now. after three month Every thing is very peaceful in here, except the politics side. My friend said, People have to go to for the politics meeting more and more. I am listen to radio on the taxi yesterday, every news about politics, I have no idea to acclimation it. I'm a person not interest the politics. But I have to take up it, because this is my country, my home. All my life; my love in here. Include Wenguang he was important for me; for my life. When I'm walking on the street, too many people too noise, very dirty, People speaking very strong and push each other. But, all this thing is very beautiful and powerful for me. It was makes me thinking and working. All it was calorigenic for my art and my heart.

I talk to Mr. Wang and Li today. They are growing corns in this week. They will go back home, Hong He in July. At intervals some music come up from other side, when we talking.

Love, Wen Hui

Date: Saturday, July 22, 2000 8:29:16 PM
From: Katherine
Subj: water and musings
To: Ralph

I thought about the comment from your Spoleto Festival friend, about wanting an explanatory dictionary in the program. I know what she's getting at but i don't think it's the answer, as funny as that would be! I'm against program notes being too much more than supplemental. They should boost or deepen what's already there on the stage, but stop short of acting as some sort of "key" which audience members must consult in order to understand.

Off the top of my head: what her comment might reflect is not that you need to explain to the audience what every term in your personal language means, but rather that you haven't yet let them see how complex and interwoven that language can be, even if they don't entirely understand it.

I'm using a metaphor to think about this all — I'm thinking about the piece in terms of language and translation, and remembering your story of how you took your headphones off while watching the Bergman piece at BAM. You didn't enjoy the simultaneous translation; you enjoyed not understanding the Swedish literally. And yet, on the other hand, you didn't understand anything of it. You could tell by listening to it that it had patterns and syntax that bore meaning, and that was what was intriguing to you — not understanding the meaning literally, but understanding the fact that it was meaningful. I don't think people on stage making random nonsense sounds would have held your attention so long. There's something in the complexity of a language that the ear can hear even if the brain can't understand.

So, to stretch this metaphor to the breaking point, I mused the following: if you want Tree to be more open to the audience, you don't need to literally translate your language for them, and in fact too much of that might kill the experience. Instead you could just make sure they get to experience more of your syntax — those patterns that indicate it has the full complexity of a language.

What could that mean? I don't know, but I imagined the following — say the sink, instead of appearing abruptly at the beginning and at the end, had a shadowy life upstage throughout the whole piece, with different dancers stopping at it to wash their faces periodically as the evening proceeds. Or, no sink upstage — say you left that as an abrupt appearance — but cups of water make an appearance throughout, and we the audience imagining that they've been filled by the sink just offstage. Thus that "vocabulary word," the sink, is brought more fully into relation to all the other "words" of the piece, and the audience understands more of your syntax.

I also imagined that the thing you liked about listening to the Swedish was listening to the relations it was spawning between different characters – language as constitutive of relationships, making them or breaking them, and language as revealing the relations that already exist – even if you didn't understand what was being said.

So to push this line of thought into Tree, that would mean that "letting the audience in" would come with letting the audience see more of the relations between things. I'm not sure what that would mean for the piece exactly, but I do know that the moment when DjéDjé comes on stage and interrupts David is important for me in this vein – I connect to what's going on like an electric flash because it tells me something, though I'm not sure exactly what, about those two performers' relation to each other. Their walking duet does that powerfully too. But I don't just mean relations in terms of relations between people, though I definitely mean that as part of what I'm saying. I mean, in a larger sense, relations between different elements of the work.

whew, enough typing for now. enjoy your retreat – xo, Katherine

Pause

August 8 Dear L

I went west for my birthday. Rocky Mountain Shambhala Center.
Here's something I wrote about the shrine room:

is that pear real?
is that fucking pear real?
it's so brilliant behind the red
behind the undulating white
the red behind the photographs
my friend said: "Trungpa looks like Clark Kent in that photograph."

P.S. The pear wasn't real.

Here's another:

the water glasses
dharma circus act waiting
where's the trick dog?
everyday I wait.

And I improvised a dance. From the Buddhist suggestion of "first thought right
thought." Acting without thinking. However, I did warm up.

There was a man at RMSC, Hamish, a meditation instructor, wheelchair bound, had to
strap himself in when doing sitting practice, his breathing challenged. He would take
the yoga classes held at 7am. It would take him 15 minutes to move unassisted from
his wheelchair to a couch in the space and then another 15 minutes to move from the
couch to the floor, joining the rest of us. I, of course, watched him non-stop throughout the day, his power, guilelessness, his determination, his ease, his faith, spending so
much struggled time wheeling his chair around, being with the rest of us, washing his
clothes by hand in the sink, using the toilet, getting a cup of tea. He made me cry at
least twice a day. The day I left I thanked him for his inspiration. He replied, "Really?
Why thank you." Smiling. Another life.

Want to hear something horrible? My daughter was robbed at gun point in Jamaica
on her way back to the US from Cuba. She's OK. Her body wasn't touched. A wake up
call for all of us. I still feel queasy. I, of course, was peacefully in the mountains when
it happened. Kinda like being in India and Japan while my father was dying.
S'pose I should break down and just stay home. Love is not freeing. A partial answer
to your question.
R

Revival

August 21
Dear Ralph
Wang Li went the American Embassy in Chengdu today. but they didn't got visa. The Embassy need original from I-797 (the visa approval notice). Wang Li have not original one. I tale Ann before Please contact with American Embassy in Chengdu as soon as possibly. Wang LI IN Changdu now.
Wen Hui

August 22
Dear Ralph
PS I'm working furiously right now to try to solve this Li and Wang problem – up all last night making calls to China without good result. Working on US calls today and will try for better results with China again tonight. This is truly a problem that needs to be solved.
A

August 22
Hello Hui,
Well I have been on this case all day. Our congressman has faxed a letter to the Chengdu embassy asking them to grant the second visa based on the copy. Also, an official from Brooklyn Academy of Music in NY did the same. We consulted an immigration lawyer here who says there is no reason at all that they should not accept the copy because they are the very same embassy that issued the visa in the first place. We asked the Immigration and Naturalization Service (INS) to send a cable again to the embassy and will pressure them to deal with it but that could take FOREVER and we do not have that kind of time. So, I will call the embassy again tonight starting at 8:30pm and see if with all of these faxes and my second round of calling they will change their stance.
I'll keep you posted.
Please make sure that Wang and Li standby. And let's all keep trying.
I am assuming of course that they in fact do have good clear copies of the original notice.
Also – could you find out if they actually saw an American consular officer or if they saw a Chinese officer at the embassy? Do they perhaps have the name of the person they saw?
Thanks.
A
P.S. I spoke with Wu today and asked him about trying to get a tourist (B-1) visa for them. I realize this would be impossible from the Chengdu embassy but what do you think about trying that from Beijing?

August 23

Hello all:

We did it! The visas were granted!! Thank you so much for your
efforts, support and suggestions. The "substitute" consular relented
and it was his last day as tomorrow (or today) the regular guy comes
back and I would have had to start all over with him and wait until they
deal with visas again which is next Monday.

One crisis down and one more to go. We still need to make sure they
have the right paperwork when they arrive at the airport in Houston.
The consular officer did tell me that they'll need the Original notice
there. I assured him we were working on that and official letters.....
so they'd get in.

So, any ideas on that front??

Jenny – please let Ellen Wallach know what happened and thank her
profusely for her help. I'm sure it had its influence. But we still
need her to call INS and see what she can do about expediting (very
quickly) our request for the duplicate. Also ask her if she has dealt
with this issue before and/or if she could write a letter to the
immigration desk at the airport....

I'm trying to get back to my vacation for today and won't be in much if
at all.

A

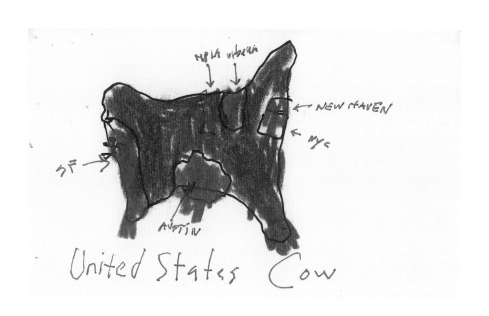

United States Cow

Austin Redux and Tour

Wang has kidney stones, is thinner.

Li is wearing all black, creased pants, dress shirt, black boots, spit shined.

Wen Hui just finished directing a work in Beijing for 100 dancers. Here, that would be a lot of choreography, not so much there.

Mano is now a father to a baby boy.

September 9

Anyway, we are barely here, don't realize anything is wrong, until the next morning when we need the company van to drive to rehearsal. Carlos had taken it to go club dancing the night before. Now, it and Carlos are nowhere in sight. We spend the morning calling, the local hospital, jail and morgue, in that order. We're not able to get through to the jail, the line always busy, but he's not in the hospital, nor the morgue. At noon, a lawyer, found in the yellow pages, we presume, calls our stage manager and solves the mystery. Carlos, drunk, was throwing up on the side of the road, had pulled the van over. After a night at a club. "Great mellow house music," he says, sadly. The football game, Texas versus Louisiana, was the next day, in six or seven hours. Party time for the police. He was taken into custody for throwing up on the side of the road. DWI. Carlos in jail. The van impounded.

The day is lost to strategizing with the lawyer, Carlos's one call, found in the yellow pages. And thank god for credit cards.

Late in the evening Carlos comes to my room, "Go ahead, hit me!"

I'm not interested in hitting him. I'm relieved. I tell him, "I thought you were dead."

Tomorrow he meets with his lawyer to arrange a plan to have the DWI charges dropped, because of "A fluke. Carlos is not that type of person. He really doesn't belong in jail." That's the story his lawyer will stick to.

September 14

Five days later. Carlos is having a good day, excited, dancing powerfully and then twists his ankle, rehearsing, my dance this time, not his. Finally. The brightest message so far. So he really cried, wept as he laid on the floor. Finished. The air clears. Something is over. Carlos's fate becomes simple for the moment. We both feel this.

September 18

So I cloud the air. Smoking cigarettes in a line, a line up, the whole cast. The scene is beautiful. Cheng-Chieh screams, crying, "No, not all Asians smoke," angrily exiting the space. I follow her. Cigarettes become ritual smoke, "that's all," I say. It's not about culture or race, it's theater. Later, I tell her that if it's impossible for her to dance after the scene, then we'll cut it, beautiful or not.

To Wen Hui, smoking represents her freedom. She loves the act, so does Asako. They tell this to Cheng-Chieh.

Yeko will stand in the middle of the line-up, not a problem, if it's OK for her to squint and tear.

There was no need to vote.

September 19

Asako says that Mr. Wang seems different. "He seems worried, concerned about something. He is much thinner than before." Wang says that, yes, he worries now, about supporting his three children through college. He says that he is also thin because he was farming corn all of the summer. There is also his kidney stone.

Mr. Li polishes his black boots daily.

Shiva day

A day off and barbecue at the tiny Studio Plus swimming pool. Carlos cooks steaks, chicken and fish. Mano and Bijaya grill vegetables. Yeko plays hostess, Djédjé eats and eats. Wen Hui repeats, over and over, how happy she is, eating in community and its performance, that would be my translation.

Mano opening bottles of Budweiser beers with his teeth. I scream. I had done this with soda pop when I was 11, 12, 13, my crooked, middle age teeth as evidence.

As usual the group is ready to perform, what makes most sense, to most of the group. Process as I know it, in this context, is perhaps "too mysterious." Mystery, as what we don't understand and how difficult a place that is to enter, why there is tradition, an evolving known.

Stephen Strawbridge is here. Tech day. I've made changes that I think help my fractured ideas. I don't feel the changes in my body. They seem abrupt and out of context. I lost the flow during the break. Most likely the changes will be perfectly fine. More flesh.

Carlos still cannot dance fully. And the work remains compromised and familiar.

September 20

Dress rehearsal. I've lost my arch. Don't understand this work any more. I've added connective tissue, broaching clarity, confusing me.

The foreigners rehearse their positions and steps. There is no audience and a great energy from their singing and dancing is naturally missing. As I try hard to find a reason to move, on a stage, pushing my physicality, with no one watching, they already understand the dark empty house. It is empty and therefore without life.

I miss my dramaturge, Katherine P. She would help guide me through this. I've lost my eye and trust. I could simplify this by just dancing.

Carlos is injured but recovering, his ankle, Yeko is injured and pissed, her ankle, Djédjé is injured and spiritual, his ankle, "I'll be fine tomorrow." He will. Oh yes, my right foot is most likely broken, a hairline fracture, metatarsus, not ankle, but it's tightly taped each night and I go on.

An interview

I mention to the radio host how extraordinary it was for me to hear Li's si xian and mountain song for the first time, that it sounded like raw American blues. The host replied, "Yes, I recently had a musician from Mali in the studio and he played an instrument that also sounded, looked like a banjo." I didn't get the reference. American blues, African music, of course. Yunnan music, American blues? Not so easy.

Maybe he thinks the world is smaller than it is. This project brings out a certain betrayal in all of us all the time.

Opening 2

Performance 23

Payne Theater

Cheng-Chieh and Yeko miss an entrance.

I jump and get stuck, locking arms with Djédjé and then fall high from his upper body, praying that my body will soften as it hits the hard floor. It softens and hits the hard floor and I continue dancing.

The scaffold is late coming on, compromising my exit cue. Instead of improvising in the empty time/space, I feel lazy and walk off stage. Call to David to enter, he might can cover the gap. Nope. "You're the choreographer," he signals from the other side of the stage. The space remains empty. Jim, our rigger, tells me it took him 4 beers later that night to get over the mistake. I tell him not to take it personally.

Around these moments the performance goes well. An audience adds reason.

Performance 24

Djédjé misses an entrance, running on stage later, looking as if he had just woken up from a deep sleep.

David comes off stage after the Translation section, walks up to me and apologizes for "ruining" my life. I have no idea what he's talking about.

I decide to put on an orange shirt in the last dance section, as David takes his orange shirt off. "I become David, he becomes me." And no one cares, certainly not the audience.

I do wish that Wang's kidney stone would pass, he's not quite present. But performs as unconcerned with his pain as he can.

September 29

Minneapolis

Of course the cold. My group complains. I complain. Not yet enough winter to quiet our complaints.

Nari is here, opened a new installation in the Walker Art Center's sculpture garden. Rites of Passage. A scaffold, a skeletal ice fishing house and more. It will be perfected in mid-winter, when ice takes over every surface of everything in Minnesota.

Performance 25

The Ted Mann Theater. A beautiful space. "You all looked nervous," Steve Cho says, coming backstage afterwards. The company picked up on my energy. I'm always so nervous here, just like I was when I first started dancing, here.

Nari hasn't seen the work since the dress rehearsal back in April at Yale. Says he likes most of the changes. But thinks the grass sink is too literal, easy, ruins the magic of the more mysterious sink, pump and water. He's right.

But I think the grass will stay, my gift to the audience, it's easy viewing and I've given them so much else to wrap their heads around.

Performance 26

My mom, dad, sister and aunt gather autographs from the entire cast, which takes an hour. They flew in from Atlanta to see the work, a work, I imagine, very far away from their lives. Later, we go out for Italian food and talk about cigarettes and buck dancing. A very engaged discussion. My family continues to surprise me. A moment when all my lives converge.

We continue to flesh out the work. Up to now the performances have seemed more to do with Tree re-development, working to recover something lost. Saturday night it hit a performance level, by all, not felt since the final week of performances at Yale, collectively understood, and a structure almost realized.

Translating our progress into new theater environments, with very little time to familiarize ourselves with those new spaces, will continue to be a big traditional challenge. The challenge of being ready on the opening night of a new venue and not having to wait until the second or third performances to get it right.

October 2-3

Heavy Rains Hit South Florida (NCDC). Abundant tropical moisture and a developing tropical system brought flooding rains to much of Miami-Dade county. The rain exceeded 20 inches in some locations. Nearly 6000 homes were damaged or destroyed, damages were estimated to be nearly $700 million, and three people were killed.

October 3

Urbana is rainy with perfect air. The plains.
Black folks here talk, act like they're from the deep South.
White folks here wear Levi's and cowboy boots.
One can also dry clean horse blankets for 8 bucks a pop, at the local dry cleaners.

Urbana. On another highway, with a swimming pool, only three feet deep from end to end, a flooded laundry room and two free passes every day to happy hour, 5:30-6:30, near a Steak n' Shake where we once ate various reincarnated forms of grease.

Li didn't go to the Steak n' Shake. Didn't want to spend any money. Wang and Li are fighting. Mr. Li thinks Mr. Wang stole ten dollars from him. Li says he counts his money first thing every morning and every night before he sleeps.
Li wants a single room, away from Wang. I tell him that that won't be possible.
Mr. Wang thinks Mr. Li is stingy, that that is the problem. So for the moment they eat and cook separately.

October 5

Asako says, "I feel sad that Mr. Wang has to resort to acting like a child, constantly playing because he can't speak deeply with the group, doesn't understand what we talk about most of the time. Rolling around on the floor like a bug gets our attention, and makes us respond, we laugh."

In my opinion, Wang enjoys the pervasive play he translates in our process, American. Perhaps his is a better process than mine, his own, and he will never tell me what it is.

October 6

TOKYO (AP) - Japan's strongest earthquake in five years struck a large region of the southwest on Friday, injuring at least 28 people and destroying buildings, homes and a Shinto shrine.

Perfromance 27

The Festival Theater. One show. Had a substantial amount of time rehearsing in the theater, on stage before. Oddly, by the time we get to the one performance, we're all, most of us, somewhat out of our bodies. Unfocused. Like the house production crew, who make us even more nervous. But the structure of Tree continues to gel and doesn't completely fall apart.

I wonder what would become of this work if we stayed together as a group, say, for two years? By then, Wang would most likely have invented a beautiful and cryptic Chinglish poetry to communicate with. And I will have been completely replaced.

A Celebration

"My first birthday party," Carlos smiles. In an airport. With a chocolate cake. He's 28. Djédjé and Wang sing happy birthday to him without a recognizable melody. "Happy birpie to you, happy birpie to you."

Inspired, Mr. Li plays the si xian.

Bijaya wonders aloud if the African djembe is a classical instrument or a folk instrument, since he now owns one, a gift from Djédjé.

Bijaya is a "classical musician" and has said that one should not play music in airports, "any just where," like Wang and Li do. At least one should not play "classical music" just anywhere.

While Li's music softens the airport's cold space. Gracefully.

October 15

San Francisco

Delirious searching for Chinese food. Found some. It's easy here, even abalone porridge. And then passed out on my bed in the room of an old hotel. Waking up a few hours later to the racket of quick lovemaking above or below or next door. Accented moaning, European style.

Hotel TV. ESPN
National Dance Team Championship (a sport competition)

What the judges look for:
1. Foot placement
2. A good arm placement
3. Good spot-rotation of the head, "Snap it around."

Eisenhower Senior High School
"Oh look at this! Ride with the music girls!"

Juneau Douglas High School
"Oh nice arm movement."
"They come all the way from the North to warm up the South."
"Great energy level."
"Very entertaining to the eye."
"What a way to kick in the new year!"

Upper St. Clair High School
"What's great is that they're using their hands to express."
"Very controlled."
"Seems all their songs are about 'dreaming,' and it looks like they've achieved their dreams."

St. Thomas More High School
"Again, we're seeing a lot of variety in music choices."
"I'm diggin it!"
"You can see that those girls are having a good time."

"Communication is worth 15 points to the judges' card. What's communication? A big smile is definitely first on the list."

October 16
What else happened?
An on-line chatroom with young dancers throughout the ether about my process. Names like DANS-D-mon and RINA2TOES.
Asako, sitting next to me says, "The speed of this exchange gives me a headache."
I find my sound-bite answers, to questions that I've spent most of my life asking, disturbing.

And then a public and live conversation with the honorable John Killacky about the process of Tree. I cry, surprised, describing how my dancing has changed and what I've learned, continue to learn from the art of Wang, Li, Mano, Asako, DjéDjé, Yeko, Bijaya, David, Cheng-Chieh, Carlos.

Performance 28

Yerba Buena Center for the Arts. Opening night, again messy. Mostly to do with the short tech time available. And then we are fine. More than fine, actually. We've found another level, since Urbana, since Mpls., since Austin. Encouraging.

Performance 29

My brothers, Mike and Robert, their wives, Sue and Val, and my sister, Anita, fly in from Atlanta and Charlotte. My little brother Robert is the last member of a family of eight to witness what it is I've done most of my adult life, perform. Afterwards, he says, "I didn't get it but I'm proud of you."

They ask the same questions that are most often asked. What do the bike wheels mean? Why the rocks, the cigarettes? Mike, of course, being my older brother, relates most of what he saw happening on stage to our boyhood acrobatics growing up in Cincinnati and Minneapolis, "Tumbling off roof tops, smoking cigarette butts (debris) behind foreign garages, concealed, and then setting fires. Remember how we used to hold each other under creek water longer than was safe?"

Once we spent a week digging a hole, 8ft deep by 4ft wide, along Minnehaha Creek, then concealing it with branches and leaves. Later, luring an unsuspecting enemy towards its cover. He sat, shaking, at the bottom of the hole for hours, but wouldn't concede.

Performance 30

The best response to Tree, so far, comes from a friend of Wen Hui's. "I don't get it. But my not getting it, here, in this context, is a more satisfying 'not getting it' than how I don't get the current Mideast crisis."

His partner then shares a conversation she'd had with a friend, another friend of Wen Hui's, a tall Chinese gentleman, who had seen the first workshop showing, of trial and error excercises, a year and a half ago, in San Francisco. He had said then, that he didn't want to come back to see the final version. That there would be no point. A year and a half ago he had said, "This work is like a necklace, the beads are beautiful but the string is not good." And, "It's like the tale of the five men racing to draw five snakes in the dirt. One of them finishes first and, while waiting for the others to finish, draws an extra line on the snake, a leg or penis, ruining the snake."

Ancient and extremely curious information. I wonder what he would think of this version of Tree.

A poem

One of the stage crew recites a poem to me, one he has written, thinking I would appreciate it. He tells me he thinks it relates to what he witnesses happening on stage. It's a good poem, about rocks, earth and dusty American barflies.

Wang and Li invite me to dinner on our last night in San Francisco. They seem to be getting along, at least they're eating together again. They want to cook all the meat they have left over in their fridge. Djédjé is also invited, is already in their hotel room when I arrive, has been there for hours, he and they, and their familiar referencing at an unspoken level, indivisible and unutterable. Another one of the many languages I fail.

October 19
HYDERABAD, India (AP) - India's military evacuated 53,000 villagers Wednesday as a cyclone took aim for the nation's southeastern coast.
The storm, centered in the Bay of Bengal, was expected to hit the southeastern state of Andhra Pradesh on Thursday, said C.V. Bhadram, director of the Indian Meteorological Department.

October 20
New York. Performance 31. The Harvey Theater.

Tree
Lotus. What the world needs now.
Rice 1. A reading, a microphone cord, a struggle, a dance.
Rocks 1. Throwing rocks at bad choreography. (Thank God it's not knives.)
Left dance. A dance made after an injury to my right ankle.
Folkdance. Wang and Djédjé dance.
Bench solo. Elaborate falling.
Translation 1. David translates Raymond Carver stories.
1. Wang on from Folkdance
2. RL enters with a bench that keeps falling
3. Asako sits on bench
4. Li enters as Wang walks to bench/waits
5. Li exits with Wang
6. Djédjé enters, interrupts
7. Wen Hui enters, interrupts.
Earthquake story. Asako learns to improvise
Girlfight. Mudrās swatting flies. Yeko beats up Carlos.
Rocks 2. Throwing rocks at the choreographer. (Thank God it's not knives.)
Translation 2. Falling up and down.
Blackface. Global minstrelsy
Collage. Simple juxtaposition: Modern, Odissi, African, modern.
Memory. Remembering Indonesia.
Pallavi. More complex juxtaposition.
Rice 2. Cigarettes and the history of rice.
Last section, which has no name. Or, what happens when you run out of time.

The end

1. Performance 32. I have not yet felt better about beginning. And then, Wang and Li argue in the middle of their opening duet, our trio. I dance btw them, stunned. Li thinks that Wang has left a movement out, Wang has not. Li stands his ground, hands on his hips, obstinately calling out, almost yelling, to Wang, in his village dialect, that he's right and Wang is wrong. Wang sits on the ground looking confused, at Li, at me. After what seems like an eternity, Li concedes and joins Wang on the floor and they continue the remainder of their duet, and exit.

In front of six hundred people, a moment of real life. The only night we videotape. The preservation copy. Perfect.

2. Performance 33. A good, tight show. With Wen Hui's coaxing, Wang and Li apologize to the cast.

Meditation

3. Yeko got up at 6:30 this morning, spent four hours having her hair braided, in Harlem.

Carlos continues to go out after performances, club dancing, wearing underwear. Certain.

Playing his music wherever he goes, cooking food, eating, Mr. Li has no other warm-up that is recognizable to me.

Putting on makeup is perhaps Wen Hui's meditation.

I was riding in a taxi with Asako on the way to the theater today. The traffic was slow and dense, the Lower East Side just before the Brookyn Bridge was gray, dirty. Asako was smiling.

"I'm happy watching the pigeon molt," detritus flying in the air because of the wind. "It reminds me of the cherry blossom season in Japan."

Clear, cheerful, no limit. Now the sky is dull and weak.
But a lot of hope.......hope of spring, billions of cherry blossoms.
Waiting for the spring.

Two millenniums left, a moment, poof.

Contradiction:
Imagination. My ability to plan/mark creatively.
Meditation. Not to imagine, to just be, quietly. No plan. Practical and physical, sitting and breathing. Of course in wonderment of my alive discursive thinking.

For me, an interesting dilemma.

I once made a dance from the Buddhist suggestion of "first thought right thought." Acting without thinking. Or perhaps what Trungpa Rinpoche called "post-practice," if one defines "practice" as sitting meditation. It was an interesting exercise. I would sit, meditate and then get up from my chair and move. Saving certain movements, repeating them, without judgement and then adding parts. It was a pleasurable experience, while not being an emotional nor intellectual excercise. That was the point.

But I love the slippery slopes of my thinking, its contradictions, neurosis, fears, recognizing my marks. Planning to throw rocks, because I know and think that they are dangerous, because danger like quiet or joy is also truth. So I hold onto discursive thought, action, life. An energetic partnership, exciting.

Sitting too long I get bored. Especially when the rest of the world is at war or drowning from some catastrophic natural disaster.

I grew up a Jehovah's Witness. Went to the Kingdom Hall four times a week. On the weekends would put on my little white shirt and black clip-on tie and go door to door, offering the Watchtower and Awake tracts/magazines. I defied it and acquired an early discipline in knocking on doors, which essentially is my creative process. It also provided a great need to believe in something.

The Geography trilogy came out of a need to work within a more collaborative process. A collaboration of conversations within the intrigue of specific foreign languages, about certain questions accumulated over the many years I've been making dances.

The trilogy, its specific cultural makeup aside, is about how my particular modern sensibility relates and/or clashes with the evolving act of refined order I find in so-called traditional forms.

The trilogy has also served my search for an integration of body, mind, and what I would describe as my more distilled nature.

Travels turned into journeys, the creative processes turned into daily insights and the performances became oridinary events. Tree is my latest attempt at the equipoise between quiet ordinariness and artificial rigorous thinking. The search for race instead found spirit, and inscrutable prayers. Now this search for spirit instead finds love, sometimes loving too much.

I will keep meditating privately, running into teachers when I'm supposed to. I will keep throwing rocks until I've finished throwing rocks.

And at some advanced point I suspect that there will not be a need to search for equipoise. Quiet ordinariness will be all that's required. I don't necessarily look forward to that day but I'm sure I will appreciate it.

Evolution

4. The rock toss dance has completely lost its danger and point. The trio on stage, dancing, have little worry that they will be hit by an out of control, tape covered, stone. The event has become as safe as is possible. Everyone but me wants it that way. There were many past accidents. Now the dancers dance. Boring, and a learning curve. "It is better to have it boring than to have a performer injured and unable to finish a

performance. No one can be replaced," says David, who tosses rocks, who should know.

5. Performance 34. Djédjé arrives at the theater at six thirty, two hours late. Stuck in traffic with friends. Djédjé is never late. No one had heard from him. I invented a few very dark scenarios. But couldn't quite bring myself to scream. Don't think I quite imagined canceling, although that most likely would have been the case if he'd not arrived. He arrives, at the precise moment Terri, our stage manager and I meet to decide what to do. Five minutes before Joe Melillo arrives in the theater to wish us a good final performance.
I'm beside myself, screaming quite freely now. Djédjé smiles, assures me that there's no problem, that he has arrived and can perform.

I think, how privileged I am to be here, to do this work. I take no notes at the end.

6. Sunday. In a taxi on the way to Kennedy airport, Mano, arm draped around my shoulder, asks me why I don't have a wife. I tell him that I almost had one, another one, but this one lost her favorite nightgown. Mano doesn't understand, so I stop talking.

7. Monday. Wang and Li are lost. Didn't arrive in Beijing as planned. My office spends the day on the phone, searching. Ignorance prevailing. We finally track down their flight, it was diverted to Seattle. Now they are in Tokyo, until tomorrow. I hope someone is feeding them.

A Series of Storms Hit the Western European Continent (NCDC). At mid-month various media sources reported that southeast England was suffering from its worst flooding in years. From the Rhone valley in France to the Po valley in northern Italy. In the US, drought conditions worsened in the southeast. Some stations in the Carolinas reported no rainfall for the entire month. Typhoon Xangsane brought death and destruction to the Philippines in late October, and whirled across the China Sea into Taiwan.

8. An Odissi student, who had seen a performance of Tree in San Francisco, informed Guru Kelucharan Mohapatra, Asako's Indian guru, that Asako had performed Odissi without a traditional Odissi costume, that she was smoking cigarettes on stage and shared Odissi choreography with a couple kissing and rolling around on the floor. Asako spoke to Kelucharan. He was outraged. Mostly because she hadn't asked for permission to use his Odissi choreography, his art. It is all that she knows to dance. In earlier discussions with Mano and Asako I was under the impression that the work they brought to the Tree process was free to process. Tradition is never simple. Kelucharan said, "You can do modern dance but not with Odissi, it's not good for the future." Years before he had told her she loved Odissi "too much." How she had left everything in her life behind to live and study for so many years in India.

Asako tells me she feels like crying at this news. But then, says she needs to cry alone, and that she needs to eat something before she can cry. And hangs up the phone.

We talk again later. "The experience I had with this whole performance is still overwhelming for me and I'm just looking at my emotion wandering around. I miss everybody I miss being that world and also I feel complete in some way. So I can see clear sky inside me."

9. Mr Wang and Li arrive safely in Yunnan and should be back to their Hong He villages in another week, if the roads are good.

November 6
JAKARTA, Indonesia (AP) - Rain-triggered landslides killed at least 52 people and officials feared more would die as the deluge continued Monday on Indonesia's main island of Java.

10. My father calls, an excited voice. Leaves a message. He's never called me before, ever. I'm shocked and call him right back.

"How did it go?" he asks.

December

Would you clarify, "Sometimes loving too much"?

"Loving too much?" Yes, maybe I can explain.
Maybe it's what happens when we don't know a part of our life, and want to know it, by any means necessary. Creating remarkable rigor. Driving dangerously fast, obscuring a point of view. Traveling a lot, being a tourist, without responsibility to the unfamiliar, a freedom. Often mistranslating. Dancing without borders, is often brilliant. Because we so need borders.
Or, maybe it's what happens when we frenetically (sometimes accidentally) scatter parts of ourselves, outside of ourselves, then furiously, or just as frenetically, pick up pieces that don't belong to our own anatomy, because they are brighter, shining exotic.
When we don't belong. And force a belonging, which creates, yes, longing, loneliness, missing ourselves.
In loving too much maybe we bypass ourselves, passing over our own innocence. Like swinging at a baseball with a bat, missing. Three times, a strike out. Mark McGuire hit 70 home runs two seasons ago, due to lots of practice and steroids. One might say that he became simultaneously the hitter, the bat, the ball and the home run. Sometimes. This year, Mark McGuire missed half the season because of chronic knee problems. He had 30 home runs at the All-Star break, two in fifteen at bats in the second half. He came in second to last place in the home run race. "Watch the video of my last four or five home runs, and you'll see I was limping around the bases," he said. Sammy Sosa stayed healthy and hit 50 home runs.
Asako's guru told her she "loved Odissi too much." Leaving all of her Japanese life behind, to study for many years in India. She's not Indian and perhaps had to love it too much, because that was the only way she would ever know it enough to dance it. So she sits at his ancient feet, in tears, in his essence and he lets her and he knows all of it and doesn't have to love it, because he was born with it, and understands that truth, perhaps never been to Japan, and has no reason to go. And better yet, maybe he has been to Japan, many times and wants to go again.
Interesting problem. It only gets more complicated. Maybe when we love too much we get seduced and lost and learn a lot and are embarrassed repeatedly. And try to talk about it.

The Mahābhārata is in storage, carefully stacked high above all the other accumulated incognizance waiting to be drawn upon. It will be there for as long as I need it to be there and it will never tell me what it is. But I own it, just like Asako owns her teacher's dances. Our human partnership, hers, mine. Where we ultimately place these foreign truths, how we give them away, is perhaps the lonely part.
It was Sogyal Rinpoche who said, "When we are lonely, we miss ourselves." He also said "Settle, just settle," many times.

Wen Hui said, "In the beginning Ralph didn't share his food with me but I watched him shift and at the end he was sharing his food with me. The experience settled him." Settled? I'm not so sure. If one can deeply miss an experience and simultaneously walk away from it, then yes, maybe.

Djédjé said, "I walk away from this experience and dream that one day I can choreograph a dance where I direct Ralph, where it will be hard for him. Where I can be more than just an African dancer."

Someday soon I must tell Djédjé that his dream came true the day we met, long before.

This morning I thought it would be nice to not judge love. But to reason it safely is useful. Krishnamurti was right, love is not knowledge, nor is it something we cherish and put on before sleeping. We are so lucky because we are not without love. It is an ocean.

AFTERMATH 2

REFUTATION

while i was with Tree,

i was traveling
i wrote every day
i drew
i walked around a lot
i meditated every day
i was singing
i was dancing
i didn't question myself about spirituality.
my spirit was shining like new leaves.

ASAKO TAKAMI

CULTURE BALANCE

I didn't think there was a balance between different cultures, because I don't think culture is something you can balance. WEN HUI

The group was generated from Ralph's own interests, so it definitely had a sense of balance for him. It was fine for me too, although I did question some of his decisions, like going to China. Why did he go there, and why did that represent something related to his spirituality? How could China be important in his tracing the roots of his blackness? India I could understand, because Africa and India have some more direct links, and Ralph's religious beliefs may be more associated with India, but China was out of the blue for me. At one point in the piece Mr. Li had the impact of an old black man, but if Ralph really wanted to use the image of an old black man on stage, why go to China to find him? CARLOS FUNN

One day in rehearsal Ralph asked Wen Hui to put blackface on Wang and Li. I was troubled by the image. It is certainly provocative to an American audience, yet why do it? Wang and Li as well as Wen Hui had no real idea about the significance of putting on blackface, even though Ralph tried to explain the history behind it. The issues were too far from their understanding. Their unawareness made me a little uncomfortable.

Ralph eventually explained it by connecting Wang and Li's blackface to the Chinese Opera's painted face. That may be sufficient in characterizing the general use of masks, but not the greater resonances of slavery and appropriation of the cultural voice involved in blackface. Wang and Li were willing to do pretty much anything Ralph asked them to do, so the whole responsibility was on Ralph. CHENG-CHIEH

In the beginning I didn't think what I was doing in the Tree workshops was anything. I didn't feel like I was working. That wasn't good. Later I enjoyed the experience. GURU MANORANJAN PRADHAN (MANO)

NATURAL DISASTERS

One section of Tree involved a trio (Mano, Djédjé, Bijiya) dancing while Cheng-Chieh, Carlos and I skipped stones across the stage. The stones' irregular edges caused unexpected trajectories, and fear for everyone involved. I hit Mano a few times. Both of us accepted the risk, but it was emotionally difficult. DAVID THOMSON

I worked alone with Ralph in the early process of creating movement. The nature of Ralph's physicality involves risk – the balance between falling/out of control movement and quietness/specificity/refinement. One has to push as far one can, until gravity starts to take over, and the next moment one has to redirect movement intention.

The sense of risk or danger was also expressed through Ralph's creative process, although he tried to provide a safety structure in which to house the risky explorations. That didn't always work. During the creation of the rock throwing section I threw a rock that landed on Djédjé's head. This accident provoked the full emotions of catastrophe that I remember from my earthquake experience in Taiwan [in 1999]. I experienced myself as a natural force gone out of control.

Many of the performers in Tree come from environments where typhoons, earthquakes, and profound social turmoil are the cruel norm of life. Whether the stage is the refuge from or continuation of that dangerous environment is a good question. I prefer to keep the stage a sacred place. CHENG-CHIEH

BEING HIT ON THE HEAD WITH A ROCK

When we were at Yale rehearsing Tree, many times the signs showed that the environment in which we were working was not good, so I decided to speak with Ralph. I was concerned about the Indian Gods he was using as points of reference. He told me about the many Gods of India, and explained he was most interested in Shiva for his particular character and the fact that he represents both destruction and creation. He also told me I had no need to worry.

After the accident happened, in the hospital, the doctor asked me to rest for three to four days without doing anything. Nevertheless I decided to reassure the others by promising them that I would join them the very next day and remain with them all the way to the end of the project. Mentally I had to quickly forget this incident in order to concentrate on what would follow.

I also made sure Ralph knew my vision and interpretation of what had just happened, by telling him this: The path that you are taking is dangerous, and I don't think you know it. When one engages an energy it should be in proportion to your ability to contain it and your knowledge of why you are engaging it. Above all you should know how to adapt it to the purposes for which you engaged it. You should pay careful attention, for in a spiritual voyage you will meet obstacles far more difficult than the wound I just received. The blood that has spilled is a sign of destruction, for Shiva has responded to your call. DJÉDJÉ DJÉDJÉ GERVAIS

RESPECT

Sometimes Ralph was missing information on traditional elements, which demand a certain amount of knowledge, and sometimes he persisted in wanting to use them nevertheless, which could cause trouble. For example, this was the situation with

the trance dancing in Geography 1 and the use of Shiva as a reference during Tree.
DJÉDJÉ DJÉDJÉ GERVAIS

Ralph liked my music, and he liked that I played other music that wasn't mine. Once he asked me to sing a song on the stage. I answered that it wasn't good because it's used when somebody dies, and then he didn't say any words. WANG LILIANG

I recall an early workshop in San Francisco in which Ralph was searching for cast members. Asako entered the process there. She then introduced Ralph to Mano. The first time that Mano visited our rehearsal Ralph showed him a videotape of an experiment where Asako did Odissi dance with Ralph dancing around her. After the video viewing, Mano disapproved very directly. He said that the juxtaposition of Odissi and Postmodern dance was "BAD." I was shocked a bit by his directness and felt my own naiveté in the assumptions I make and intercultural ease I have as a Postmodern practitioner. We mix and match with great license but may be actually insensitive about the outcome of viewing from the other side. Ralph might not have been as shocked as I was, but he certainly didn't expect such direct criticism.

Ralph convinced Mano and Bijiya to come to Austin, Texas for some test rehearsals. I witnessed many intense conversations. In time Ralph encouraged Mano's will to experiment further and further with the Odissi form.

Within the group, I felt somewhat privileged, or enabled, because my own work and experience had more in common with Ralph's aesthetic. CHENG-CHIEH

At one point during Tree, Mano was dancing Odissi with Asako. During the same moment I was dancing with David on the same stage. I showed my leg to the audience at that moment. Mano felt uncomfortable about this because of his religion. Ralph asked me how can we fix this, and said we needed to think about it. I agreed and changed the movement. WEN HUI

I think Ralph tried to be respectful but he was also very Ralph in asking for as much as he could! This became an issue with Mano & Asako. In Ralph's efforts to edit or abstract the traditional form of Odissi for use in the project, Mano tried to be as accommodating as possible. But there were limits, and in my opinion Mano's culturally prescribed relationship to Ralph (as his employee) made him defer more that he might have under other circumstances.

Another moment of discomfort was Ralph & Djédjé's duet during which Djédjé would dance (African) while Ralph would improvise around him and jump on him. It created a strange sense of imperialism. It was disturbing to watch and I'm not sure if that was supposed to be the point of the duet. DAVID THOMSON

Because I felt Ralph was aware of what he was doing (how risky it was) and trying to be respectful and responsible, I could trust and work with him.

Some people in India were very angry when they heard that we smoked a cigarette and danced Odissi on the same stage. It was difficult for a while because of that.

It's like wearing shoes inside the house in Japan,
   like putting books down on the floor in Tibet,
   like eating steak with your hands in this country(...maybe)

For them, no matter what, smoking a cigarette in the same space you dance Odissi was beyond their...what is the right word???...in Japanese, RIKAI WO KOERU. [Tr: beyond their comprehension]. It is considered something completely wrong. ASAKO TAKAMI

Ed. note: Guru Manoranjan Pradhan (Mano) declined to be interviewed on the subject of the cigarette-smoking.

WHAT HAPPENED NEXT

The December after the show closed, my father almost died. We sent him to a nursing home to recuperate. I took over his affairs and the massive renovation of his Bronx home, where I grew up. I have been working on it for the last three years. I feel like I have returned to rebuild the places of my memory. DAVID THOMSON

After working in the USA, I had money to build my house. People here always say I'm great because I got money from the USA. I'm glad that they say that. Here life is still hard, there's no money, and not many chances to help my household. After I got back home I still needed to work for my family, like I do carpentry if someone asks me. I still want to earn money with my music if there is any opportunity. WANG LILIANG

MOST AT HOME / MOST STRANGE

I feel at home with my husband, and family. Yes, I could probably say that I feel most at home when I'm in Ghana, but I have grown so much in love with my [American] husband over the years that without him there is no home. YEKO LADZEKPO-COLE

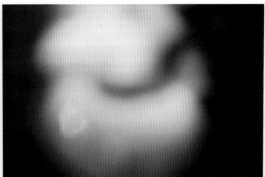

Home is a constantly shifting idea for me.

Home has multiple definitions. Home is Monkey Cave, a remote Taipei County village, where my childhood memory resides.

Home is the semitropical, where 2 out of 3 days are rainy, where all kinds of weeds and insects are exultantly happy.

Home is busy bustling Taipei City where you and many others sweat in traffic jams and choking hot polluted air.

Home is New York City when I fly over it.

Home is where my parents are and where my husband is.

Home is where I was and where I left behind.

Home is where I choose, and sometimes it chooses me.

Home is where I can reinvent myself.

The place I feel the strangest is anywhere my difference becomes a problem. CHENG-CHIEH

I feel at home in a dark room, with a nice floor, and house music playing. That's my sanctuary. When I feel most troubled I need to go out dancing, to that environment with people I can share that energy with, and I feel replenished.

As for feeling strange or foreign — I guess I feel out of place if I'm being looked at a certain way, labeled as just one thing, or considered simply "urban." That would be more likely to happen at European-American functions. It was also my beef with the folks who did publicity for Ralph, who were quick to label and categorize me, which I think cheapens what I have to offer. On this earth, that's what makes me feel most out of place. CARLOS FUNN

At home:
I remember the first time I went to India. I was at the airport in Calcutta in the middle of the night. The smell of the air, the darkness, the temperature... I never felt that comfortable before. My body was open fully.

Foreign:
I remember when I came to the United States, there was no smell in the air... I felt that there was no life in the air. I couldn't get from one place to another by walking. I couldn't function for a long time.
ASAKO TAKAMI

At home: in China. Strange: in China. WEN HUI

IF YOU WERE THE DIRECTOR/CHOREOGRAPHER AND RALPH WERE ONE OF YOUR PERFORMERS, WHAT WOULD YOU ASK HIM TO DO FOR YOU?

I would like him to do what he wants to do. But the only thing I wouldn't want him to do is dance too much, because his dancing is too beautiful. WEN HUI

I wouldn't take the job! DJÉDJÉ DJÉDJÉ GERVAIS

Interviews conducted and edited by Katherine Profeta

Thank you:

Suzanna Tamminen and Rina Drucker Root, for the portal and the art.

The heroic staffs at Wesleyan University Press and University Press of New England.

The Performers who make up this book and propelled the great shift: Bijaya Barik, Carlos Funn, Djédjé Djédjé Gervais, Yeko Ladzekpo-Cole, Li Wen Yi, Manoranjan Pradhan, Asako Takami, David Thomson, Wang Liliang, Wen Hui, Cheng-Chieh Yu, and all our teachers.

My Saviors at MAPP: Ann Rosenthal, Jordana Phokompe, Cathy Zimmerman, Lisa Phillips, Joyce Lawler and Jenny Tool (who now resides in Korea).

For the boat and compass: Stan Wojedwodski Jr., Victoria Nolan, Mark Bly, Ben Sammler and The Yale Repertory Theatre.

The Collaborators: Katherine Profeta, James Lo, Nari Ward, Anita Yavich, Stephen Strawbridge, David Budries, Rick Sordelet, Richard Gold, Terri Anne Ciofalo, Chelsea Lemon Fetzer, Steve Cho, Kraig Blythe, Takeshi Kata, Izumi Bernadette Ashizawa.

For Asian travel guidance and support: Ralph Samuelson, Cecily Cook, Rachel Cooper, David Roche.

The Presenters, for the safety of their theaters: Neil Barclay, Philip Bither, Ruth Felt, John Killacky, Nancy Martino, Joseph Melillo, Cynthia Quinn, Mike Ross, Pebbles Wadsworth.

Molly Davies and Polly Motley for all the Vermont retreats. The staff of the Atlantic Center for the Arts for all the Florida retreats. And Akiyoshidai International Art Village.

Sam Miller and Cynthia Mayeda, for the beginning.

Marcia Sullivan, Jennifer Goodale, Stephanie French, Marilynn Donini at Altria for their consistent support.

My Board: Norton Owen, Baraka Sele, Stanley Smith, Jack Kupferman, Elissa Bernstein.

Christopher Reardon for the interview text.

David Gere for the reader's report that forced a different book.

Tara Fallaux and T. Charles Erickson and their cameras.

For the invaluable support and new friendships in and out of Asia, I want to thank: Wu Wenguang (Wenguang, I cannot thank you enough), Wen Bin, Ellen Wallach in the Office of Congressman Jerrold Nadler, Douglas Kelly, Consular Officer at the US Embassy in Chengdu, China. Oba Taido Roshi, Minh Tran, I Madé Subandi, Dr. I Wayan Dibia, Ida Ayu Sinaryati, Anna Wong Lee, Mindy Yim, Ming Yin, Victor Ma Choi Wo, Paulo Nunes-Ueno, Dr. Fred C. Tillis, Nan Golden, Yumi Kawashima (for all the stories), Kakuya Ohashi, Kenzo Kusada, Takiko Iwabuchi, Mikuni Yanaihara, Paz Tanjuaquio, Robin Stiehm, Nicolas Conroy, Dorji Wangd. And Rajesh for keeping me safe.

Kelly McDonald for the partnership, that last drive and the beginning and end of this book, the search.

I thank MY FAMILY. MY FAMILY. And my father for his recovery. Nuff said.